Patty Nancy Carol Martin Cheryl William Deborah Sharon
Anne Dwayne Karen Gwen Delia Tom Jule Helen Ellen
Barbara Rex Michael Gordon Barbara Norton Sheila Susan
Lester Sue Richard Clifford Diane Yolanda Stacie Betty Joan
Kathy Evelyn Carol Arthur Harriet Paulene Ruth Eugene
David Erica Nettie Pat Bill Beverly Missy Roger Lynn
Glenda Cynthia Charles Ira Ellen Margaret Frank Mark
Robert Sid Peter Steven Sonia Judith Kate Linda Michael
Janet Elise Trinita Linda Astrid Shelby Nina Donna John
Douglas Lisbeth Ann Ralph Louise Alexandra Judy Deanna
Marsha Larry Bettye Sarah Kenji Mary Luis Samuel Janice
Kristin Frederic Craig Diana Valora Sheldon Emily Nicholas
Eugene Michelle Gregg Jack Gary James Urie Elinor Julius
June Docia Edward Elaine Shelly Sandra Katy Mary Ann
Toni Rosalie Yasmina Caroline Martha Lynson Mary Beth
Patrick Andrea Bruce Mary Kay Darlene Candice Claudia
Bernice Hedy Elizabeth Theresa Meredith Ernesto
Rutherford Diane Beverly Christopher Eliza Katherine
Jennifer Sarit Julia Jean Jane Murial Fern Stephen Patty
Nancy Carol Martin Cheryl William Deborah Sharon Anne
Dwayne Karen Gwen Delia Tom Jule Helen Ellen Barbara
Rex Michael Gordon Barbara Norton Sheila Susan Lester
Sue Richard Clifford Diane Yolanda Stacie Betty Joan Kathy
Evelyn Carol Arthur Harriet Paulene Ruth Eugene David
Erica Nettie Pat Bill Beverly Missy Roger Lynn Glenda
Cynthia Charles Ira Ellen Margaret Frank Mark Robert Sid
Peter Steven Sonia Judith Kate Linda Michael Janet Elise
Trinita Linda Astrid Shelby Nina Donna John Douglas
Lisbeth Ann Ralph Louise Alexandra Judy Deanna Marsha
Larry Bettye Sarah Kenji Mary Luis Samuel Janice Kristin
Frederic Craig Diana Valora Sheldon Emily Nicholas Eugene
Michelle Gregg Jack Gary James Urie Elinor Julius June
Docia Edward Elaine Shelly Sandra Katy Mary Ann Toni
Rosalie Yasmina Caroline Martha Lynson Mary Beth Patrick
Andrea Bruce Mary Kay Darlene Candice Claudia Bernice
Hedy Elizabeth Theresa Meredith Ernesto Rutherford Diane
Beverly Christopher Eliza Katherine Jennifer Sarit Julia Jean
Jane Murial Fern Stephen Patty Nancy Carol Martin Cheryl
William Deborah Sharon Anne Dwayne Karen Gwen Delia

This volume is dedicated to our colleagues

Reinventing Early Care and Education

Reinventing Early Care and Education

A Vision for a Quality System

Sharon L. Kagan

Nancy E. Cohen

Editors

Jossey-Bass Publishers • San Francisco

Substantial discounts on bulk quantities of Jossey-Bass books are available to corporations, professional associations, and other organizations. For details and discount information, contact the special sales department at Jossey-Bass Inc., Publishers (415) 433–1740; Fax (800) 605–2665.

For sales outside the United States, please contact your local Simon & Schuster International Office.

 Manufactured in the United States of America on Lyons Falls Pathfinder Tradebook. This paper is acid-free and 100 percent totally chlorine-free.

Library of Congress Cataloging-in-Publication Data

Reinventing early care and education : a vision for a quality system /
  Sharon L. Kagan, Nancy E. Cohen, Editors. — 1st ed.
      p.   cm.
  Includes bibliographical references and index.
  ISBN 0-7879-0319-1 (cloth : perm. paper)
    1. Education, Preschool—United States.   2. Child care—United
States.   I. Kagan, Sharon Lynn.   II. Cohen, Nancy. E.
LB1140.23.R55   1996
372.21—dc20   96-25323
                                                                    CIP

FIRST EDITION
HB Printing   10 9 8 7 6 5 4 3 2 1

Contents

Preface

Throughout the history of our nation, America's rhetorical commitment to young children has been one of beneficence. Its policy commitment, however, has been one of neglect. This policy stance has produced early care and education programs of undeniably questionable quality (Cost, Quality & Child Outcomes Study Team, 1995; Galinsky, Howes, Kontos, & Shinn, 1994), doing little to promote the development of our youngest citizens (Hayes, Palmer, & Zaslow, 1990). Why, despite verbal commitment, has the lack of dedication to American youngsters prevailed? More important, given burgeoning numbers of children entering early care and education programs as their parents join the workforce and attend training and school, what can be done about such neglect? *Reinventing Early Care and Education* tackles these questions head on, challenging conventional assumptions, revisiting important social events, and bringing fresh knowledge to bear on one of the country's most important social problems—the crisis of quality in American early care and education.

A National Crisis of Quality

Even to casual onlookers, America's neglectful policy commitment toward its young children is readily apparent. Episodic national investments in early care and education have been made in response to economic and defense crises, such as the Great Depression and World War II. But these efforts have not been sustained, and there has been no broad-based universal action to meet the day-to-day needs of young children and their families for quality, supportive services to promote children's basic health, safety, and development.

Early care and education—unlike education for older children—has never been considered an entitlement. Periodic investments by federal, state, and local governments and by business, coupled with marginal commitments to quality, have resulted in programs that are often poorly staffed, poorly housed, and poorly run. Trends suggest an even bleaker future, as research documents the deterioration in the quality of programs over the past fifteen years (Hofferth, Brayfield, Deich, & Holcomb, 1991; Kisker, Hofferth, Phillips, & Farquhar, 1991).

Beyond concerns that most early care and education programs provide custodial care at best and place children at the risk of harm at worst, little attention has been directed to the quality of the early care and education system as a whole. The hesitant, fragmented evolution of early care and education efforts in the United States has resulted in a system characterized by uncoordinated services, significant unmet needs, and limited capacity for data gathering, planning, or evaluation (Gardner, 1990)—a veritable nonsystem. Inequitable access is another hallmark of the nonsystem: whereas almost three-quarters of three- and four-year-olds in families with annual incomes ranging from $50,000 to $75,000 were enrolled in preschools, child care centers, or prekindergarten programs in 1995, fewer than half the children in poor or working class families were enrolled in preschool programs, including Head Start (U.S. Department of Education, 1995).

Such weaknesses in our national approach to the early care and education system is perhaps most distressing because they occur despite a rich knowledge base that suggests clear and implementable policy solutions. Research in child development and early childhood education, for example, converges on several indicators of quality programs that are predictive of children's healthy development, including practitioner training and education, higher salaries, child-to-staff ratios, and smaller group size (Hayes, Palmer, & Zaslow, 1990; Phillips & Howes, 1987). Research has linked the stringency of state regulations of early care and education to the quality observed in regulated programs (Cost, Quality & Child Outcomes Study Team, 1995). In short, the quality crisis is amenable to policy intervention, yet very little has been done to convert good intentions and valuable knowledge into action.

This is not to say that nothing has been done. Policy makers, foundations, and corporations, hand in hand with the early care and education field, have set in motion numerous stopgap measures in the form of limited interventions, research, and evaluation. Over the past half decade, the federal government has infused some new dollars into early care and education targeted to lower-income working families, either to help them get off welfare or to help them keep from needing public assistance. There has also been expansion of federal dollars in the Head Start and Chapter I programs. The future of these federal commitments is ambiguous as this volume goes to press, because the federal role and responsibility in social services are being hotly debated in Congress. It is also true that an increasing number of states have enlarged their investments in early care and education. Fueled in part by the first National Education Goal, that by the year 2000 all children in the United States will start school ready to learn, state-level political activity on behalf of young children is on the rise. This goal is part of eight educational goals shaped in 1989 at the bipartisan Charlottesville Education Summit. The goals were designed to guide a national education agenda.

Though early care and education have gained some momentum in recent years, serious shortfalls in quality and coverage are still pervasive. Inconsistencies, contradictions, and a lack of systemic cohesion prevail. Some programs promote children's development but do not support working parents; other programs provide the hours of care working parents need but do not promote children's development. Piecemeal categorical legislation is proffered without addressing the coordination of funding streams, quality standards, planning, governance, or administration. Programs target poor families, heightening racial and income segregation in the process. Head Start is transformed from a demonstration project to a large-scale national program, with little serious examination of its structure or place in the array of social and educational programs for children. Funding levels that rely on the hidden subsidy of poverty-level wages for the staff who work with young children are tolerated. And perhaps most distressing, we often fail to realize that all of these issues not only are crucial to quality but also are intimately linked to one another and must be addressed as part of a comprehensive solution, rather than in a set of isolated responses.

The dilemma is not related to policy alone. The early care and education field has not developed an integrated, long-range vision for a quality early care and education system. There has been little opportunity to examine and challenge conventional assumptions; to commandeer knowledge from other fields, disciplines, and countries; or to convene a range of scholars and practitioners to consider alternatives. The *Quality 2000* initiative, funded by the Carnegie Corporation of New York, with additional support from the Ewing Marion Kauffman, W. K. Kellogg, and David and Lucile Packard Foundations, provided such an opportunity.

Launched in 1992, *Quality 2000* embarked on an ambitious journey involving over 250 researchers, advocates, and practitioners from fields that included early care and education, public education, special education, higher education, nursing, social work, family support, community organizing, and the environment; from disciplines that included early childhood education, developmental psychology, political science, economics, and communications; and who are experts on practice in countries from around the globe. Together, via task forces, working groups, and meetings, a new vision for early care and education was crafted. This vision, and the seminal thinking that led to it, are presented in *Reinventing Early Care and Education*.

A New Approach to a Quality System

Reinventing Early Care and Education takes an analytical approach to creating a comprehensive vision of a quality early care and education system. It strives to address historical, social, and political factors that have led to and perpetuated the quality problem. We ask: Why does this situation exist and what can be done about it? In response, the volume scrutinizes some of the accepted wisdom of the early care and education field, as it broadens the dialogue by using knowledge from other fields, disciplines, and nations as a springboard for a fresh conceptualization of quality in early care and education. Designed to take a bird's eye view of the field and to make recommendations for its improvement, *Reinventing Early Care and Education* synthesizes and integrates a range of perspectives, ideas, and approaches into a cohesive vision for a quality early care and education system.

Chapter One provides the context for the volume. Kagan, Cohen, and Neuman set the stage, painting a backdrop of the history of the field and the nature of the dilemmas, against which any reform must be considered.

In Part One, a range of perspectives on quality are advanced. This section begins from the premise that our conventional definitions of quality have been too narrow and have omitted key voices. Larner (Chapter Two) begins by focusing on how parents think, learn, and make decisions about early care and education for their young children, as well as on how parents themselves experience programs. She recommends what should be done for early care and education to work better for families and to reflect more closely parents' ideas about quality. In Chapter Three, Phillips continues to expand conceptions of quality, exploring how the *context* in which quality is defined and implemented and *who* does the defining and implementing both color the definitions. She concludes that too often quality has been considered a static construct and suggests that it be regarded as a process, closely aligned with continuity and social equity. Bush and Phillips (Chapter Four) extend the discussion by drawing from international conceptions of quality. They review a range of approaches to quality from across the globe and consider what the United States can learn. In Chapter Five, Cohen and Pompa present multicultural conceptions of quality, suggesting the need for universal goals for child outcomes, but also the necessity for staff practices to be tailored to respond to multicultural variation.

Whereas Part One heralds a clarion call to broaden the definition of quality for programs, Part Two extends the conception of quality to embrace elements of the infrastructure. Part Two suggests that a quality early care and education system must include the essential functions of the infrastructure, such as licensing, training, regulation, governance, and funding and financing. Each chapter discusses selected elements of the infrastructure. Mitchell (Chapter Six) provides a comparative analysis of licensing, preparation systems, and credentialing in eight occupations and professions in the United States. She concludes that an individual license for early childhood professionals could greatly enhance quality in the field. In Chapter Seven, Pritchard examines approaches being used in other nations to train early care and education workers, concluding that more coherence, accessibility, and rigor are needed in the training of staff in this country. Presenting a set of alternatives to traditional regulation, Scurria (Chapter Eight) considers the experiences in a range of fields in the United States and suggests that the regulation of early care and education would benefit if it moved from a "command-and-control" approach to one that uses incentives to motivate regulatory compliance. In Chapter Nine, Gormley discusses how early care and education might be governed and funded, delineating distinct roles for localities, states, and the federal government. Gerry (Chapter Ten) reviews the principles of how children's services are currently funded in this country, poses a set of alternatives for funding a quality early care and education system, and explores the pros and cons of different options. In Chapter Eleven, Miller targets family child care and discusses how several components of the infrastructure—including training, regulation, and funding—can best promote quality in these programs. Taken together, these chapters suggest that though much attention has been paid to programs, there is an urgent need to commandeer support for the infrastructure because the actual quality of programs is contingent on the quality of that infrastructure.

Turning from discussions of the quality of programs and the infrastructure, Part Three acknowledges that the reforms called for in Parts One and Two will demand significant alteration of the national commitment to and investment in young children. Social-change efforts in several fields are explored, with the goal of extracting lessons for early care and education. In Chapter Twelve, Bonk and Wiley discuss the role of the media and mass communications in affecting policy and social change. They suggest ways that early care and education might harness the power of the media to commandeer support for a quality system. Howard (Chapter Thirteen) turns to a discussion of how citizens can accelerate social change by taking advantage of opportunities for the public influence of policy making set forth in the U.S. Constitution. In Chapter Fourteen, Cortés outlines how entire communities can mobilize for change, relating concrete examples from the experience of the Industrial Areas Foundation. Lieberman, Wood, and Falk (Chapter Fifteen) present a panorama of educational reform, discussing how schools can change. This discussion reviews some of the difficulties of changing institutions as well as some of the strategies that have been successful. Finally, few social reforms have been as broad-based and successful in this country as the policies that created a system to serve children with disabilities and their families. In Chapter Sixteen, Turnbull and Turnbull discuss the evolution of special education legislation, addressing the role of parents and courts in social reform. Each of the chapters in this section considers the ingredients necessary for broad-based social change and explores the implications for early care and education.

Combining the lessons concerning program quality, infrastructure quality, and effective change strategies, Part Four presents a vision for quality early care and education programs and infrastructure that would meet the needs of children, families, and the nation (Chapter Seventeen). In Chapter Eighteen, the process of change as well as the players to be involved are discussed. In these chapters, Kagan and Cohen distill the ideas presented earlier in the volume, offering specific recommendations for the construction of a quality early care and education system and for the allocation of responsibility. Recognizing the challenges inherent in such fundamental change, the year 2010 is the target. The consolidation of ideas is bold and complex; it is designed to be provocative. Many of the ideas presented are carefully delineated; others need more study. All need more debate and discussion. This volume, though marking the end of the *Quality 2000* initiative, denotes the beginning of a long process of change.

The editors would like to dedicate *Reinventing Early Care and Education* to our wonderful colleagues who have been willing to travel the *Quality 2000* journey with us and with whom we will continue to work for a quality early care and education system. We wish to thank our funders and friends—Michael Levine and Vivien Stewart of the Carnegie Corporation of New York, Valora Washington of the W. K. Kellogg Foundation, Deanna Gomby of the David and Lucile Packard Foundation, and Stacie Goffin of the Ewing Marion Kauffman Foundation. Without their vision and faith, the project would not have been possible. We owe a debt of gratitude to Deborah Phillips, whose inspiration and conceptualization during the early stages of *Quality 2000* helped lay a solid foundation. We also thank Rima Shore for her way with words and her insightful conceptual support. We thank our colleagues at Yale who have put much time and effort into making this project a reality. Special thanks to Jane Murray for her patience and tact and to

Katherine Scurria for her thoughtful analyses. In the course of editing a volume, the work of one or two people always stands out; this case is no exception. We would like to thank Michelle Neuman and Eliza Pritchard for their unending assistance in editing the material in this volume. With tenacity, care, and the highest standards, they have paid attention to content and details, and their excitement and dedication kept us fresh. Finally, we wish to thank our families, whose patience and insights have nourished our spirits.

New Haven, Connecticut   SHARON L. KAGAN
September 1996   NANCY E. COHEN

References

Cost, Quality & Child Outcomes Study Team. (1995). *Cost, quality and child outcomes in child care centers.* Denver: Department of Economics, University of Colorado.

Galinsky, E., Howes, C., Kontos, S., & Shinn, M. (1994). *The study of children in family child care and relative care: Highlights of findings.* New York: Families and Work Institute.

Gardner, S. (1990). Failure by fragmentation. *Equity and Choice, 6*(2), 4–12.

Hayes, C. D., Palmer, J. L., & Zaslow, M. (Eds.). (1990). *Who cares for America's children? Child care policy for the 1990s.* Report of the Panel on Child Care Policy, Committee on Child Development Research and Public Policy, National Research Council. Washington, D.C.: National Academy Press.

Hofferth, S. L., Brayfield, A., Deich, S. G., & Holcomb, P. (1991). *The national child care survey 1990.* Washington, D.C.: Urban Institute.

Kisker, E. E., Hofferth, S. L., Phillips, D., & Farquhar, E. (1991). *A profile of child care settings: Early education and care in 1990.* Washington, D.C.: U.S. Department of Education.

Phillips, D., & Howes, C. (1987). Indicators of quality in child care: Review of the research. In D. Phillips (Ed.), *Quality in child care: What does the research tell us?* Research monograph of the National Association for the Education of Young Children, Vol. 1. Washington, D.C.: National Association for the Education of Young Children.

U.S. Department of Education, National Center for Education Statistics. (1995). *National household education survey.* Washington, D.C.: U.S. Department of Education.

The Editors

Sharon L. Kagan, senior associate at the Bush Center in Child Development and Social Policy, Yale University, is recognized nationally and internationally for her work related to the care and education of young children and their families. She is a frequent consultant to the White House, Congress, the National Governor's Association, the U.S. Departments of Education and Health and Human Services, and numerous national foundations, corporations, and professional associations. Formerly chair of the Family Resource Coalition board of directors, and a member of the governing board of the National Association for the Education of Young Children (NAEYC), President Clinton's education transition team, and National Commissions on Head Start and Chapter I, Kagan has received numerous awards, among them an honorary doctoral degree from Wheelock College and the Distinguished Alumna Award from Teachers College, Columbia University. She received her bachelor's degree from the University of Michigan, a master's degree from Johns Hopkins University, and a doctorate from Teachers College, Columbia University.

Presently, Kagan serves on more than forty national boards and panels. A prolific author, she has written more than one hundred publications, including authoring or editing ten volumes and guest editing numerous journals. In these, Kagan has investigated such issues as policy development for children and families, family support, early childhood pedagogy, strategies for collaboration and service integration, and the evaluation of social programs. Augmenting her scholarship with field work, she has been a Head Start teacher and director, a fellow in the U.S. Senate, an administrator in the public schools, and director of the New York City Mayor's Office of Early Childhood Education.

Nancy E. Cohen was a research associate at the Bush Center in Child Development and Social Policy at Yale University during the writing and editing of this volume. She has participated in and researched the implementation, dissemination, replication, and institutionalization of innovative programs and infrastructure services for young children and their families. She has studied and evaluated a variety of initiatives, including community-based family support programs, training and accreditation programs for family child care providers, consumer education for parents, and projects implemented by volunteers to improve the quality of early care and education. In addition, her writing on early care and education policy and infrastructure has appeared in several edited volumes and journals. Cohen is currently a doctoral student in clinical and developmental psychology at the University of California at Berkeley, studying parenting, family functioning, and couple development. She received her bachelor's degree in social anthropology from Harvard University in 1988, where she studied parenting and family functioning cross-culturally.

The Contributors

Kathy Bonk is the founder and executive director of the Communications Consortium Media Center (CCMC), a nonprofit media group based in Washington, D.C., that specializes in developing communications strategies for policy change. CCMC works with numerous foundations that specialize in reinforcing the child welfare system. Bonk is on the advisory board of the Harvard Divinity School's Center for the Study of Values in Public Life, and the national boards of the National Women's Hall of Fame in Seneca Falls, New York; the International Women's Center in Moscow; and Women, Men, and Media, a project of the School of Journalism, University of Southern California. She was awarded a W. K. Kellogg Foundation Leadership Fellowship in 1989. She received her bachelor's degree from the University of Pittsburgh in 1973.

Jennifer Bush is a freelance writer in northern California. She has contributed to *The Washington Post* and worked as a staff reporter at a daily newspaper in central California. She received her bachelor's degree in English from Wesleyan University in 1987, and has completed graduate course work focusing on child care and social policy at Georgetown University's Graduate Public Policy Program.

Ernesto Cortés, Jr., is the Southwest regional director of the Industrial Areas Foundation and the director of the Texas Interfaith Education Fund, an organization that provides leadership training and technical support to the Southwest Industrial Areas Foundation network. Cortés is recognized nationally for his work in community organizing, including being named a MacArthur Foundation Fellow in 1984. He serves on several national committees for education reform, and his work has been highlighted in many national publications. He received his bachelor's degree in English and economics from Texas A&M University in 1963. He did graduate work in economics at the University of Texas in Austin, but left to pursue his interest in community organizing.

Beverly Falk is associate director for research at the National Center for Restructuring Education, Schools and Teaching (NCREST) at Teachers College, Columbia University. She has taught in settings from early childhood through graduate education, and currently teaches at Teachers College and City College of New York. She has been the director of an early childhood center, the founding principal of a public elementary school, a program coordinator, and a consultant for several school districts; and she has been a speaker at numerous conferences and workshops. Falk's present work focuses on supporting learner-centered teaching practices through authentic assessment design and development. She is currently involved in helping the state of New York redesign its curriculum and assessment system. She is coauthor, with Linda Darling-Hammond and Jacqueline Ancess, of the recently released book, *Authentic Assessment in Action* (1995), and is the author of several other articles and monographs about learner-centered education reform initiatives. She received a bachelor's degree from Sarah Lawrence College in 1970, a master's degree in education from City College of New York in 1975, and a doctorate in education from Teachers College, Columbia University, in 1993.

Martin H. Gerry is the founding director of the Center for the Study of Family, Neighborhood and Community Policy at the University of Kansas at Lawrence. He holds a university appointment as a senior research professor and serves as a member of the faculties of the University's Law School and School of Education. Gerry has served as the executive director of the Austin Project at the L.B.J. School of Public Affairs, University of Texas at Austin. He was formerly the assistant secretary for planning and evaluation of the U.S. Department of Health and Human Services. Gerry received his bachelor's degree in English literature in 1964 and his law degree in 1967 from Stanford University. He is the author of numerous monographs, articles, and reports.

William T. Gormley, Jr., is a professor of government and public policy at Georgetown University. He received his bachelor's degree in political science from the University of Pittsburgh in 1972 and his doctorate in political science from the University of North Carolina at Chapel Hill in 1976. He taught for ten years at the University of Wisconsin at Madison prior to joining the Georgetown faculty. He is the author of several books, including *Taming the Bureaucracy: Muscles, Prayers, and Other Strategies* (1989), which won the Louis Brownlow Book Award from the National Academy of Public Administration. His latest book is *Everybody's Children: Child Care as a Public Problem* (1995).

Christopher Howard is an assistant professor of government at the College of William and Mary and also teaches in the college's Thomas Jefferson Program in Public Policy. He received his bachelor's degree in history from Duke University in 1983, his master's degree in 1990 and his doctorate in 1993, both in political science, from the Massachusetts Institute of Technology. He has published in the *American Political Science Review, Journal of Policy History, Political Science Quarterly,* and *Public Administration Review.* His forthcoming book concerning tax incentives as social policy will be published by Princeton University Press.

Mary Larner is a policy analyst and editor at The Center for the Future of Children, The David and Lucile Packard Foundation. She develops and edits issues for the center's journal, the *Future of Children,* which summarizes knowledge relating to the well-being of children for policy makers. Previously at the National Center for Children in Poverty, Columbia University, she studied child care issues that face low-income families. After receiving a bachelor's degree in French literature from Swarthmore College in 1972, she began working in child care and family support programs. She completed a master's degree in child study at Tufts University in 1976, and received a doctorate in human development and family studies from Cornell University in 1985. She has coauthored two books and several reports and articles concerning programs for children and families, including most recently *Linking Family Support and Early Childhood Programs* (1995), *In the Neighborhood:*

Programs That Strengthen Family Day Care for Low-Income Families (1994), and *Fair Start for Children: Lessons Learned from Seven Demonstration Projects* (1992).

Ann Lieberman is professor and codirector of the National Center for Restructuring Education, Schools and Teaching at Teachers College, Columbia University. She is currently chair of the Program Committee of the American Educational Research Association (AERA), for which she served as president in 1992. She is widely known for her work in the areas of teacher leadership and development, collaborative research, school-university partnerships, educational reform networks, and schools in the process of change. She is currently researching educational reform networks. She has written numerous books and articles on teacher development and school change. Her recent books include *Building a Professional Culture in Schools* (1988); *Staff Development for the 90's: New Demands, New Realities, New Perspectives* (with Lynne Miller) (1992); and *The Work of Restructuring Schools* (1995). Her publications represent her ongoing work in studying and making accessible to the field the changing body of knowledge on organizing for school restructuring, as well as the effects and new social realities these changes present to teachers. Lieberman received her bachelor's degree in English literature from the University of California, Los Angeles, in 1957, a master's degree in educational psychology from California State University, Northridge, in 1966, and a doctorate from the University of California, Los Angeles, in the sociology of education in 1969.

Shelby H. Miller is an independent consultant to foundations and to national and statewide nonprofit organizations. She specializes in early childhood and adolescent program and policy development, program evaluation, and long-range planning. From 1986 to 1991, she was the program officer at the Ford Foundation, responsible for grant making in early childhood development and related services and policies. Miller received her bachelor's degree in psychology from Smith College in 1975 and her master's degree in child study from Tufts University in 1977. She has completed all but the dissertation requirements for her doctorate in developmental psychology at Emory University.

Anne Mitchell has been the president of Early Childhood Policy Research, an independent consulting firm specializing in policy research and planning for government, foundations, and national nonprofit organizations, since 1991. Previously, she was associate dean of the Research Division at Bank Street College of Education in New York City. She founded the college's graduate program in Early Childhood Leadership and has been the director of child care centers in Massachusetts and Vermont. She received her bachelor's degree in astronomy from Wellesley College in 1972 and her master's degree in educational leadership from Bank Street College of Education in 1988.

Michelle J. Neuman is a research assistant at the Bush Center in Child Development and Social Policy at Yale University. Her research has focused on issues related to children and families, including leadership in early care and education, child care policies for low-income working families, education of homeless children and adolescents, and government programs for children and families in France. In 1995, she received a bachelor's degree from the Woodrow Wilson School of Public and International Affairs, Princeton University, where she also received a certificate in French language and culture. Her senior thesis on lessons for the United States from French family policy was awarded the Senateur Andre Maman and Woodrow Wilson School prizes.

Deborah Phillips is currently director of the Board on Children and Families of the National Research Council's Commission on Social and Behavioral Sciences at the Institute of Medicine. Prior to this, she was an associate professor of psychology at the University of Virginia. As a congressional science fellow of the Society for Research in Child Development, she served as an analyst at the Congressional Budget Office and on the personal staff of Congressman George Miller. She has also been a midcareer fellow at the Bush Center in Child Development and Social Policy, Yale University, and was the first director of the Child Care Information Service of the National Association for the Education of Young Children (NAEYC). A member of numerous task forces and advisory groups that address child and family policy issues, Phillips has continued to focus her research on child care quality. She received her bachelor's degree in psychology from Stanford University in 1975, her master's degree in developmental psychology from Yale University in 1978, and her doctorate in developmental psychology from Yale University in 1981.

Delia Pompa is director of the U.S. Department of Education, Office of Bilingual Education and Minority Languages Affairs (OBEMLA). She has also been director of education and adolescent pregnancy prevention and youth development for the Children's Defense Fund; the principal of an educational consultation firm, Pompa and Associates, for which she conducted work in policy and program development for universities, educational agencies, and nonprofit organizations; and a member of the Stanford Working Group, the National Clearing House for Bilingual Education Advisory Panel, the New Standards Project, and the National Board for Professional Teaching Standards Committee on English as a New Language. Locally she has been the executive director for bilingual programs and early childhood education for the Houston Independent School District, as well as a Title VII Fellow, a bilingual kindergarten teacher, and a Title VII teacher-trainer. She received a bachelor's degree in sociology and early childhood education from Trinity University in San Antonio in 1972 and a master's degree in early childhood education from the University of Texas at San Antonio in 1974, and she has completed work toward a doctorate at the University of Houston.

Eliza Pritchard recently served as a research assistant at the Bush Center in Child Development and Social Policy, Yale University. In her work and writing, she has focused on service integration, international child care systems, infrastructure development in early care and education, and social change. She received a bachelor's degree in English from Wesleyan University in 1993.

Katherine L. Scurria practices law as an associate at Simpson Thacher & Bartlett in New York. She received her bachelor's degree in history from Princeton University in 1988, where she was awarded the C. O. Joline Prize in American history, and her juris doctor from Harvard Law School in 1992. Scurria has been a teaching fellow at Harvard University and a postdoctoral associate at Yale

University. Her professional interests are focused on education, government roles, public-private ventures, and not-for-profit issues.

Ann P. Turnbull is the codirector of the Beach Center on Families and Disability and a professor in the Department of Special Education, University of Kansas. Her research focuses on family systems and family-centered services. She has been the principal investigator on more than twenty federally funded research grants, and has authored twelve books and more than one hundred articles, chapters, and monographs. In 1988, she was a Joseph P. Kennedy, Jr., policy fellow working with the U.S. House of Representatives Select Committee on Children, Youth, and Families. In 1990, she received the Rose Fitzgerald Kennedy Leadership Award. She has served in leadership positions in professional and family organizations. She received her bachelor's degree in education from the University of Georgia in 1968, her master's degree in special education from Auburn University in 1971, and her doctorate in education from the University of Alabama in 1972, in the field of special education–mental retardation.

H. Rutherford Turnbull is the codirector of the Beach Center on Families and Disability and a professor of special education and courtesy professor of law at the University of Kansas. He concentrates his research and training in special education law and policy, mental disability law and policy, public policy analysis, and ethics as related to disability policy and service provision. He has been "of counsel" on amicus briefs in two disability cases heard by the U.S. Supreme Court, has authored and drafted North Carolina's special education and limited guardianship laws, has drafted the Assistive Technology for Individuals with Disabilities Act of 1988, and has testified before the U.S. Civil Rights Commission and the North Carolina and Kansas legislatures on disability policy and law. He received his bachelor's degree in political science from Johns Hopkins University in 1959, his bachelor of law–juris doctor degree from the University of Maryland Law School in 1964, and his master of law from Harvard University Law School in 1969.

Meredith Wiley has extensive experience in political campaign planning and communications. She is director of strategic planning and communications for Focus on Parenting, a nonprofit institute based in Portland, Oregon. She is coauthor of a book to be published in 1997 that shows links between maltreatment during the first thirty-three months of life and growth imbalance. She was a consultant to the School of Journalism, Columbia University on design and development of the Prudential Fellowship on Children and News. As chief of staff to the Oregon speaker of the house, she ran a thirty-person task force, which made recommendations for redesigning the state social service system to create more preventive, integrated, and acceptable services for children and families. She received a master's degree in public administration from John F. Kennedy School of Government, Harvard University, in 1993 and a law degree from Willimatt University in Salem, Oregon, in 1980.

Diane Wood is an assistant professor at the Institute for Educational Transformation, George Mason University. After working for twenty years in schools, she now teaches in a master's program for practicing teachers. Her research interests include building collaborative cultures in schools, networks, and electronic conferences, and teaching narratives as sources of faculty development. She received a bachelor's degree in education from the University of Nebraska, Omaha, in 1973, a master's degree in English from the University of Nebraska, Omaha, in 1982, and a doctorate in education from Teachers College, Columbia University in 1996.

Reinventing Early Care and Education

Chapter One

Introduction

The Changing Context of American Early Care and Education

Sharon L. Kagan
Nancy E. Cohen
Michelle J. Neuman

> *Of all the civil rights for which the world has struggled*
> *and fought for 5,000 years, the right to learn is*
> *undoubtedly the most fundamental.*
> —W.E.B. Du Bois (1970)

The world approaches the year 2000 amidst the recognition that we are on the cusp of a profoundly new era. Long-held conventional beliefs are being challenged; new knowledge surfaces daily; and major reforms—be they in business, technology, or human services—abound. Today, America is the preeminent world power; tomorrow, perhaps a cog in the wheel of a new global economy. Yesterday, we were a land of hope and optimism; today, the lives of many seem stagnant, and we remain a nation fragmented by race and inequality of opportunity. Yesterday, we were a land that took pride in our government; today, we denigrate government as intrusive, cumbersome, and inefficient, and we are skeptical of public investments in children, unless they are our own.

Not mere sentimental observations, these developments represent major shifts in how we define our commitments, how we determine our national and personal priorities in general, and how we do so with respect to young children and families in particular. Indeed, these trends represent a changed social context. It is this new context that we examine in this chapter.

Quality Matters

In past eras, America was committed to production—fast, efficient, and plentiful. The assembly line and the mentality that surrounded it—disengagement and routinization—prevailed. Quality was seen more as a luxury than a necessity, merely a handmaiden to quantity. With the advent of postmodern methods of communication and transportation, combined with the emergence of a global market and global competition, a secondary emphasis on quality is no longer sufficient or acceptable (Naisbitt, 1982). Quality matters, and it matters a lot. On the heels of this realization, quality-enhancement efforts are sweeping through U.S. business and industry, bringing with them revitalized commitments to workers, to collaboration, and to a new culture of quality.

Those concerned with human services in general, and with young children in particular, are seeing similar developments. Although the need for human services has reached an all-time high, it is clear that human services are not of sufficient quality to meet these needs. Task forces, commissions, and think tanks are addressing quality in the human services, and new approaches are emerging that realign structures, incentives, and relationships (Dunst, 1995; Farrow & Bruner, 1993; Gardner, 1992; Wynn, Costello, Halpern, & Richman, 1994).

At the same time, new knowledge regarding the quality of early care and education—the out-of-home programs used by young children—has emerged. We know that young children are in many types of programs—child care centers, Head Start, preschools, nursery schools, and family child care. Moreover, we have learned that the quality of these programs is important to the cognitive and socioemotional development of all young children (Cost, Quality & Child Outcomes Study Team, 1995). Children who develop reasoning and problem-solving skills within a quality early care and education environment are likely to be more cooperative and considerate of others and to have better self-esteem. Many of these positive effects linger and contribute to children's increased cognitive abilities, positive classroom-learning behaviors, long-term school success, and even improved likelihood of long-term social and economic self-sufficiency (Phillips, 1995; Poersch, Adams, & Sandfort, 1994; Schweinhart & others, 1993). On the other hand, children attending lower-quality programs are more likely to encounter difficulties with language and social development and are less likely to master age-appropriate behaviors or expected levels of development (Whitebook, Howes, & Phillips, 1989). Furthermore, there is some preliminary evidence that lower-quality programs are more harmful to the development of children from lower-income families than to their more advantaged peers, particularly with respect to prereading development (Peisner-Feinberg, 1995); quality may matter even more for low-income children (Phillips, 1995).

We have also learned that quality services for young children are rare, deteriorating, and inequitably distributed. Indeed, recent multisite studies indicate that the typical quality of programs, whether based in centers or homes, is substandard. The Cost, Quality & Child Outcomes Study (1995) found that 86 percent of the centers studied in four states were rated poor to mediocre in quality; specifically, seven in ten centers provided mediocre care, and one in eight actually threatened the health and safety of children. The quality of infant and toddler care seems to be particularly poor, with fully 40 percent of infant and toddler rooms in this study found to be endangering children's health and safety (Cost, Quality & Child Outcomes Study Team, 1995) and over 60 percent in a smaller study (Burchinal, Roberts, Nabors, & Bryant, 1995). Another recent multisite quality study found 89 percent of the family child care homes observed to be only inadequate to adequate and merely custodial in quality (Galinsky, Howes, Kontos, & Shinn, 1994).

Adding to this, there are serious concerns regarding quality deterioration and equity across family income. Data indicate that the quality of early care and education in the United States has seriously deteriorated over the past fifteen years (Hofferth, Brayfield, Deich, & Holcomb, 1991; Kisker, Hofferth, Phillips, & Farquhar, 1991; Whitebook, Howes, & Phillips, 1989). Children without access to either government or business subsidies and without a high family income are at particular risk of being in low-quality programs. Working-class and lower-middle-income families end up relying on poorer-quality programs (Hofferth, 1995; Phillips & others, 1994; Whitebook, Howes, & Phillips, 1993), as do low-income families without access to subsidies (Phillips, 1995). The combined crises of lack of quality and lack of equity make the early care and education challenge formidable.

Though the low quality of programs for young children from birth to age five is deeply disturbing, the even more rampant poor quality of programs for our youngest citizens—infants and toddlers—is particularly frightening. Indeed, increasing numbers of very young children are being cared for outside the home. More than half of mothers return to work within a year of their babies' births, and most of their children are being cared for by someone else for thirty or more hours per week (Hofferth, Brayfield, Deich, & Holcomb, 1991).

History Matters

The settlement of this nation had its origins in the unsettlement of Europe—the dissolution of a feudal economy and the rise of capitalism, the intellectual turbulence of the Renaissance and the Reformation, and the political turmoil of the Thirty Years' War and its aftermath (Cremin, 1977). Seeking refuge and innovation, pioneers came to this land with the hope of creating a democracy.

Ensconced early in this nation were values of industry, independence, and religious freedom and toleration, as well as the belief that the family had the lion's share of responsibility for nurturing and educating offspring. Social institutions—for all children and families—were of secondary importance. Indeed, with the exceptions of schools and libraries, other public (and to a lesser extent private) institutions rendered support only when families failed. Such history has profoundly shaped the delivery of social services in general, leaving a legacy of a deficit approach. The nation's social services systems are designed as institutions of last resort, to be used when personal and familial supports fail. Cast in this light, human services have come to be regarded as a necessary evil, the "gift" of a caring democracy to its less fortunate citizens.

Not immune from this history, early care and education in the United States is infused with these assumptions. The first infant schools were established in the early nineteenth century, with the mission of offering personal and moral lessons to the children of the indigent, providing what their parents could not or did not (Infant School Society of Boston, 1828). Later, during the depression of 1873–1877, public kindergartens were established for the children of the needy to provide nutrition, cleanliness, good health, and work habits (Ross, 1976). Child care continued on this track for many years, receiving federal attention and funding infusions during times of national crises such as the Great Depression and World War II.

Child care continues to be provided for the needy today, via public efforts that support children of the poor, infirm, and unemployed. In addition, child care serves the needs of working parents regardless of income. As such, child care is typically a full-day service operated in the private nonprofit, private for-profit, and public sectors. A second kind of support for young children takes the form of part-time services that are often associated with greater emphasis on early education. These services are funded by parents, schools, and community organizations. A third form of program, generally called comprehensive services, includes Head Start and strives to meet the educational and social service needs of children and their parents; comprehensive services tend to be part-day and publicly funded.

Operationally, these historic splits in types of programs have been fueled by varying legislative mandates, funding streams, regulatory standards, and administrative agencies. Rife with fragmentation, some programs fall under the jurisdiction of state departments of education, others are controlled by departments of health, and still others by departments of welfare or social services (Kagan, Goffin, Golub, & Pritchard, 1995). In reviewing federal subsidy programs, a recent U.S. General Accounting Office analysis found that different requirements produced serious discrepancies in who could participate and for how long (Ross, 1995). Taken together, ninety federal programs funding early care and education sit in eleven federal agencies and twenty offices (U.S. General Accounting Office, 1995b). The highly fragmented delivery system (U.S. Advisory Committee on Intergovernmental Relations, 1994) focuses more on the quantity and affordability of services than on their quality; programs compete for space, resources, and even children (Goodman & Brady, 1988; Sugarman, 1993; U.S. General Accounting Office, 1995a, 1995b). In a climate characterized by piecemeal attention to young children, the mere existence of services, not their excellence, has been considered enough.

Infrastructure Matters

Quality is not achieved easily or quickly. Fields and organizations that have pursued quality have devoted considerable time, energy, and other resources to discern what elements of an infrastructure are necessary, as well as how to secure durable commitments for supporting such infrastructure. For example, in education, the preparation and credentialing of teachers, the regulation of school facilities, the governance by school boards, and the funding by states and localities—components of the infrastructure that support quality in schools—have been given considerable attention in recent decades. In early care and education, by contrast, there has been much less attention to the infrastructure, though it is essential to supporting quality programs.

Specifically, a quality early care and education infrastructure would include the establishment of durable mechanisms to provide or carry out:

- Parent information and engagement
- Professional development
- Facility licensing, enforcement, and accreditation
- Funding and financing
- Governance

The following is a brief description of each component of the infrastructure:

Parent information and engagement—mechanisms to provide parents necessary information and to engage them purposefully in programs, services, and policy making (Cost, Quality & Child Outcomes Study Team, 1995; Galinsky, Howes, Kontos, & Shinn, 1994; Shinn & others, 1992)

Professional development—mechanisms to ensure that staff are qualified to work with young children, including requirements for preservice and ongoing training, a series of licenses and certificates, and a range of training and educational opportunities to meet and exceed requirements (Copple, 1990; Mitchell, 1995; Morgan & others, 1993)

Facility licensing, enforcement, and accreditation—mechanisms to ensure that facilities promote health, safety, and development, including facility licensing and enforcement, as well as program accreditation (Adams, 1990, 1995; Gormley, 1995)

Funding and financing—mechanisms to generate, distribute, and coordinate funds that adequately support the early care and education system

Governance—mechanisms to make decisions about what needs will be met, for whom, by whom, at what cost, and in what order; that create short- and long-term plans to implement decisions; that authorize and administer funds and may also raise funds; that create accountability to promote effectiveness; and that collect and utilize data for planning and evaluation

Government Involvement Is Important but Not a Panacea

Throughout the nation, citizens increasingly view government as part of the problem, not part of the solution. In a recent poll, 72 percent of the public thought that the federal government created more problems than it solved, and 57 percent believed this criticism also held true for state government (Hart & Teeter, 1995). Some believe that the problem is functional: by realigning management practices, streamlining procedures, devolving authority to states, and providing incentives tied to outcome achievement, government can function more effectively. For others, the problem is far more fundamental: government engagement is inherently intrusive, expensive, and expansive; it should be curtailed, leaving individual citizens free from interference. Whichever explanation one accepts, such disaffection with government is leading to numerous cuts and reforms.

Disaffection with government also reverberates through the early care and education community, with criticism emanating both from those who believe that government involvement has been too intrusive and from those who believe it has been insufficient. The former regard early care and education as a free-market commodity that should be left to the invisible hand of market competition and consumer choice for adjustment. This segment of the field is particularly concerned with the uneven application of regulations across the sectors.

Another segment of the early care and education field argues that government has a responsibility to provide basic protections for children and families in the form of regulations and financial investment. Indeed, there has been a long history of attempts to secure quality protections via national standards in federal legislation (Phillips & Zigler, 1987), efforts that were revived during the debate leading to the 1990 Child Care and Development Block Grant, but to little avail. Joining these concerns are criticisms that government does not use existing knowledge about child development to enhance the quality of early care and education services. For example, research has converged on several indicators of quality programs, defined in terms of their predictive significance for children's development, including practitioner training and education, salaries, child-to-staff ratios, and group size (Hayes, Palmer, & Zaslow, 1990; Phillips & Howes, 1987). Research has repeatedly linked the stringency of state facility licensing on these and other factors to the quality of care and education that is observed in regulated settings (Whitebook, Howes, & Phillips, 1989, 1993; Cost, Quality & Child Outcomes Study Team, 1995). Yet, this research has had little discernible impact on social policy.

As the nature of government involvement in early care and education is debated, few if any suggest that government alone can guarantee a quality system. The investment and support of parents, business, and community organizations are necessary for quality early care and education. Parents, for example, currently pay the bulk of early care and education costs, more than $17 billion in 1993 (Casper, 1995). Parents also play the consumer role, and all concerned benefit when they are engaged in their children's programs. Clearly, parents must be key partners in a quality early care and education system.

The business community has become increasingly involved in early care and education. Although corporate investments still benefit only the minority of employees, business efforts have identified best practices and quality-improvement models. In some cases, corporate investments in programs and the infrastructure (particularly in the development and maintenance of child care resource and referral agencies) have directly benefited entire communities (Committee for Economic Development, 1993). In less publicized efforts, the leaders in the business community have strived to make their workplaces family friendly—including part-time and flextime work, paid days to care for sick children, and supervisors who understand how to help employees balance work and family responsibilities (Galinsky, Friedman, & Hernandez, 1991). Investing in quality programs and infrastructure and making workplaces family friendly are key roles for business in a quality early care and education system.

In addition, community organizations, including houses of worship, United Ways, and volunteer and civic organizations, contribute funding and in-kind resources to early care and education (Cost, Quality & Child Outcomes Study Team, 1995). Their continued involvement is important both because the contributions make a difference for some children and parents and because these collaborations knit the fabric of strong communities.

The point is that government involvement in early care and education is necessary, but it is not a panacea. Early care and education must be a shared responsibility.

Paradoxes in Attitude Prevail

Mothers with young children are returning to work in ever increasing numbers, yet the country remains ambivalent about the role of women and who should care for young children. On the one hand, family life and home are revered. The primacy and privacy of the mother's traditional domain—the home—is upheld as the ideal. So strong is this belief that many Americans still believe—despite research to the contrary (Phillips & Howes, 1987)—that the development of children is damaged by early care and education programs. Full-time motherhood is venerated.

Simultaneously—and contradictorily—mothering and nurturing are not valued roles. Linked to the devaluation of women's work, there is a widespread perception that mothering and child rearing are simple, elemental tasks requiring little knowledge, intellect, or skill (Powell, 1989; Grumet, 1988). The job of mothering is denigrated.

These paradoxical beliefs affect how the populace regards (or "ill-regards") those who work in early care and education. Seldom viewed as professionals, early care and education staff are undervalued, underpaid, and overworked. Indeed, early care and education staff subsidize the early care and education market in the form of forgone wages and benefits. For example, given their levels of experience and education, teachers in early care and education centers would earn an average of $5,238 more a year in other fields, and assistant teachers would earn an average of $3,582 more annually (Cost, Quality & Child Outcomes Study Team, 1995). Bearing this burden, early childhood workers seldom have the financial means or incentives to pursue training. They frequently leave their jobs for better-paying employment, thereby fueling staff turnover and the reputation of early care and education staff as nonprofessionals.

With both mothering and early care and education devalued by our society, one might expect sympathy between mothers and caregivers. Though this may sometimes be the case, it is also true that many practitioners do not actively approve of mothers leaving their children to go to work and disapprove of the parenting skills of the parents for whose children they care. In turn, it is not uncommon for practitioners to feel unsupported by the parents of the children with whom they work (Galinsky, 1990). In addition, parents and practitioners often have different expectations about the need for their communication. Whereas many parents do not think that it is necessary to keep staff informed about family issues, staff do feel it is important. Low levels of parent-practitioner communication are the norm (Powell, 1989).

Such chasms fuel tensions between parents and practitioners, probably adding to the separation anxiety many mothers experience when leaving their children in the care of another. In essence, Americans seem to resent early care and education staff for usurping mothers' nurturing roles and moving the care and education of young children out of the home, and early care and education staff resent the mothers for leaving their children to go to work.

America's Children and Families Are Suffering

The state of American young children and their families is dismal. More than one out of every four children under six—approximately six million of the youngest Americans—lives in poverty. Over four million other young children are near poor, meaning that a total of more than ten million young children—44 percent—live in low-income families (National Center for Children in Poverty, 1994).

To understand this crisis better, it is important to examine the major demographic changes in the American family over the past decades—the increase in marital instability, the delay and decline of marriage, the increase in births outside of marriage, and the increase in maternal employment. Soaring numbers of single-parent families, reconstituted families, and working mothers dot the social landscape. Contemporary families look and behave differently than those of eras past. The traditional American family—married parents with the mother caring for children full-time—is no longer the norm.

Children are not faring well, in part due to changes in family structure and in part due to extensive economic and social dislocations in recent years. Children's well-being has declined as the percentages of children in poverty have soared. Low-income children are two times more likely than other children to die from birth defects and three times more likely to die from all causes combined (Children's Defense Fund, 1995). As economic hardship interferes with adequate human growth and development, low-income children are not the only ones suffering. Nearly half of all infants and toddlers face one or more major risk factors, (National Education Goals Panel, 1993) including the following:

- Nearly a quarter of all pregnant women in the United States receive little or no prenatal care, jeopardizing the healthy development of their young children.

- Increasing numbers of single-parent families, higher divorce rates, and less family and community support have left the parents of young children more isolated than ever before.
- Only half of infants and toddlers are routinely read to by their parents, and many parents do not engage in other activities to stimulate their young children's development.

Given this context, it is not surprising that 35 percent of American kindergarten children arrive at school unprepared to learn (Boyer, 1991). This country has failed to implement the knowledge of what matters for young children and their families to improve their well-being.

The Time for Change Is Now

Early care and education, along with other human services, sits at the vortex of the social, technological, and economic revolutions that are sweeping the nation. First and most prominent, increasing workforce participation by mothers with young children means that the number of children in nonparental care has and will likely continue to rise, with infants and toddlers constituting the fastest-growing subgroup of children in early care and education programs. More children in programs and the low quality of most programs means that increasing numbers of children are exposed to poor-quality care year after year. These factors accelerate the need for attention to young children now.

Second, as the global economy takes hold, politicians and business leaders—heretofore largely uninterested in young children—are voicing concern and demonstrating readiness for action. Facing an increasingly competitive global economic market, they are worried about economic productivity. Employee turnover, particularly the cost of training new employees, is an expensive proposition that has made worker retention and satisfaction an important issue. Given this climate, quality early care and education services have been advocated as a cost-effective approach to maintaining a stable, well-prepared workforce today—and preparing such a workforce for the future (Committee for Economic Development, 1993; Fernandez, 1986). Further, U.S. business and industry, striving for quality in their own organizations, recognize the need for emphasizing quality in early care and education.

Third, fueled by concerns of the business and political communities, national education reform now includes a focus on the early years. The first National Education Goal, that all children will start school ready to learn, which has been endorsed by all the governors and two presidents, has highlighted the important relationship between early care and education and later educational achievement. Due to this emphasis, more and more Americans are realizing that *all* programs for young children are about education. Early care and education professionals are taking the opportunity to illustrate the kind of programs from which young children benefit, emphasizing the multiple dimensions of children's readiness for school and the importance of providing quality services to address multiple developmental domains (Kagan, Moore, & Bredekamp, 1995).

Fourth, in part generated by the school readiness debate, there is growing understanding in the field of the urgent need for change. Early care and education administrators and practitioners are recognizing that as more children require early care and education, the current pressures on the field are mounting. The field, already characterized by high-turnover rates and poor and declining compensation, recognizes that the supply of qualified practitioners has diminished by crisis proportions. The field is also recognizing that early care and education programs are more alike than different and that a shared agenda for improving quality holds tremendous potential for impact.

Beyond receptivity to change, significant professional advances have provided concrete strategies for change, particularly in pedagogical and developmental areas. For example, the field has developed strong, widely recognized program and curricular models, including Head Start, developmentally appropriate practice, and accreditation standards emanating from the National Association for the Education of Young Children and the National Child Care Association for Family Child Care. Early childhood researchers have gained in-depth understanding of children's early years, identifying developmental milestones in the physical, emotional, social, and cognitive domains. In particular, the importance of early brain development is increasingly being understood (Carnegie Task Force on Meeting the Needs of Young Children, 1994).

Looking beyond individual children and programs, many in the early care and education field are now beginning to address the system. Comprehensive visions of what an early care and education system should include have been developed (Kamerman & Kahn, 1995; Sugarman, 1993), and systemic efforts to actualize such visions have been launched by a variety of national groups and state and local organizations.

Taken together, these lessons regarding quality, infrastructure, the roles of government, and the imminent need for change suggest that the lack of quality in early care and education programs cannot be attributed to a lack of knowledge about the status of quality or about how to provide higher-quality services. The problem is far more complex: it is the reflection of ingrained ideology, history, and practice. Without attention to the social, conceptual, organizational, and political structures, as well as to the deepseated values that have obstructed efforts to improve quality, the mere generation of additional knowledge will, in and of itself, not be a successful strategy for advancing a quality agenda. It is time to put our knowledge to work in new ways. This volume was designed to do just that.

References

Adams, G. (1990). *Who knows how safe? The status of state efforts to ensure quality child care.* Washington, D.C.: Children's Defense Fund.

Adams, G. (1995). *How safe? The status of state efforts to protect children in child care.* Washington, D.C.: Children's Defense Fund.

Boyer, E. (1991). *Ready to learn. A mandate for the nation.* Princeton, N.J.: Carnegie Foundation for the Advancement of Teaching.

Burchinal, M. R., Roberts, J. E., Nabors, L. A., & Bryant, D. M. (1995). *Quality of center child care and infant cognitive language development.* Unpublished manuscript. Chapel Hill, N.C.: Frank Porter Graham Child Development Institute, University of North Carolina.

Carnegie Task Force on Meeting the Needs of Young Children. (1994). *Starting points: Meeting the needs of our youngest children.* The report of the Carnegie Task Force on Meeting the Needs of Young Children. New York: Carnegie Corporation of New York.

Casper, L. M. (1995). What does it cost to mind our preschoolers? *Current population reports: Household economic studies*. Washington, D.C.: U.S. Department of Commerce. (P70–52).

Children's Defense Fund. (1995). *The state of America's children yearbook, 1995*. Washington, D.C.: Children's Defense Fund.

Committee for Economic Development. (1993). *Why child care matters: Preparing young children for a more productive America*. New York: Committee for Economic Development.

Copple, C. (1990). *Quality matters: Improving the professional development of the early childhood work force*. Washington, D.C.: National Institute for Early Childhood Professional Development.

Cost, Quality & Child Outcomes Study Team. (1995). *Cost, quality and child outcomes in child care centers*. Denver: Department of Economics, University of Colorado.

Cremin, L. (1977). *Traditions of American education*. New York: Basic Books.

Du Bois, W.E.B. (1970). The freedom to learn. In P. S. Foner (Ed.), *W.E.B. Du Bois Speaks!* New York: Pathfinder.

Dunst, C. (1995). *Key characteristics and features of community-based family support programs*. Chicago: Family Resource Coalition.

Farrow, F., & Bruner, C. (1993). *Getting to the bottom line: State and community strategies for financing comprehensive community service systems*. Falls Church, Va.: National Center for Service Integration.

Fernandez, J. (1986). *Child care and corporate productivity*. Lexington, Mass.: Heath.

Galinsky, E. (1990). Why are some parent/teacher partnerships clouded with difficulties? *Young Children, 45*(5), 2–3.

Galinsky, E., Friedman, D. E., & Hernandez, C. A. (1991). *The corporate reference guide to work-family programs*. New York: Families and Work Institute.

Galinsky, E., Howes, C., Kontos, S., & Shinn, M. (1994). *The study of children in family child care and relative care: Highlights of findings*. New York: Families and Work Institute.

Gardner, S. (1992). A commentary. *Serving children and families effectively: How the past can help chart the future*. Washington, D.C.: Education and Human Services Consortium.

Goodman, I. F., & Brady, J. P. (1988). *The challenge of coordination*. Newton, Mass.: Education Development Center.

Gormley, W. T. (1995). *Everybody's children: Child care as a public problem*. Washington, D.C.: Brookings Institution.

Grumet, M. R. (1988). *Bitter milk: Women and teaching*. Amherst, Mass.: University of Massachusetts Press.

Hart, P. D., & Teeter, R. M. (1995). *Survey of the role and effectiveness of government.* Survey conducted for the Council for Excellence in Government by the survey research firms of P. D. Hart & R. M. Teeter. Washington, D.C.: Council for Excellence in Government.

Hayes, C. D., Palmer, J. L., & Zaslow, M. (Eds.). (1990). *Who cares for America's children? Child care policy for the 1990s.* Report of the Panel on Child Care Policy, Committee on Child Development Research and Public Policy, National Research Council. Washington, D.C.: National Academy Press.

Hofferth, S. L. (1995). Caring for children at the poverty line. *Children and Youth Services Review, 17*(1/2), 1–31.

Hofferth, S. L., Brayfield, A., Deich, S. G., & Holcomb, P. (1991). *The national child care survey 1990.* Washington, D.C.: Urban Institute.

Infant School Society of Boston. (1828). *Constitution and by-laws.* Boston: T. R. Marvin.

Kagan, S. L., Goffin, S. G., Golub, S. A., & Pritchard, E. (1995). *Toward systemic reform: Service integration for young children and their families.* Falls Church, Va.: National Center for Service Integration.

Kagan, S. L., Moore, E., & Bredekamp, S. (Eds.). (1995). *Reconsidering children's early development and learning: Toward shared beliefs and vocabulary.* Washington, D.C.: National Education Goals Panel.

Kamerman, S. B., & Kahn, A. J. (1995). *Starting right: How America neglects its youngest children and what we can do about it.* New York: Oxford University Press.

Kisker, E. E., Hofferth, S. L., Phillips, D., & Farquhar, E. (1991). *A profile of child care settings: Early education and care in 1990.* Washington, D.C.: U.S. Department of Education.

Mitchell, A. (1995). *A proposal for licensing individuals who practice early care and education.* New Haven, Conn.: *Quality 2000,* Bush Center in Child Development and Social Policy, Yale University.

Morgan, G., & others. (1993). *Making a career of it: The state of the states report on career development in early care and education.* Boston: Center for Career Development in Early Care and Education, Wheelock College.

Naisbitt, J. (1982). *Megatrends.* New York: Warner Books.

National Center for Children in Poverty. (1994). *Young children in poverty: A statistical update.* New York: National Center for Children in Poverty.

National Education Goals Panel. (1993). *Building a nation of learners: The national education goals report: Executive summary.* Washington, D.C.: National Education Goals Panel.

Peisner-Feinberg, E. S. (1995). *Effects of child care on children by family income level: The costs, quality, and child outcomes in child care centers study.* Paper presented at a workshop sponsored by the Board on Children and Families, February 21, 1995. Chapel Hill: Department of Psychology, University of North Carolina.

Phillips, D. (Ed.). (1995). *Child care for low-income families: Summary of two workshops.* Washington, D.C.: National Academy Press.

Phillips, D., & Howes, C. (1987). Indicators of quality in child care: Review of the research. In D. Phillips (Ed.), *Quality in child care: What does the research tell us?* Research monograph of the National Association for the Education of Young Children, Vol. 1. Washington, D.C.: National Association for the Education of Young Children.

Phillips, D., & Zigler, E. (1987). The checkered history of child care regulation. In E. Rothkopf (Ed.), *Review of research on education: Vol. 14.* Washington, D.C.: American Educational Research Association.

Phillips, D., & others. (1994). Child care for children in poverty: Opportunity or inequity? *Child Development, 65,* 440–456.

Poersch, N., Adams, G., & Sandfort, J. (1994). *Child care and development: Key facts.* Washington, D.C.: Children's Defense Fund.

Powell, D. R. (1989). *Families and early childhood programs.* Washington, D.C.: National Association for the Education of Young Children.

Ross, E. D. (1976). *The kindergarten crusade: The establishment of preschool education in the United States.* Athens: Ohio University Press.

Ross, J. L. (1995). *Child care: Recipients face service gaps and supply shortages.* Testimony before Committee on Labor and Human Resources, U.S. Senate, March 1, 1995.

Schweinhart, L. J., & others. (1993). *Significant benefits: The High/Scope Perry preschool study through age 27.* Ypsilanti, Mich.: High/Scope Press.

Shinn, M., & others. (1992). *Correspondence between mothers' perceptions and observer ratings of quality in child care centers.* New York: Department of Psychology, New York University.

Sugarman, J. (1993). *Building local strategies for young children and their families.* Washington, D.C.: Center in Effective Services for Children.

U.S. Advisory Committee on Intergovernmental Relations. (1994). *Child care: The need for federal-state-local coordination.* Washington, D.C.: U.S. Advisory Committee on Intergovernmental Relations.

U.S. General Accounting Office. (1995a). *Early childhood centers: Services to prepare children for school often limited.* Washington, D.C.: U.S. General Accounting Office. (95–21).

U.S. General Accounting Office. (1995b). *Early childhood programs: Multiple programs and overlapping target groups.* Washington, D.C.: U.S. General Accounting Office (95–4FS).

Whitebook, M., Howes, C., & Phillips, D. (1989). *Who cares? Child care teachers and the quality of care in America: Final report of the national child care staffing study.* Oakland, Calif.: Child Care Employee Project.

Whitebook, M., Howes, C., & Phillips, D. (1993). *National child care staffing study revisited: Four years in the life of center-based child care.* Oakland, Calif.: Child Care Employee Project.

Wynn, J., Costello, J., Halpern, R., & Richman, H. (1994). *Children, families, and communities: A new approach to social services.* Chicago: Chapin Hall Center for Children at the University of Chicago.

Part One

Quality Programs
The Case for an Expanded Definition

Chapter Two

Parents' Perspectives on Quality in Early Care and Education

Mary Larner

Quality counts in early care and education—on that, parents and professionals agree. But who defines what quality is? The views of early childhood professionals have dominated discussions of what constitutes quality in programs for young children, whereas the voices of parents have gone mostly unheard. Yet, no one who is a parent or knows a parent who has used child care would suggest that parents are uninterested in the quality of care. Their perspectives are not integrated into prevailing definitions of quality because they have seldom been asked their views. In recent years, however, researchers have begun to examine the choices parents make and have asked them to explain their decisions. A small but growing body of literature on parent perspectives on child care quality now exists, and it provides the foundation for this chapter.

Parents and professionals share an interest in assuring that young children who spend time in child care are safe, nurtured,

Note: Portions of this text are reprinted by permission of the publishers from a chapter titled "Valuing Quality as a Parent," by Mary Larner and Deborah Phillips, in P. Moss and A. Pence (Eds.), *Valuing Quality in Early Childhood Education* (pp. 43–60). © 1994 by Teachers College Press, Columbia University, New York, and Paul Chapman Publishing Ltd, London. All rights reserved.

and given opportunities to learn and grow, yet the two groups of adults differ in their relationships to children and to child care programs and providers. Parents use child care programs for service and support; professionals work as child care providers, or train them, study them, or supervise their work. Parents focus on particular child care arrangements, avoiding those that might be harmful and finding one that will serve the family well; professionals more often focus on the quality of child care in general, working to improve it by using the tools of management, training, regulation, research, and advocacy.

Professional concepts of quality are designed to apply across a wide range of programs and may be used as research indicators, regulatory requirements, or accreditation criteria. To judge early care and education settings fairly, professionals need criteria that are concrete, objective, and quantifiable, such as child-to-adult ratios, group size, and staff training. These measures have been the foundation for decades of research on child care quality, and they are stressed in the regulatory standards that govern child care in most states (Hayes, Palmer, & Zaslow, 1990). These structural features of quality create the conditions in which positive interactions between adults and children can take place. Research has shown that child-to-adult ratios and the formal education of staff are associated with caregiving that is more developmentally appropriate, more sensitive, and less harsh. In turn, in settings where the caregiving is more supportive, children have more secure attachments, engage in more purposeful activity and complex play, and have higher language scores (Phillips, 1987).

For parents, it is their personal images of children's daily experiences, not objective standards that can be applied to many settings, that they use to define child care quality. Parents need only find one child care arrangement, but their stake in the quality of that arrangement is immense. Averages and probabilities are not reassuring to parents who must entrust their child's safety, happiness, and development to a single caregiver or program. Most parents have little control over the child care that is available to them, and some are painfully aware of how ignorant they are about the quality of the care they actually use. As one New Jersey parent said, "My children being babies, they can't really come home and tell me, well she did this and she did that. So I don't really know what's going on when I leave them" (Porter, 1991, p. 20).

Another important difference between parents and professionals is that parents experience child care as a multidimensional service that focuses on the child but affects the entire family. Arranging child care usually involves balancing requirements imposed by the family's schedule and resources with advantages offered to the child (Larner & Mitchell, 1992). Parents care about child care quality, but when they define it in relation to the particular needs of their own child and family, they often make choices that differ from those endorsed by professionals.

This chapter examines parents' views about child care and child care quality, intentionally using the term "child care" to refer to the regular arrangements parents make during periods when they cannot be with the child. (In addition, throughout this chapter, we refer to parents' "work" but mean to include commitments to education or job-training programs as well.) Part-day early care and education programs like preschool and Head Start are not discussed because they are designed and used primarily as an educational service for children. The chapter reviews what is known about how parents make decisions regarding child care—the initial decision to use nonparental care and the subsequent choice among child care settings. It focuses on the preferences families bring to this decision, explores the constraints that limit the options available to many families, and discusses tensions in the relationship between families and early childhood professionals. Finally, the chapter proposes steps that the professional child care community can take to learn more about parental perspectives on child care and to create an early care and education system that is more responsive to the interests and concerns of parents.

Parents as Child Care Consumers

Parents' judgments concerning child care quality are important not only for ethical reasons but also for practical and political reasons. Professionals have begun to acknowledge that parents are not only partners in programs that serve children but also consumers seeking to maximize their purchasing power in the child care marketplace. Indeed, marketplace pressures have brought the interests of professionals who seek resources to improve program quality into direct conflict with the interests of parent-consumers who cannot (or will not) pay more to purchase care. Awareness of these competing interests is reflected in professional references to the "trilemma" of problems that beset child care in the United States—availability, affordability, and quality. High-quality care exists but is expensive. Do parents care enough about quality to pay what it costs? Many cannot afford to. Recognizing that parents who have to work necessarily worry most about availability and affordability, many professionals have argued that employers and public agencies should invest in the child care system, so improvements in quality can be made without increasing the burden on parents (Eichman & others, 1992).

Awareness of the extent to which parents' choices diverge from professional recommendations has also increased as federal child care assistance programs for low-income families in the 1990s have begun to focus on parents as consumers and have sought to protect parent choice. In the past, most subsidies were paid directly to programs that offered care free to eligible children. Since the early 1990s, an increasing amount of subsidy funding has been provided in the form of vouchers that parents may use to secure any legal form of child care (Kagan & Neville, 1993). Such subsidy programs make the child care choices of low-income parents visible in a way they never were before, and they have forced the professional community to take parent values and needs more seriously.

The fresh interest in parents as child care consumers comes at the same time as research findings that illuminate how parents think about and choose child care have become available. The most significant is the National Child Care Survey of 1990, for which researchers interviewed a nationally representative sample of 4,392 parents of children under thirteen years of age to determine what child care arrangements they had made, what factors had influenced their choices, and how satisfied they were (Hofferth, Brayfield, Deich, & Holcomb, 1991). Because it included families who used all types of child care, this study provides a strong research basis for statements about the child care choices of American parents, and throughout this chapter it is referenced as "the national survey."

Deciding to Use Child Care

The first child care choice a family makes is the determination that the demands of work or education require that the child be cared for by someone other than the parents. Choices about parental versus out-of-home care force many parents to weigh the family's financial security against child-rearing and family values, especially given the lack of a strong policy on parental leave to enable parents to remain at home with a new infant (Bond & others, 1991). A 1986 study found that 55 percent of a sample of 1,302 mothers of preschool-aged children considered care by the parents to be the ideal for children from infancy through five years of age (Mason & Kuhlthau, 1989).

Along with the family's values and preferences, the practical availability of child care—the cost and suitability of nearby alternatives—affects decisions about parental employment. Research has shown that low-income parents, who earn relatively little and find it almost impossible to secure good child care they can afford, can become so discouraged by child care problems that they give up their employment and training plans and return to welfare (Meyers, 1993; Siegel & Loman, 1991).

Searching for Child Care

When the decision to use nonparental child care is made, most families begin their search by seeking advice from those close at hand—friends, relatives, and neighbors. The national survey indicated that 66 percent of parents who arranged child care outside the family relied on such informal sources of information about child care, whereas 13 percent used advertisements, and 9 percent turned to resource and referral agencies (Hofferth, Brayfield, Deich, & Holcomb, 1991). A similar pattern was found among parents living in low-income communities (Kisker, Maynard, Gordon, & Strain, 1989) and among parents of higher socioeconomic status (Powell & Eisenstadt, 1982). Child care experts may be seen as strangers who have a vested interest in promoting a particular form of child care, whereas friends and relatives may seem more likely to share the family's basic values and a primary interest in the well-being of the child and the family. Moreover, kin and friends are free to recommend or criticize child care options that they know from experience or by reputation, which community service organizations like resource and referral agencies do not currently do, to avoid liability and charges of favoritism.

Whatever sources of information they seek, many parents actively consider several child care alternatives. The national survey found that of the employed mothers using child care for children from birth to thirteen years of age, 43 percent seriously considered more than one type of child care—by a relative, a center, or a family child care provider, and nearly half investigated more than one provider of the same type (Hofferth, Brayfield, Deich, & Holcomb, 1991). Those parents spent an average of seven weeks searching for care, attempting to find options that fit the family's budget and work hours, to screen out those that might be untrustworthy, and to imagine how the child would fare in each setting. Despite the time spent on their search, few parents feel confident that they are informed consumers, able to make child care choices that will meet their requirements, expectations, and hopes (Zinsser, 1987).

Choices Among Child Care Settings

Whether or not they feel well informed, parents are the ones who must trust and invest in a particular child care arrangement. Most families' choices are constrained in some way: wealthy parents may be unable to arrange care with relatives, and middle- and low-income parents cannot afford many desirable programs. Nevertheless, one good way to examine parents' preferences and values is through the arrangements they make to place a child in a particular type of care and through their expressions of interest in changing from one type of care to another.

The national survey found that in families with an employed mother and a child under five, nearly half the children were cared for within the family network—28 percent by the parents themselves and 19 percent by relatives. Just over a fourth of the children were in center-based care, and almost a fifth were in family child care homes.

Assessing parents' satisfaction with their arrangements is more difficult. To a direct survey question, 96 percent of parents answered that they were satisfied or very satisfied. The national survey researchers also asked parents who were using child care whether they would now prefer a different type of care if there were no constraints on their choice. To that question, over one fourth of the reportedly satisfied parents said they would like to make a change (Hofferth, Brayfield, Deich, & Holcomb, 1991). When the question is posed that way, parents may find it easier to acknowledge doubts about their child care arrangements. Others may want a change because their child has outgrown a particular arrangement that was once satisfactory. The complex interplay of choice, satisfaction, and desire to change can be seen in the following description of parents' reactions to different types of child care.

Reliance on Relatives

When the employed mothers in the national survey were asked about the most important factor behind their choice of care, 22 percent responded that they preferred having a relative as a caregiver. Many parents believe that relative care is, next to parental care, the most appropriate and nurturing environment for children, especially for very young children. Relatives are trusted to look after the child with vigilance, attentiveness, and warmth, whereas strangers may seem potentially threatening. Care by relatives is often affordable as well. Although 36 percent of employed mothers in the national survey paid their relative caregivers, the amounts of money that changed hands were modest compared with the cost of care purchased in the open market (Hofferth, Brayfield, Deich, & Holcomb, 1991). Parents who paid for relative care in 1990 spent an average of $31 per week, compared with $45 per week for family child care and $53 per week for center-based care.

Despite the appeal of relative care, however, it is not available to everyone. Many parents do not have kin living nearby who are able or willing to offer child care. Moreover, relative care appears to work better for short periods of time than as a long-term, full-time child care solution. A study of Illinois welfare recipients who used child care revealed that informal arrangements were often unreliable, in part because the relatives or friends were likely to quit if they were offered other employment, became ill, or lost interest in child care (Siegel & Loman, 1991).

The national survey found that 27 percent of the parents using relative care would prefer another arrangement, perhaps because of its unreliability and perhaps because it offers a less structured learning environment than other forms of child care. Of course, families who can do so are likely to turn to relatives as a first child care option, especially for very young children. The desire to change could reflect problems in the relationship, or it could simply attest to the increasing appeal of formal child care settings as the child enters the preschool years.

Family Child Care

Family child care, broadly defined to include all care in the home of a nonrelative, is as prevalent as care by relatives and has recently been taken more seriously by professionals (Galinsky, Howes, Kontos, & Shinn, 1994; Kontos, 1992). Family child care has practical advantages for many parents. Child care homes are more likely than centers to accept children under one year of age: 96 percent of regulated homes and 85 percent of unregulated homes in a national sample reported that they serve infants, compared with just 55 percent of the center-based programs (Willer & others, 1991). Further, family child care providers are more likely than centers to care for children part-time, to offer hourly rates, and to take children who need care early and late in the day; 35 percent of the licensed providers in an Illinois sample cared for children after 6 P.M., compared with only 8 percent of the centers (Siegel & Loman, 1991).

Family child care appears to have two disadvantages in the eyes of parents—an uncertainty about its trustworthiness and a perception that it does not offer structured learning experiences. Mistrust is likely to be most salient at the outset, when the parent is trying to determine whether the provider will truly offer a safe environment for the child. One parent described how assertively she grilled the provider on whom she decided to rely: "I went all into her life, all into her business, you know. I asked her who lived in her house and who didn't live in her house. I asked her if she did drugs and everything" (Porter, 1991, p. 12). Once the parent feels confident about the safety and emotional warmth of the home, all may be well until the preschool years, when concerns about the child's preparation for school often make center environments seem preferable. In the national survey, 30 percent of the parents who used family child care said they would prefer to change to another form of care.

Child Care Centers

The most striking change in patterns of child care over the past twenty-five years has been parents' growing reliance on child care centers. Once children pass their third birthdays, many parents are eager for their youngsters to benefit from the social expectations and structured learning experiences that they believe centers are likely to provide. Center-based programs are often seen as an educational resource that complements what the parents can offer at home. It is worth noting, however, that the strong interest many parents have in instruction for their preschoolers can place them at odds with many of the early childhood professionals they encounter in centers, who often believe in child-directed learning and emphasize self-esteem, problem solving, and well-rounded development instead of academic instruction.

From the perspective of convenience for adults, centers have reliable, albeit rigid, schedules. Their predictability is welcomed by working parents whose hours coincide with a center's. Many anxious parents also feel reassured by the very institutionalism of the center environment, with its director's office and staff of busy teachers (Porter, 1991). For these and other reasons, 49 percent of the parents in the national survey who were not center users but were unhappy with their child care arrangement reported that they would prefer a center-based program.

Criteria That Guide Parents' Choices

What factors do parents weigh as they make these choices? The national survey asked parents two open-ended questions: "Why did you choose the [current arrangement] for your youngest child? What was the most important thing you considered?" (Hofferth, Brayfield, Deich, & Holcomb, 1991, p. 227). Interviewers then grouped the parents' responses into six categories—quality (including class size, provider warmth or training, curriculum, and the setting's safety and equipment); general preference for a relative; availability; cost; hours; and location. The parents most often mentioned factors that relate to the child's experience in child care. Fully 42 percent of employed mothers with a child under five stressed the quality of the arrangement, especially the characteristics of the caregiver. The next most prevalent response (given by 22 percent of employed mothers) was a general preference for care by a relative. Only 12 percent mentioned the location of the child care arrangement, and 10 percent cited reasonable cost as an important consideration.

A study of parents who used home-based child care (provided by family child care providers and relatives) asked parents to rate the importance of nineteen factors one might consider when judging the quality of child care (Galinsky, Howes, Kontos, & Shinn, 1994). These parents stressed safety, communication with the provider, cleanliness, the attention children receive, and the provider's warmth toward children. Factors related to adult needs, like cost and convenience, came near the middle of the ranking. Very similar patterns emerged in studies involving low-income families in California, Illinois, and New Jersey (Meyers, 1993; Porter, 1991; Siegel and Loman, 1991). Those parents gave top priority to safety and trust, closely followed by the quality of the care, described by the parents in phrases like "taking the time for each child," and "really caring about them and their well-being," and "teaching them" (Siegel and Loman, 1991, p. 15).

Role of Convenience

As mentioned above, when parents answer questions about the factors they consider when choosing child care, they seldom emphasize logistical factors like location and cost—even though these factors certainly drive their behavior. Social desirability is one reason: interview respondents tend to shade the truth in answering researchers' questions, either to please the questioners or to flatter themselves. Parents may also consider location and cost to be unavoidable constraints, rather than characteristics among which they actively choose. A third explanation is that the convenience factors play their part at the very start of the parents' decision-making process, when they define the set of options that can be considered at all. After all, why bother visiting a center that costs far more than you can afford to spend? Few parents are pleased that their choices must reflect not only the child's well-being but also the fit between a given arrangement and their financial resources and work obligations. Nevertheless, those factors influence child care choices and affect the ability of the parents to manage the demands they face as workers.

Attitudes Toward Regulation

The research on child care choices also indicates that parents pay relatively little attention to the structural indicators of quality that professionals often stress, such as regulatory status and caregiver training. Over 40 percent of the low-income parents in the Illinois study did not consider it important that their child was cared for by a provider with a license from the state (Siegel & Loman, 1991). Few parents understand where the boundary between unregulated care and regulated family child care is drawn. (In some states, anyone caring for even one unrelated child must be regulated; in other states, regulations do not apply until the home includes six or more unrelated children.) Parents more often realize that centers should be licensed, but some assume that any open center is licensed, or it would not be operating.

Although some parents believe that licensing may offer safety protections, they doubt that licensing has much to do with the positive interactions they want their children to have with caregivers. One parent commented, "Getting a license may be hard, but it doesn't mean you know any more about children than the lady next door" (EDK Associates, 1992, p. 9). In fact, at a time when budget cuts have slashed the capacity of state regulatory departments to monitor child care programs' compliance even with health and safety requirements, parents may be wise to place more weight on their own observations than on the presence or absence of a framed license on the wall.

Disregard for Training

Many parents are also skeptical about the importance of specialized child care training, explaining that "you can't teach someone to love children." Whereas professionals argue that training gives caregivers the skills that make it easier to keep loving groups of children all day long, parents hope to find one special person who "will care for my child the way I would."

However, as children grow older, their parents focus more on academic and social skills and place more stock in the expertise of specially trained caregivers or teachers. One parent commented, "If it's a little baby, I don't care if they have a degree in something. If they're going to hold that child and love it and nurture it, then that is good enough for me. But on the other hand, if I have a three- or four-year-old, then I want to know what kind of activities they're going to be doing" (EDK Associates, 1992, p. 10). This increasing shift in appreciation of professional credentials fits with parents' perceptions that programs for children of preschool age should be more like schools and less like homes.

Contextual Factors That Influence Choices

A variety of contextual factors (including the child's age and the family's cultural background and socioeconomic status) affect parents' beliefs about the experiences that are most important for their children, their attitudes toward work and family roles, and the supply of child care that is available to them. These factors also influence the choices those parents face in the child care market. For instance, center-based infant care and programs in languages other than English are scarce, and low-income families are unable even to consider many child care arrangements.

Children of Different Ages

The age of the child for whom care is needed is a critical determinant of the options that are available and of the characteristics of care that matter most to parents. The national survey found that only 14 percent of children under one year of age whose mothers are employed were in center-based care, whereas 43 percent of the children between three and four attended centers (Hofferth, Bray-field, Deich, & Holcomb, 1991). Center-based infant care is expensive and scarce, largely because of the child-to-adult ratios that are necessary to keep children safe. Moreover, many parents of children under three would prefer to be home with the child, and therefore they are likely to search for child care that is as similar to parental care as possible—care in the child's own home or another home setting that surrounds the child with the language, values, and foods that are present in the family's home. The national survey found that relatives cared for 22 percent of the infants whose mothers worked, and another 20 percent of infants in child care were in family child care homes.

Parents with children over three have the luxury of choosing from a wider variety of programs in homes and centers. They are also likely to view child care as an important educational opportunity for the child, a setting in which children become independent and learn social, verbal, and academic skills that will be needed in school. Many whose children spent their earliest years in home settings want to shift to a center or preschool as the child's third birthday nears. Even 30 percent of mothers in the national survey who were not employed enrolled their three- and four-year-old children in center-based programs, presumably believing that the programs offered beneficial learning experiences.

Families with Different Cultural Backgrounds

The influence of a family's cultural and ethnic values on its choice of and comfort with child care has only recently drawn the attention of researchers. Serious study of this area is long overdue, given the escalating diversity of the population of the United States. Twenty percent of the children enrolled in Head Start speak a language other than English (Kagan & Garcia, 1991). In California, a recent study of 434 child care centers revealed that 77 percent of the centers included at least one child who was not a fluent English speaker, and 40 percent of the teachers reported that they had difficulty communicating with parents with whom they did not share a common language (Chang, 1993).

The capacity of child care programs to provide culturally and linguistically appropriate care to the diverse children who now make up the child care population is uncertain. Cultural values influence the expectations of both parents and professionals for how such issues as infant care, discipline, and academic instruction will be handled. Parents and infant caregivers can easily come into conflict over infant caregiving practices, such as feeding, comforting, and toilet training (Gonzalez-Mena, 1993). Parents of older children often disagree with professionals about how children learn (Bredekamp & Willer, 1993; Stipek, Rosenblatt, & DiRocco, 1994): "Generally speaking, Black parents and providers are very committed to programs with strong discipline and control as well as heavy academics. . . . By contrast, typical White standards for developmentally appropriate child care programs would put far greater emphasis on exploration, freedom, and socialization" (Hill-Scott, 1989, p. 210).

It is perhaps not surprising that many parents avoid doing battle with their child care providers over these emotionally charged issues by looking, from the outset, for child care that is consistent with the family's values—relying on relatives or family child care providers who share the family's background or seeking center-based programs that explicitly espouse the family's orientation toward education.

Families Varying in Economic Resources

Family income determines the context in which parents make child care choices, perhaps more significantly than any other single factor. Its effect derives not from preferences and values but from the constraints that face low- and even middle-income families as they consider the type of child care they need (Larner & Mitchell, 1992). Child care costs are more consistent across neighborhoods of varying socioeconomic status than are, say, prices charged in restaurants. In a national poll taken in 1989, the Philip Morris Companies found that business executives reported paying an average of $244 per month for child care, whereas the single mothers polled paid $221 per month—a difference of only $23 per month (Harris & Associates, 1989). Forced to pay the same child care fees though they earn so much less, low-income families allocate an average of 25 percent of their household incomes for child care (Hofferth, Brayfield, Deich, & Holcomb, 1991). Economic pressures often force those families to take the least-expensive child care alternative they can find.

The jobs held by many low-income working mothers also pose problems for them when it comes to making child care arrangements. Low levels of education consign many to pink collar jobs in the service industries, where they are expected to work shifts that extend beyond the traditional work hours between 8 A.M. and 6 P.M. In one study of welfare mothers, close to 30 percent of the child care users needed care either before 6 A.M., after 7 P.M., or on weekends (Sonenstein & Wolf, 1991). When nonnegotiable adult requirements confront rigid child care policies, low-income parents are likely to stop working or drop out of training programs (Meyers, 1993).

Low-income families also tend to live in impoverished neighborhoods that cannot support an array of high-quality child care services—aside from Head Start or publicly funded child care programs. Although those programs typically offer excellent care to the children and families they serve, their capacity is limited and waiting lists are often long. The shift toward vouchers in the public subsidy programs that help low-income parents pay for child care has made the financial situation of many programs in poor neighborhoods even more precarious (Kagan & Neville, 1993). Previously, in many states, selected programs serving low-income children received guaranteed contracts from public agencies that gave them the financial security to plan investments in quality. Vouchers allow eligible parents to choose care in another neighborhood or in a friend's home, so they provide less stable funding streams to programs than do contracts. In many states and communities, a mix of vouchers and contracts appears to provide the flexibility many parents want and need and also assures the survival of selected programs in economically devastated neighborhoods.

Low-income parents recognize that their children often do not get the quality of care that they deserve, or need. Whereas surveys of the general population of employed mothers show that over 90 percent are very or mostly satisfied with their child care arrangements, only 70 percent of the welfare mothers in one study felt that way (Sonenstein & Wolf, 1991). One mother who received welfare and had to find child care when she began attending job training commented, "The care I can afford . . . is not up to my par" (Siegel

& Loman, 1991, p. 97). The values and aspirations of low-income parents are not different than those of more advantaged parents, but low-income parents face many more obstacles when they attempt to find satisfactory care.

The Experience of Using Child Care—as a Parent

The recent interest in parents' views of child care quality has focused heavily on the choice of what type of child care to use, but that is only the starting point of an ongoing relationship between the family and the child care provider or program. We know far less than we need to know about how that relationship develops over time. Several studies suggest that parents and child care providers communicate relatively little. (See Powell, 1989, for an excellent review of this literature.) Conversations tend to occur at the start and end of the day, when parents and providers are rushed and distracted. Parents and staff also hold different views of the type of communication that they consider appropriate, beyond greetings and the exchange of factual information about the child. Parents may not want to discuss what is going on in the family or receive advice on parenting from the staff (Shimoni & Ferguson, 1992). However, staff members are sometimes offended when they feel their expert advice is not valued by parents (Kontos & Wells, 1986).

The triangular relationship between providers, parents, and the child is often complicated by tensions. Some parents press for a greater focus on academic instruction than caregivers believe is appropriate for young children, and a struggle for control over program content may ensue. For instance, a center director who was instituting a new play-oriented curriculum in her program encountered resistance from parents. She persisted in spite of their protests, arguing: "They don't know what the children need. They think they need to know the alphabet at two years old. So I can't go by what the parents think is right; I have to go by what I know is right. What they think and what I think are two different things" (Zinsser, 1991, p. 115). As this example shows, it is the professionals who control the programs they operate. Parents who disagree strongly with the professional's practice are left to exercise their one basic right as consumers—voting with their feet to seek another child care program, if they can find one more to their liking.

Several researchers have found that a surprising proportion of child care professionals have negative attitudes toward the parents who use their services—sometimes exactly because those parents work outside the home and leave the child in care (Galinsky, 1990; Nelson, 1989). Caregivers disapprove when job demands force parents to arrive late to pick up their children or to bring sick children to child care. However, from the perspective of parents, these problems are partly caused by the rigidity of the child care program. Too seldom do programs that offer high-quality experiences to children also design their services to meet the parents' needs for long hours and flexibility. Often, the parents who are the most stressed by their dual roles also face the most criticism from the staff who are their partners in caregiving (Kontos & Wells, 1986).

Making Child Care Work for Children and Parents

All families want care that is good for their children, that meets their needs as workers, and that they can trust to support their child-rearing efforts, but almost no child care arrangements are truly ideal from the parents' perspective. A relative may offer attentive care to an infant for several hours a day but may be unable to keep up with the curiosity of an older child all day. Center-based programs are reassuringly school-like, but their cost and rigid policies can cause problems for parents. Parents worry that family child care homes, though convenient, may be unsafe, and they may refuse to pay high fees for care that seems so "homelike." Moreover, a substantial proportion of families (such as those with infants and toddlers and those who speak languages other than English) find they must choose among very few options. Parents with limited incomes can only access a small slice of the child care system— a slice that is usually of most questionable quality.

No one has a greater stake in the quality of child care than parents. They are the ones who will share their child-rearing role with the programs or individuals they choose as caregivers. It is time that the early childhood field—professionals, policy makers, researchers, and advocates—pay more attention to the concerns parents have about child care quality. There are a number of concrete steps these groups can take to draw parents into the effort to understand and improve child care quality.

Directions for Research

Although initial studies relating to the parental perspective on quality in early childhood programs have been conducted, this area of research is still in its infancy. Key issues that should be addressed in future research are suggested:

1. We must continue and build on the research on parents' child care choices to clarify inconsistencies and to provide a more dynamic understanding of how different types of parents make decisions about child care. Research studies linking qualitative and quantitative methods are needed to document the thinking of parents and to offer representative findings.

2. Parents' concerns about the quality of child care must be reflected in the measures employed in research on child care quality, which currently stress what professionals define as developmentally appropriate practice. Reliable measures are needed that can assess the safety of the environment, the levels of communication and value consensus between parent and provider, and the program's responsiveness to parents' needs.

3. Longitudinal studies are needed to track changes in parent evaluations of the quality of a given child care setting, as the parent becomes more familiar with the actual characteristics of the care and as the child grows older. Such studies could help clarify the conflicting findings concerning parent satisfaction with child care mentioned earlier. (Over 90 percent of parents say they are satisfied, yet 24 to 40 percent would prefer to change to a different type of care.)

4. Research should systematically explore parents' knowledge of, reliance on, and satisfaction with services that are designed to assist them, including child care regulations, consumer education, resource and referral services, and the assistance offered by family and friends.

Directions for Policy and Practice

As research on parents accumulates, recommendations for changes in policy and practice can be made on an increasingly solid empirical foundation. The research reviewed in this chapter constitutes a strong beginning that suggests the following steps to improve policy and practice:

1.   Promote a varied policy and program agenda to support parents who choose different ways of balancing work and child-rearing roles. Resources must be sought simultaneously to support paid parental leave, a system of child care subsidies that mixes vouchers and program contracts, and efforts to develop the quality of all child care alternatives.

2.   Target efforts to build the supply of child care to create the types of care that are most critically needed, by gathering data that link the characteristics of the child care supply in given neighborhoods (ages served, hours available, home-versus-center setting, language spoken, fees charged) to assessments of child care needs in those same neighborhoods.

3.   Review the purposes that the regulation of child care can best serve to guide revisions of state standards and state investments in information, oversight, and enforcement of those regulations. If regulation is intended to protect children from harm, requirements must be universally applied and enforced. By cutting back the scope of the standards encompassed by regulations and simultaneously placing the full power of the state and its budget behind the enforcement of the remaining requirements, it may be possible to make regulation more meaningful—effectively achieving a more modest set of goals.

4.   Take the parent perspective on child care quality seriously. This means that high-quality programs must address the needs of both children and parents. Making child care work for families means creating more programs that have strong developmental curricula as well as flexible hours, age ranges, and policies; and it means improving the ability of relatives and informal caregivers to nurture and teach the children in their care.

5.   Include a focus on parents and the parent-caregiver relationship within all training for caregivers to counteract the strained relationships between parents and child care providers revealed in recent research. The content of that training should prepare providers to communicate and negotiate with parents as equals, and it should address the implications of cultural diversity for program practices and relationships with families.

6.   Finally, encourage parents to articulate what they want and need for their children, taking their concerns and suggestions seriously. Within specific child care programs, the steps that empower parents include providing formal and informal opportunities for parents and staff to exchange ideas and views and establishing parent boards or advisory councils with the power to suggest or review key decisions that shape the program, such as personnel and curriculum.

Mobilizing parents as a constituency for child care in the larger political arena is more difficult, in part because most parents use child care for a few years in their lives, when they are busiest, most anxious, insecure, and overwhelmed. Nevertheless, there are practical steps professionals can take to support parent advocacy: "To enable parents to become involved in the child care delivery system, and not just in individual programs, we must include parent representation in an official capacity at every opportunity, pay for this participation, schedule meetings at convenient times and locations, improve notice and outreach by providing information in multiple languages through minority media outlets, and ensure accessible locations. And even with these supports, it will undoubtedly prove to be difficult" (Cohen & Stevenson, 1992, p. 87).

The importance of a task is not diminished by its difficulty, however, and it is well past time that the professionals involved in child care open the doors to involve parents in discussions of what quality child care is and of how to create and support it.

References
Bond, J. T., & others. (1991). *Beyond the parent leave debate: The impact of laws in four states.* New York: Families and Work Institute.

Bredekamp, S., & Willer, B. (1993). Professionalizing the field of early childhood education: Pros and cons. *Young Children, 48*(3), 82–84.

Chang, H. (1993). *Affirming children's roots: Cultural and linguistic diversity in early care and education.* San Francisco: California Tomorrow.

Cohen, A., & Stevenson, C. (1992). *Caring for the future: Meeting California's child care challenges.* San Francisco: Child Care Law Center.

EDK Associates. (1992). *Choosing quality child care: A qualitative study conducted in Houston, Hartford, West Palm Beach, Charlotte, Alameda, Los Angeles, Salem and Minneapolis.* New York: Child Care Action Campaign.

Eichman, C., & others. (1992). *Investing in the future: Child care financing options for the public and private sectors.* New York: Child Care Action Campaign, and Washington, D.C.: Center for Policy Alternatives.

Galinsky, E. (1990). Why are some parent/teacher partnerships clouded with difficulties? *Young Children, 45*(5), 2–3, 38–39.

Galinsky, E., Howes, C., Kontos, S., & Shinn, M. (1994). *The study of children in family child care and relative care: Highlights of findings.* New York: Families and Work Institute.

Gonzalez-Mena, J. (1993). *Multicultural issues in child care.* Mountain View, Calif.: Mayfield

Harris, L., & Associates. (1989). *The Philip Morris Companies Inc. family survey II: Child care.* New York: Philip Morris.

Hayes, C. D., Palmer, J. L., & Zaslow, M. (Eds.). (1990). *Who cares for America's children? Child care policy for the 1990s.* Report of the Panel on Child Care Policy, Committee on Child Development Research and Public Policy, National Research Council. Washington, D.C.: National Academy Press.

Hill-Scott, K. (1989). No room at the inn: The crisis in child care supply. In J. Lande, S. Scarr, & N. Gunzenhauser (Eds.), *Caring for children: Challenge to America* (pp. 197–216). Hillsdale, N.J.: Erlbaum.

Hofferth, S. L., Brayfield, A., Deich, S. G., & Holcomb, P. (1991). *The national child care survey 1990.* Washington D.C.: Urban Institute.

Kagan, S. L., & Garcia, E. (1991). Educating culturally and linguistically diverse preschoolers: Moving the agenda. *Early Childhood Research Quarterly, 6,* 427–443.

Kagan, S. L., & Neville, P. R. (1993). *Parent choice in early care and education: Myth or reality?* White Plains, N.Y.: Mailman Family Foundation.

Kisker, E., Maynard, R., Gordon, A., & Strain, M. (1989). *The child care challenge: What parents need and what is available in three metropolitan areas.* Princeton, N.J.: Mathematica Policy Research.

Kontos, S. (1992). *Family day care: Out of the shadows and into the limelight.* Washington, D.C.: National Association for the Education of Young Children.

Kontos, S., & Wells, W. (1986). Attitudes of caregivers and the day care experiences of families. *Early Childhood Research Quarterly, 1,* 47–67.

Larner, M., & Mitchell, A. (1992). Meeting the child care needs of low-income families. *Child and Youth Care Forum, 21*(5), 317–334.

Mason, K., & Kuhlthau, K. (1989, August). Determinants of child care ideals among mothers of preschool-aged children. *Journal of Marriage and the Family, 51,* 593–603.

Meyers, M. K. (1993). Child care in JOBS employment and training program: What difference does quality make? *Journal of Marriage and the Family, 55,* 767–783.

Nelson, M. (1989). Negotiating care: Relationships between family day-care providers and mothers. *Feminist Studies, 15*(1), 7–33.

Phillips, D. (Ed.). (1987). *Quality in child care: What does research tell us?* Washington, D.C.: National Association for the Education of Young Children.

Porter, T. (1991). *Just like any parent: The child care choices of welfare mothers in New Jersey.* New York: Bank Street College of Education.

Powell, D. R. (1989). *Families and early childhood programs.* Washington, D.C.: National Association for the Education of Young Children.

Powell, D. R., & Eisenstadt, J. W. (1982). Parents' searches for child care and the design of information services. *Children and Youth Services Review, 4*(3), 239–253.

Shimoni, R., & Ferguson, B. (1992). Rethinking parent involvement in child care programs. *Child and Youth Care Forum, 21*(2), 105–118.

Siegel, G. L., & Loman, L. A. (1991). *Child care and AFDC recipients in Illinois: Patterns, problems, and needs.* St. Louis, Mo.: Institute of Applied Research.

Sonenstein, F., & Wolf, D. (1991). Satisfaction with child care: Perspectives of welfare mothers. *Journal of Social Issues, 47*(1), 15–31.

Stipek, D., Rosenblatt, L., & DiRocco, L. (1994). Making parents your allies. *Young Children, 49*(3), 4–9.

Willer, B., & others. (1991). *The demand and supply of child care in 1990: Joint findings from the national child care survey 1990 and a profile of child care settings.* Washington, D.C.: National Association for the Education of Young Children.

Zinsser, C. (1987). *Over a barrel: Working mothers talk about child care.* New York: Center for Public Advocacy Research.

Zinsser, C. (1991). *Raised in East Urban: Child care changes in a working class community.* New York: Teachers College Press.

Chapter Three

Reframing the Quality Issue

Deborah Phillips

Research in child development and early childhood education has identified several clear indicators of quality care, defined in terms of their predictive significance for children's development. Among the indicators are several that are amenable to regulation and thus able to be influenced by policy mechanisms. Yet, this research has had relatively little impact on social policy. "Quality" has admittedly become a rather entrenched, if not stale, concept in the field of early care and education. Indeed, as a basis for influencing social policy, existing conceptions of quality have been almost entirely ineffective. A new language for talking about quality, grounded in clear perceptions of what needs to be achieved over the course of the coming decade, is in order. The challenge we face is how to reframe this issue so as to reinspire hope that a quality vision can be realized. This chapter is intended to provide the conceptual groundwork for meeting this challenge.

Note: The author would like to acknowledge the contributions made to her own thinking by the other authors and task force members involved in the *Quality 2000* initiative. Special thanks are due to William Gormley, Marcy Whitebook, Sharon Lynn Kagan, and Nancy Cohen who provided important substantive feedback. The views presented in this chapter, however, are the sole responsibility of the author. They do not have the endorsement of the National Research Council or the Institute of Medicine.

Critique of Prevailing Definitions

An important point of departure for this task is to examine the shortcomings of the existing knowledge base as they might bear on policy uses of the literature on quality early care and education. Although factors far beyond the control of the early care and education field have played a role (for example, funding shortages in the face of increasing pressures to expand supply and the profound lack of appreciation and support for nurturing roles in our society), other factors more in the control of the field warrant careful scrutiny.

First, the correlational evidence that predominates in this field, indicating that better inputs reap better outputs, has provided important clues to the factors within early care settings—mostly center-based—that are advantageous to children. What the field lacks is clear evidence of thresholds below which children's development is compromised or above which children thrive. Without persuasive evidence confirming that quality requirements a little bit better than those that exist will produce better outcomes or that requirements a little bit worse will harm children, it is difficult to sustain momentum for incremental improvements in quality, particularly when such initiatives compete with efforts to extend care to larger numbers of young children.

Second, both field-based and research-based definitions of quality remain somewhat parochial, focused predominantly on features of care that reside within the early care and education setting. Minimal attention has been paid to aspects of quality that are found beyond the classroom door; for example, the importance of community infrastructure, which provides opportunities for training, resource and referral; and the need for adequate health care services, on which early care and education—both home-based and center-based—is dependent. Relatedly, the policy context of early care and education has received scant attention. This includes regulations, political structures, and broader financing mechanisms that either support or fail to support quality care and education. Although evidence from interstate comparisons of center-based care has demonstrated that regulatory stringency is associated with higher-quality care (Galinsky, Howes, Kontos, & Shinn, 1994; Phillips, Howes, & Whitebook, 1992), it is impossible to discern whether this association is causally linked to regulatory stringency or to some other factor that affects both program quality and the stringency of state regulations. Absent compelling links between program quality and other community and policy-level influences on quality, the range of supportable actions to improve quality is seriously limited.

Third, the frameworks that have guided developmentally appropriate practice and empirical efforts to define quality focus on inputs rather than outputs. Quality consists of various factors that predict positive outcomes for children. The recent ground-swell of concern about accountability in education, including early education, raises the possibility of conceptualizing quality as an output. In other words, quality *is* positive developmental outcomes, not merely the ingredients that produce these outcomes (Kagan, Moore, & Bredekamp, 1995). Outcome assessment at the pre-school level is, however, a somewhat more daunting undertaking than at the elementary level. Not only is the state of the art with respect to measuring improvements in the cognitive and social development of preschoolers relatively less advanced (Love, Aber, and Brooks-Gunn, 1994), but the smaller scale of early care and educational establishments in comparison with elementary edu-cational establishments poses major logistical challenges to the sys-tematic assessment of preschool outcomes.

Fourth, although early care and education has a long philo-sophical commitment to parent involvement and parent partner-ships—evidenced in nursery cooperatives, Head Start, parenting education, and family support—only certain sectors of the market have regarded parents as consumers. Parents have not been the primary force in defining quality, they have not been a force for accountability, and all parents have not had the freedom to exer-cise choice. Only recently have serious efforts been made to under-stand parents' conceptions of quality (Larner, 1994; Powell, 1994). Further, this work has not yet been integrated into field- and research-based efforts to define quality. A major challenge is posed by the fact that parents are not monolithic in their views and can-not be approached as such.

Fifth, despite strong adherence to a developmentally appro-priate pedagogical orientation within the mainstream early child-hood field, there remains ample debate about its espoused advantages. Further, issues regarding the generalizability and cultural appropriateness of various instructional approaches require much more empirical attention, given the controversy that surrounds efforts to prepare children from disadvantaged environments for elementary school (Kagan & Zigler, 1987; Laosa, 1991). Even the term "cultural appropriateness" remains largely undefined. Yet, early childhood settings are now serving as a harbinger of the rapidly growing diversity of the school age population—a demographic fact of life that poses substantial challenges to our nation's educators. In our increasingly pluralistic society, it is incumbent on those who conceptualize and institutionalize quality to incorporate differing cultural norms and values about the attributes of quality early care and education.

Sixth, prevailing definitions of quality are static in two senses. Quality is conceptualized as a product that is characterized by particular criteria—pedagogy, structures, and interactions. Relatively little attention has been paid to the processes that create and sustain high-quality settings for children, including processes for community and parent input. Relatedly, from the child's perspective, quality has been defined and measured setting by setting. Researchers, inspectors, and parents alike see quality as a snapshot—a set of features that characterizes a setting. Continuity of care across settings and over time is rarely considered as a core dimension of quality early care and education. Although staff turnover has been identified as an important dimension of quality (Hayes, Palmer, & Zaslow, 1990; Whitebook, Howes, & Phillips, 1989), and some investigators include the total number of care settings that children experience during their early childhood years among the variables that they examine (Hofferth, Brayfield, Deich, & Holcomb, 1991), minimal attention has been paid to factors that either promote or undermine advantageous transitions for children from home to care settings and from one care setting to another.

In sum, there is ample room for expanding the frameworks in which the prevailing definitions of quality in early care and education have been developed. New conceptions, new constituencies, and new frameworks that hold the potential to revitalize public and political support for improving quality in early care and education settings are needed. This is the focus of this chapter.

Contextualizing Quality

The importance of *contextualizing* conceptions of quality in early care and education draws heavily on ecological models, which explicitly acknowledge the multiple levels of environmental influence on development and seek to identify systems that promote positive development (Bronfenbrenner, 1979).

Ecological models hold several important implications for the frameworks in which we consider issues of quality. Most fundamentally, they widen the lens through which we capture attributes of quality. The community context of early care and education is viewed as a central feature of quality, not just as a set of conditions that either support or constrain quality. Quality, in other words, becomes a community-level construct. Notions of community stewardship are central to considerations of quality care. Along these lines, substantial thought has been given to the functions that are essential to supporting quality early care and education services (Kagan, 1993). These include an equitable and coordinated financing structure, collaborative planning and cross-system linkages, consumer and public engagement (discussed again in the section on who defines quality), a regulatory structure, and systems for staff and leadership development.

Carefully examining the functional entities and the structural considerations required of a workable system poses a conceptual challenge to formulating definitions of quality—that of reframing the unit of analysis that is to be considered when assessing and discussing quality. Take, as an example, the model of an early care and education infrastructure proposed by Gormley, Kagan, & Cohen (1995) and by Kagan (1993). According to this model, each of the following elements should be embraced by definitions of quality and should be central to initiatives aimed at improving quality:

- The presence, effectiveness, and inclusiveness of a community-wide planning system for early care and education
- Widespread, accessible consumer education about what to look for in early care settings, including information about regulation and regulatory enforcement, and the penetration of this information across neighborhoods within a community, which would offer a very useful marker of quality

- Adequate, coordinated, and equitable financing systems that expand rather than constrain the choices available to families
- A local-employer community that demonstrates active involvement in efforts to improve the quality of early care and education services
- Accessible, rigorous, and publicly recognized training opportunities and credentials for those who work in early care and education settings

Initiatives aimed at including the community surrounding early care and education settings in conceptions of quality can build on numerous related efforts in other areas. Neighborhood-level variables are increasingly being included in research aimed at understanding variation in developmental outcomes (Duncan, Brooks-Gunn, & Klebanov, 1994; Mayer & Jencks, 1989). Substantial energy and resources are now being devoted to designing evaluations that are appropriate for assessing community-wide interventions (Connell, Kubisch, Schorr, & Weiss, 1995). A key issue in these evaluations is how best to assess the existing political, economic, and social conditions that produce variation in the delivery, and hence the effects of, these interventions. Finally, the literature on assessing school readiness has highlighted the critical need to conceptualize the capacity of schools to receive and educate the children who are now entering our nation's kindergartens (Kagan, Moore, & Bredekamp, 1995).

Quality as Process

In addition to expanding the unit of analysis that is encompassed by definitions of quality, considering early care and education in a community context highlights the importance of considering quality not as a product that can somehow be achieved once and for all, but rather as an ongoing process. Indeed, each of the community-level quality indexes proposed above implies a process that will be vital to the strength of the community infrastructure for early care and education. Inclusive planning processes, outreach efforts, public education initiatives, regulatory enforcement, and the sustained involvement of community employers constitute procedural dimensions of quality that have been overshadowed by definitions and data collection efforts that focus on products—the provisions of regulations, the levels of funding, the numbers of employer-sponsored programs, and the substance of parents' definitions of quality.

Comparative research has revealed that other countries place much greater emphasis on processes of consensus building as integral to advancing a high-quality early care and education system (see Chapter Four). New Zealand, for example, has initiated a "chartering system," wherein local communities apply for a charter to start a child care system. The programs that are supported within the local system must abide by national standards on ratios, group size, and caregiver training. But the localities are free to construct a broader system that meets their unique needs. Determining these needs involves a consensus-building process among parents, policy makers, and professionals that is an essential step toward submitting a charter for approval.

As Pence has noted based on his research with the First Nation's community in Canada, "Given lack of agreement on 'quality,' perhaps the process of involvement should take precedent over the product of definition" (1992, p. 5). In an environment where early care and education is explicitly discussed from several vantage points, although disagreement is inevitable, the process raises the profile of the field, heightens awareness of various viewpoints, and distills goals and priorities.

Quality as Continuity

Finally, attention to context must include a temporal dimension that also has been examined only quite cursorily in the quality-of-care literature, despite the longstanding attention to the importance of continuity of care as a guiding theme in developmental psychology (Rutter, 1979; Wachs & Gruen, 1982). This literature has promoted understanding of the continual and progressive accommodation of the child to the environment that successful development entails.

The practical implications of this literature are wide-ranging, and two are particularly important to this discussion. The first is the demonstrated importance of integrating programs over time to provide a continuum of services. Periodic and isolated interventions are ineffective in combating the debilitating consequences of ongoing disadvantage. The second is the attention that this literature has directed to environmental transitions as developmentally significant events. Here the issue is one of the degree of articulation across settings and of the degree to which transitions are carefully planned.

Even a cursory examination of the early care and education field makes it abundantly evident that concern for continuity of care has influenced neither policy nor practice. Quality is typically assessed at a single point in time, whether by researchers, inspectors, or accreditation mechanisms. In addition, numerous obstacles exist to assuring young children well-articulated and predictable patterns of care over the first several years of life. At the policy level, early care and education services and benefits have evolved over time in piecemeal fashion, with new programs layered onto preexisting programs with little regard for coordination. As a consequence, families confront a system characterized by gaps in coverage, splintered jurisdiction, and arcane funding structures.

The extent to which continuity is undermined by these systemic features of care has recently been documented in a study of state and local efforts to coordinate preexisting child care programs with the new federal child care programs enacted in the early 1990s (Ross & Kerachsky, 1993). Significant discontinuities were found between welfare-based programs, such as Aid to Families with Dependent Children (AFDC) Child Care and Transitional Child Care, and other child care programs targeted to low-income populations, such as Child Care and Development Block Grant and At Risk Care. Parents leaving the AFDC or transitional programs are not necessarily picked up by other subsidies. Loss of child care subsidies can force unanticipated changes in arrangements as a family's eligibility or capacity to pay for a particular program is suddenly lost. It can also disrupt parents' abilities to prepare for and sustain employment (Phillips & Bridgman, 1995).

At the program level, salaries that only minimally reward higher levels of professional preparation, combined with the absence of an effective support infrastructure for early care and education, fuel discontinuity in the form of staff turnover and program closings. These events are highly disruptive to families and expose children to the loss of loved caregivers. Recent evidence has revealed that even during the first year of life, children in care typically experience over two changes in their care arrangements (Hofferth, Brayfield, Deich, & Holcomb, 1991). It is not surprising that in a recent study, staff continuity (low turnover) was the strongest predictor of mothers' satisfaction with child care (Shinn & others, 1992).

In this context, it is critical that notions of developmental continuity infuse our efforts to define and assess the quality of existing early care and education systems. Increasingly, we are asking questions about the long-term consequences of children's early care settings, particularly for their school readiness and social adjustment. Answers to these questions require that patterns of stability and change in the context of development be assessed alongside patterns of stability and change in the context of children's behavior.

Who Defines Quality?

Efforts to articulate the meaning of quality in early care and education have been the special reserve of researchers, professional organizations, and advocates. Within the field, it is members at the highest level of the profession—not direct service providers—who have shaped discussions of quality early care and education. Further, these groups have been largely dominated by white, middle-class voices, despite efforts to be more inclusive of a range of cultural perspectives on quality (Head Start Bureau, 1991; National Association for the Education of Young Children, 1989; National Association for Family Day Care, 1990; National Association of State Boards of Education, 1988).

Efforts to extend the cultural appropriateness of the field's definitions of quality have failed to include the voices of parents as a critical source of input regarding how we consider and seek to improve quality in early care and education. Those providers who are struggling to survive on very modest salaries, a high proportion of whom are women of color, are not at the table when quality is discussed. In this section, we first examine the role of parents in efforts to reframe definitions of quality and then turn to the cultural inclusiveness of prevailing definitions. Our underlying premise is that the most challenging and the most critical aspect of reframing the quality debate may not involve reconsidering the *content* of prevailing definitions, but rather extending the reach of *who* defines, and therefore feels personal responsibility for, quality in early care and education.

The Consumer Voice

Turnbull and Turnbull (1994) assign substantial responsibility to an empowered-parent movement for the successful enactment of the Individuals with Disabilities Education Act. Parents have also played a very prominent role as effective advocates for the Head Start program (Zigler & Muenchow, 1992). Beyond the Head Start constituency, however, consumer voices have been conspicuously absent in efforts to improve the quality of early care and education services. As noted by Larner (1994), professionals, not parents, "determine the content of training for those who establish and staff child care programs; they set criteria for recognizing excellence within the profession; their expert judgments inform the policy-makers who set child care regulatory policies; and their insights into child development steer the efforts of researchers to assess how programs affect the children who attend them" (p. 2). Yet, in the context of an early care and education system characterized by relatively lax regulation, substantial variation in form and quality of care, and an entrepreneurial provider base, parents are not only consumers but also important watchdogs of quality of care.

Parents also have the most immediate personal stake in any effort to improve quality and may offer the single most effective and credible constituency for the purpose of advocating for this goal. Absent their direct involvement, the consumer voice has been manipulated in policy debates by those who have argued that parents' priorities are demonstrated by the actual early care and education choices they make—what they use is what they want. As long as there is no uproar from parents, there is no need to improve quality. Indeed, numerous studies reveal high levels of parent satisfaction with their care arrangements (Hofferth, Brayfield, Deich, & Holcomb, 1991), lending additional weight to the assertion that parent choice is an operative and effective mechanism for assuring quality care.

Some fledgling efforts have been made to gain a systematic understanding of parental perspectives on quality care (Larner, 1994; Larner & Phillips, 1994; Powell, 1989). By asking parents to explain their decisions and to discuss their experiences with early care and education, researchers are beginning to uncover the priorities, anxieties, compromises—and many readjustments—that characterize parents' efforts to provide for the care of their children. Findings from this literature offer particularly important insights for efforts to gain consumers an active voice in the national debate about quality.

Parents balance a range of needs, interests, and constraints when selecting early care and education and invariably compromise certain criteria in the interest of maximizing others. Quality considerations consistently surface as the element of care that parents seek most adamantly to protect (Phillips, 1995).

Parents do not, however, emphasize the same features as do professionals and researchers when asked to define quality (Zinsser, 1987). They pay relatively little attention to the structural indicators that the field often stresses, such as licensing and caregiver training. They have only a vague sense of what licensing involves. They also equate regulation with bureaucracy and, accordingly, as irrelevant if not antithetical to the nurturance they seek in their care providers. Many parents are also skeptical about the importance of specialized training, asserting that you can't teach someone to love children. Instead, parents emphasize safety, cleanliness, nurturance, and, particularly, the trustworthiness of the provider (Larner, 1994). Parents from minority and immigrant groups often stress the importance of finding caregivers who will honor and reinforce the values that they uphold in their homes (Chang, 1993).

Those seeking to reconceptualize quality in the early childhood field need to be cognizant of this knowledge base of parents' views of quality in early care and education and to appreciate its potential for advancing efforts to improve quality. It offers a clear means of both operationalizing and seizing the debate about parent choice. Parent choice becomes a reality when gaps between what parents want and what they are using for early care and education are minimized. Exercising this choice is part of being a responsible parent. Parents having the opportunity to exercise choice is a fundamental right that, like the ideology of equal treatment in the disability movement (Turnbull & Turnbull, 1994), could provide an unchallengeable basis for reframing debates about quality of care. To the extent that parents' reliance on early care and education is compulsory, as is the case when its use is mandated by welfare reform, this premise becomes particularly compelling.

Capitalizing on the themes of parent choice and responsibility affords the opportunity to establish coalitions of support across the family leave and early care and education advocacy constituencies. If one considers the decision about *when* to initiate the family's reliance on nonmaternal care as the first in a series of early care and education decisions—and perhaps the most constrained of decisions given the lack of a paid-leave policy in the United States—then the debate about early care and education can be contextualized within a continuum of care choices.

Notions of parent choice and responsibility may also offer a particularly effective lever for enlisting parents as partners in quality-improvement initiatives. It is important, however, to be realistic about both the opportunities and the constraints that will characterize any effort to increase the volume of the parent voice in efforts to improve quality. Unlike the chronic nature of the pressures and anxieties that face parents of a child with special needs, the need for quality early care and education is temporary—one can grin and bear it if need be, knowing that this particular source of anxiety will come to an end. Time for advocacy is also a precious commodity, and especially so for working parents of young children. And, there is not yet a clear, single, shared purpose around which to mobilize parents.

Perhaps the greatest barrier, however, derives from how little parents appear to demand from their care arrangements. Of necessity, they must find arrangements; their choices are constrained by place, time, and money; and their standards for quality are simple and straightforward. To turn the acknowledged misgivings of some parents into an effective, empowered-consumer movement for quality is among the biggest challenges facing the early care and education field. The proposals for accomplishing this, provided by Larner (1994) and Turnbull and Turnbull (1994), nevertheless warrant the serious attention of the field.

A first step for the field is to agree to take on the significant task of nurturing an effective parent constituency for child care quality, of considering a variety of participation structures by which parents can join existing advocacy communities, and of insisting on and supporting parent representation in an official capacity at every opportunity (Cohen & Stevenson, 1992). Future parents and grandparents may provide important additions to this constituency. A variety of organizations at the local level (for example, resource and referral agencies) and the national levels (for example, Parent Action, Child Care Action Campaign, Child Care Law Center) are strategically placed to play a central organizing role if this task is prioritized by the field.

Incorporating Cultural Diversity

Not since the 1930s has the ethnic composition of the nation's children been so diverse. Nonwhites now account for almost one-third of the U.S. population of children and youths (to age eighteen), with recent growth accounted for predominantly by Latinos and Asians, two groups that are themselves extremely diverse. These trends pose new opportunities, but also serious challenges, to U.S. educational institutions, starting with the early care and education services that lay the foundation for children's school experiences and achievement. In California, for example, a recent study of more than four hundred child care centers revealed that only 4 percent enrolled children from a single racial group (Chang, 1993). Nationwide, estimates suggest that 20 percent of the children enrolled in Head Start speak a language other than English (Kagan & Garcia, 1991). Parents seeking child care providers from their own culture often cannot find them. Teachers are confronted with classrooms of children they feel ill-prepared to teach.

Many are left wondering how to assure that the first exposure to a school-like setting—often child care—is a positive one for all children. Whether this experience makes a child feel accepted or alienated is believed to set the stage for subsequent attitudes about and performance in school. The prevailing orientation within the early childhood community assumes that children whose language or cultural background does not correspond to the typical practices of most American schools will feel accepted only to the degree that their classroom experiences are compatible with their home culture and language. Others, however, hold the belief that instructional programs must employ general and universal principles of learning and instruction for all students. Fundamental questions are raised by this debate regarding appropriate and effective educational practices in a pluralistic society (Phillips & Crowell, 1994).

In this context, it is egregious that those in the early care and education field who construct definitions of quality pay, at most, cursory attention to the multilingual and multicultural aspects of children's earliest care and education settings. Too often, relatively superficial and unproven features of diversity, such as a match between teacher and student ethnicity or attention to non-Christian holidays, are used as yardsticks of cultural sensitivity. Prevailing theory and practice in early care and education are perceived by African American and Hispanic leaders in the field to reflect European American middle-class values (Cohen & Pompa, 1994). And, often, multicultural dimensions of early care and education are viewed as pertinent only to members of the nonmajority culture, ignoring, for example, the influence of values and belief systems on the behaviors of providers and teachers from the majority culture. The fact that all preschoolers are growing up in a world characterized by the rapid globalization of economic and geopolitical activity lends a new urgency to assuring that all children benefit from multicultural learning environments. Incorporating issues of cultural sensitivity and appropriateness into prevailing definitions of quality is a fundamental first step toward this goal.

Numerous issues are the focus of efforts to reformulate definitions of quality in early care and education toward greater cultural inclusiveness, only three of which will be considered here. First, it is abundantly evident that notions regarding the importance of "home and school" compatibility require substantial refinement. It is not necessarily the case that quality equals consistency. Under some circumstances, consistency across home and school environments may not be desirable. Some degree of complementarity may be desirable and may even be sought deliberately by parents. Some parents, for example, seek out preschool settings that will expose their children to educational experiences, including English instruction, that they know they cannot provide at home.

From the child's standpoint, the process of adjusting to different practices at home and at school may even be beneficial, particularly in a multicultural society such as ours. The goal should be one of enabling these two contexts to complement and reinforce each other.

Second, there is growing discussion in the literature of a major reorientation in the thinking about how best to create environments, away from a focus on environments that may mirror what children are accustomed to at home, and toward a focus on multicultural environments, in which they feel challenged and encouraged to interact with children from a range of cultures (Cocking, 1994; Tharp, 1989). As noted by the individuals interviewed by Cohen & Pompa (1994), a multicultural environment for all children, rather than an environment that makes it easier for nonmajority children to adjust to the majority culture, may be best suited to the demands that today's preschoolers will face as adults and may actually foster the development of flexible cognitive and social strategies that will benefit them in the long run. Greenfield recently expressed this notion in terms of instructional practices that "are designed to 'wean children to the majority culture' and those that are designed to promote a 'true cultural exchange,'" thereby preserving the heterogeneity of cultural orientations that children bring to the classroom (as quoted in Phillips & Crowell, 1994, p. 28).

Third, this literature challenges both practitioners and researchers in the early childhood field to supplement prevailing definitions of quality attributes with indicators of high-quality, culturally appropriate, and multicultural environments for young children. The process by which this is accomplished will be as important as the outcome and must incorporate both professional and parent voices.

Quality in the Context of Social Equity

There is growing documentation of the striking inequities that characterize virtually every aspect of our nation's early care and education system. Parent choice is inequitably distributed such that mothers who are poor, single, and working are most likely to acknowledge that they wish they could change their care arrangements (Phillips & Bridgman, 1995). Evidence is also clear regarding inequities in the financial burden that early care and education services constitute for families of differing means. Among families who pay for these services, those with lower family incomes spend a substantially higher share of their weekly family incomes than do higher-income families, despite the fact that higher-income families pay higher fees. Among employed mothers, those with an annual family income of $50,000 or more spend about 6 percent of their incomes on care for their children (averaging $85 weekly); those with incomes under $15,000 spend about 23 percent of their incomes (averaging $63 weekly) (Hofferth, Brayfield, Deich, & Holcomb, 1991).

Beyond issues of equity in choice and costs, what is known about equity of access to high-quality child care? An extensive literature on compensatory early education programs has documented positive consequences for low-income children of attending high-quality center-based programs (Barnett, 1985; Lazar & others, 1982; Lee, Brooks-Gunn, Schnur, & Liaw, 1990; McKey & others, 1985). A parallel, but independent, literature that has included low-income families in studies of more typical child care programs not only has failed to document positive outcomes but also has revealed detrimental effects of center-based care on children living in poverty (Baydar & Brooks-Gunn, 1991; Vaughn, Gove, & Egeland, 1980).

Taken together, this evidence suggests that low-income children in center-based programs are receiving both the best and the worst early care and education. The rare studies that have compared low-income children attending intervention and nonintervention programs have reported positive outcomes only for those children in centers that were explicitly designed to provide compensatory education (Lee, Brooks-Gunn, & Schnur, 1988; McCartney, Scarr, Phillips, & Grajek, 1985). Further, several studies of center-based care and some small-scale studies of family child care, particularly in urban settings, have indicated that stressed, less educated, and low-income families tend to rely on poorer-quality arrangements (Goelman & Pence, 1987; Howes & Stewart, 1987; Phillips, McCartney & Scarr, 1987).

Most recently, a small set of studies has explicitly compared the quality of care that children from low-, middle- and high-income families receive (Galinsky, Howes, Kontos, & Shinn, 1994; Layzer, Goodson, & Moss, 1993; Phillips & others, 1994). The portrait that emerges is one in which high-income families, with few resource constraints on the care that they can purchase, are able to obtain significantly higher-quality care than are families with fewer financial resources. The situation for middle- and low-income families varies by type of care. Among those using center-based arrangements, there is some evidence that low-income families can obtain arrangements that are higher in quality, on some dimensions, than can middle-income families. Middle-income families may be at a particular disadvantage because they have neither the financial resources to purchase high-quality care nor access to public subsidies that, at least in the case of government intervention programs, appear to provide some assurance of quality.

Among families using home-based arrangements, however, children in low-income families receive the poorest-quality care. This may be explained by the fact that the United States has made a substantial investment in improving the quality of center-based care for children in poverty (particularly in Head Start and other early-intervention programs) but has not made a comparable investment in family-based arrangements (Galinsky, Howes, Kontos, & Shinn, 1994). Indeed, low-income children in Head Start, and to a lesser extent in school-based programs, receive relatively high-quality care (Layzer, Goodson, & Moss, 1993).

Taken together, these data about inequities in parental choice, financial burden of care, and access to quality arrangements point to a particularly compelling framework in which to cast efforts to improve the quality of our nation's early care and education settings, namely the framework of social equity. As a nation, we have maintained unwavering allegiance to the equal protection doctrine and its extension to notions of equal access to political processes, education, and workplaces. Early care and education may offer the next domain in which to assert the applicability of legal protections based on these notions. An equity-based framework not only embeds debates about early care and education within a long-standing legal tradition—one that offers a basis for arguing that quality of services can no longer be a privilege for high-income families—but it also holds the potential to enlist a much broader coalition on behalf of quality initiatives, including those who have previously advocated on behalf of civil rights and special education. It may also offer a particularly appealing message, which can enlist the participation of parents and frontline care providers.

Conclusion

Effective political change requires good timing, compelling justifications, and a broad constituency of support. In recent years, efforts to improve the quality of our nation's early care and education system have lacked each of these ingredients. Although we cannot manipulate good timing, we can consider how to reframe the quality issue so as to reinspire hope that a quality vision can be realized, and we can enlist a diverse constituency on behalf of this goal. It is hoped that this chapter has offered a first step in this direction and that it will provoke creative feedback as we seek to make tangible improvements in the quality of care and education that our nation's youngest citizens receive.

References

Barnett, W. S. (1985). Benefit-cost analysis of the Perry preschool programs and its long-term effects. *Educational Evaluation and Policy Analysis, 7,* 333–342.

Baydar, N., & Brooks-Gunn, J. (1991). Effects of maternal employment and child-care arrangements on preschoolers' cognitive and behavioral outcomes: Evidence from the children of the national longitudinal survey of youth. *Developmental Psychology, 27,* 932–945.

Bronfenbrenner, U. (1979). *The ecology of human development.* Cambridge, Mass.: Harvard University Press.

Chang, H. (1993). *Affirming children's roots: Cultural and linguistic diversity in early care and education.* San Francisco: California Tomorrow.

Cocking, R. R. (1994). Ecologically valid frameworks of development: Accounting for continuities and discontinuities across contexts. In P. M. Greenfield & R. R. Cocking (Eds.), *Cross-cultural roots of minority child development* (pp. 365–392). Hillsdale, N.J.: Erlbaum.

Cohen, A., & Stevenson, C. (1992). *Caring for the future: Meeting California's child care challenges.* San Francisco: Child Care Law Center.

Cohen, N. E., & Pompa, D. (1994). Multicultural perspectives on quality in early care and education: Culturally-specific practices and universal outcomes. New Haven, Conn.: Quality 2000, Yale University.

Connell, J. P., Kubisch, A. C., Schorr, L. B., & Weiss, C. H. (Eds.). (1995). *New approaches to evaluating community initiatives: Concepts, methods, and contexts.* Washington, D.C.: Roundtable on Comprehensive Community Initiatives for Children and Families, Aspen Institute.

Duncan, G. J., Brooks-Gunn, J., & Klebanov, P. K. (1994). Economic deprivation and early childhood development. *Child Development, 65,* 296–318.

Galinsky, E., Howes, C., Kontos, S., & Shinn, M. (1994). *The study of children in family child care and relative care: Highlights of findings.* New York: Families and Work Institute.

Goelman, H., & Pence, A. (1987). Effects of child care, family and individual characteristics on children's language development: The Victoria Day Care Research Project. In D. Phillips (Ed.), *Quality in child care: What does research tell us?* (pp. 89–104). Washington, D.C.: National Association for the Education of Young Children.

Gormley, W. T., Kagan, S. L., & Cohen, N. E. (1995). *Options for government and business roles in early care and education: Targeted entitlements and universal supports.* New Haven, Conn.: Quality 2000, Yale University.

Hayes, C. D., Palmer, J. L., & Zaslow, M. (Eds.). (1990). *Who cares for America's children? Child care policy for the 1990s.* Report of the Panel on Child Care Policy, Committee on Child Development Research and Public Policy, National Research Council. Washington, D.C.: National Academy Press.

Head Start Bureau. (1991). *Information memorandum: Multicultural principles for Head Start programs.* Log No. ACYF-IM-91–03. Washington, D.C.: Head Start Bureau, Administration for Children, Youth, and Families, U.S. Department of Health and Human Services.

Hofferth, S. L., Brayfield, A., Deich, S. G., & Holcomb, P. (1991). *The national child care survey 1990.* Washington, D.C.: Urban Institute.

Howes, C., & Stewart, P. (1987). Child's play with adults, toys, and peers: An examination of family and child care influences. *Developmental Psychology, 23,* 423–430.

Kagan, S. L. (1993). *The essential functions of the early care and education system: Rationale and definition.* Essential Functions and Change Strategies Task Force. New Haven, Conn.: Quality 2000, Yale University.

Kagan, S. L., & Garcia, E. (1991). Educating culturally and linguistically diverse preschoolers: Moving the agenda. *Early Childhood Research Quarterly, 6,* 427–443.

Kagan, S. L., Moore, E., & Bredekamp, S. (Eds.). (1995). *Reconsidering children's early development and learning: Toward shared beliefs and vocabulary.* Washington, D.C.: National Education Goals Panel.

Kagan, S. L, & Zigler, E. (Eds.). (1987). *Early schooling: The national debate.* New Haven, Conn.: Yale University Press.

Laosa, L. M. (1991). The cultural context of construct validity and the ethics of generalizability. *Early Childhood Research Quarterly, 6,* 313–321.

Larner, M. (1994). *Parent perspectives on child care quality.* New Haven, Conn.: Quality 2000, Yale University.

Larner, M., & Phillips, D. (1994). Valuing quality as a parent. In P. Moss & A. Pence (Eds.), *Valuing quality in Early Childhood Education.* New York: Teachers College Press.

Layzer, J. I., Goodson, B. D., & Moss, M. (1993). *Life in preschool. Final report of the observational study of early childhood programs. Vol. 1* Washington, D.C.: U.S. Department of Education.

Lazar, I., & others. (1982). Lasting effects of early education: A report of the Consortium for Longitudinal Studies. *Monographs of the Society for Research in Child Development, 47* (2–3, Serial No. 195).

Lee, V. E., Brooks-Gunn, J., & Schnur, E. (1988). Does Head Start work? A 1-year follow-up comparison of disadvantaged children attending Head Start, no preschool, and other preschool programs. *Developmental Psychology, 24,* 210–222.

Lee, V. E., Brooks-Gunn, J., Schnur, E., & Liaw, F. (1990). Are Head Start effects sustained? A longitudinal follow-up comparison of disadvantaged children attending Head Start, no preschool, and other preschool programs. *Child Development, 61,* 495–507.

Love, J. M., Aber, L., & Brooks-Gunn, J. (1994). *Strategies for assessing community progress toward achieving the first national educational goal.* Princeton, N.J.: Mathematica Policy Research.

Mayer, S. E., & Jencks, C. C. (1989). Growing up in poor neighborhoods: How much does it matter? *Science, 243,* 1441–1446.

McCartney, K., Scarr, S., Phillips, D., & Grajek, S. (1985). Day care as intervention: Comparison of varying quality programs. *Journal of Applied Developmental Psychology, 6,* 247–260.

McKey, & others. (1985, June). *The impact of Head Start on children, families, and communities.* (Final report of the Head Start Evaluation, Synthesis and Utilization Project.) Washington, D.C.: CSR.

National Association for the Education of Young Children. (1989). *The anti-bias curriculum: Tools for empowering young children.* Washington, D.C.: National Association for the Education of Young children.

National Association for Family Day Care (1990). *Helping children love themselves and others: A professional handbook for family day care providers.* Washington, D.C.: National Association for Family Day Care.

National Association of State Boards of Education (1988). *Right from the start: The report of the NASBE task force on early childhood education.* Alexandria, Va.: National Association of State Boards of Education.

Pence, A. (1992). *Quality care: Thoughts on R/rulers.* Paper presented at a workshop on defining and assessing quality. Seville, Spain.

Phillips, D. (Ed.). (1995). *Child care for low-income families: Summary of two workshops.* Washington, D.C.: National Academy Press.

Phillips, D., & Bridgman, A. (Eds.). (1995). *New findings on children, families, and economic self-sufficiency: Summary of a research briefing.* Washington, D.C.: National Academy Press.

Phillips, D., & Crowell, N. A. (Eds.). (1994). *Cultural diversity in early education: Report of a workshop.* Washington, D.C.: National Academy Press.

Phillips, D., Howes, C., & Whitebook, M. (1992). The social policy context of child care: Effects on quality. *American Journal of Community Psychology, 20,* 25–51.

Phillips, D., McCartney, K., & Scarr, S. (1987). Child care quality and children's social development. *Developmental Psychology, 23,* 537–543.

Phillips, D., & others. (1994). Child care for children in poverty: Opportunity or inequity? *Child Development, 65,* 440–456.

Powell, D. R. (1989). *Families and early childhood programs.* Washington, D.C.: National Association for the Education of Young Children.

Powell, D. R. (1994). Parents, pluralism, and the NAEYC statement on developmentally appropriate practice. In B. L. Mallory & R. S. New (Eds.), *Diversity and developmentally appropriate practices: Challenges for early childhood education.* New York: Teachers College Press.

Ross, C., & Kerachsky, S. (1993). *Strategies for child care program integration: Parent and provider perspectives.* Unpublished manuscript. Princeton, N.J.: Mathematica Policy Research.

Rutter, M. (1979). Maternal deprivation, 1972–1978: New findings, new concepts, new approaches. *Child Development, 50,* 283–295.

Shinn, M., & others. (1992). *Correspondence between mothers' perceptions and observer ratings of quality in child care centers.* New York: Department of Psychology, New York University.

Tharp, R. G. (1989). Psychocultural variables and constants: Effects on teaching and learning in school. *American Psychologist, 44,* 349–359.

Turnbull, H. R., & Turnbull, A. P. (1994). *The Individuals with Disabilities Education Act: The synchrony of stakeholders in the law reform process.* New Haven, Conn.: Yale University.

Vaughn, B. E., Gove, F. L., & Egeland, B. (1980). The relationship between out-of-home care and the quality of infant-mother attachment in an economically disadvantaged population. *Child Development, 51,* 1203–1214.

Wachs, T. D., & Gruen, G. E. (1982). *Early experience and human development.* New York: Plenum.

Whitebook, M., Howes, C., & Phillips, D. (1989). *Who cares? Child care teachers and the quality of care in America: Final report of the national child care staffing study.* Oakland, Calif.: Child Care Employee Project.

Zigler, E., & Muenchow, S. (1992). *Head Start: The inside story of America's most successful educational experiment.* New York: Basic Books.

Zinsser, C. (1987). *Over a barrel: Working mothers talk about child care.* New York: Center for Public Advocacy Research.

Chapter Four

International Approaches to Defining Quality

Jennifer Bush
Deborah Phillips

The issue of quality in early care and education has become a major topic for debate around the world. As early care and education has become a normative experience for children in most countries, the focus of discussion has progressed from whether parental or non-parental care is superior, to the quality of the nonparental programs. This chapter examines international perspectives on quality in early care and education with the goal of broadening the debate about quality in the United States.

Conceptions of quality early care and education vary throughout the world, with different countries considering different combinations of factors to be important. We consider a variety of factors in this chapter, including the structural aspects of programs; the outcomes and goals programs help children achieve, such as health and safety, socioemotional development, or preparation for school; and the degree to which programs have a homelike environment, have a community orientation, provide coherence and continuity, or embody consensus building. We also consider how conceptions of quality vary according to the particular stakeholder, the socioeconomic status and culture, the age of the child, and whether early care and education is seen as a right or a privilege.

To gather information for this chapter, we relied heavily on unstructured interviews with U.S. experts who study other countries' early care and education systems, as well as interviews with researchers from other countries. We also drew on the relevant English-language literature. Our observations are most appropriately viewed as constituting a conceptual model that awaits more systematic, empirical testing.

Attention to Quality

Before we explore how different countries conceive of quality, it is important to note that quality is not a salient goal for all countries. Whereas Scandinavian and other Western European countries pay much attention to quality, it is much less of a focus in Brazil and other developing nations. In many countries, early care and education systems originate as custodial care only for those children deemed to be at risk economically or socially and then gradually evolve into more universal coverage with more developmental or educational curricula.

It is this evolution toward more universal coverage from which the quality discussion has arisen. As Cochran notes, "Societies further along in policy and program development, with a longer public child care tradition, are now focused more on quality. Societies recently entering the field (last 20 years) are still more preoccupied with coverage" (1993, p. 640). Active discussion of quality, therefore, is more likely to occur in those regions where supply is more extensive, suggesting that sufficient quantity of services may be a necessary condition for concerted attention to the quality of programs. It appears that quality concerns move to the forefront when more of the population, especially the middle and upper classes, rely on early care and education.[1]

Once attention does turn to quality issues, the subcultures and plurality of values in societies often mean that no one definitive definition of quality exists. It is a relative concept that varies depending on one's perspective. Kamerman and Kahn write that "countries have multiple goals, and these goals may be inconsistent at the same time or over time. The ultimate policy choice a country makes represents a compromise—an amalgam of responses to complex and diverse factors within the context of historical and ideological elements" (1981, p. 246). Indeed, quality is both a dynamic and a relative concept so that perceptions of quality change as a variety of factors evolve. In many countries, early care and education that provided daily meals was once considered quality care, whereas now, many industrialized nations have standards of living that have caused quality expectations to encompass much more than the provision of adequate nutrition. Changing social situations, such as immigration rates, also affect definitions of quality. For instance, at a given time, quality early care and education may include the ability of a program to acculturate immigrants to the dominant culture.

Conceptions of Quality

As noted, different countries conceive of quality in early care and education in different ways. The following factors characterize aspects of how quality is thought about throughout the world.

Quality as Structural Variables

There is wide agreement in countries around the globe that certain structural conditions, at least in theory, contribute to quality in early care and education. These conditions include such elements as child-to-staff ratios and group sizes that ensure adequate child supervision and interaction, levels of staff training and education that help qualify staff for their work, staff compensation that both attracts qualified caregivers and combats high rates of caregiver turnover, and proper physical conditions that promote safe and comfortable environments for children. These indicators are relatively easily measured and thus are commonly codified in early care and education regulations. As such, they are often relied on as indicators of quality themselves.

Nevertheless, these indicators vary widely across and within countries in terms of what are thought to be appropriate levels as well as the relative emphasis placed on each. For example, France is very concerned with quality early care and education but has higher child-to-staff ratios in preschool programs than other European countries. Though superficially, higher ratios appear to be associated with lower quality of care, France teams higher ratios with highly qualified practitioners (usually with a master's degree in education), who have at least one assistant aiding them in nonacademic tasks (Marx & Richardson, 1989). Countries manipulate structural variables to work toward quality.

Some researchers have pointed to the danger of a strict focus on structural variables, as they can become ceilings for quality rather than starting points on which to build. Those countries that define quality largely in terms of structural components tend to focus less on the quality of the processes occurring in the programs or on the outcomes the programs are achieving with children and families.

Quality as Outcomes and Goals

Definitions of quality can be extrapolated from the desired outcomes—short-term or long-term—of early care and education. Common goals or outcomes of early care and education programs include health and safety, socioemotional development, school preparation, or some combination of these.

Health and Safety

Some industrialized nations consider the nature of quality early care and education to be remedial; the locus of government control of early care and education in these cases usually resides in health and social services agencies. In these countries, publicly provided early care and education is usually only justified for those children deemed at risk economically or socially. This attitude is typical of many English-speaking countries in which traditional gender roles persist, and parents who must purchase programs rely on the free market. Government involvement is warranted only in extreme cases when the family cannot provide for the child adequately. The presumption is that economically disadvantaged parents cannot fully provide for their children's basic needs; therefore, basic health and safety provisions are considered improvements, or quality outcomes, for the small target group eligible for public provision of early care and education. Those countries that focus on health and safety do so in order to satisfy the need for specific, tangible results to justify governmental involvement in social services.

Developing countries frequently locate early care and education administration in their health departments because many of their immediate demands are related to health. Life in these countries is, in general, more survival oriented. Health concerns are often the most pressing problems, and in the absence of an adequate health delivery system, early care and education programs are forced to concentrate their efforts in this area. Most developing countries do not have the luxury to focus on developmental or educational needs and find the delivery of care focused on basic needs to be challenging enough. According to Tolbert and his colleagues, "The quality of child care services must be defined in terms of the community's available alternatives, taking into account minimum standards and optimal care" (1993, p. 369).

Socioemotional Development

Other countries define quality early care and education as that which promotes socioemotional development. Examples of this approach are found primarily in the Scandinavian countries (Ruggie, 1984). Compulsory education does not start until age seven in these countries and, as a result, early care and education services do not emphasize preparation for school until around age six, at which point academic curricula become increasingly prominent. Prior to age six, Scandinavian countries stress social learning and emotional development. They require lower child-to-staff ratios to suit these developmental goals than a country like France, for example, which stresses academic learning. As Broberg and Hwang explain, "Quality of care must be defined and measured differently if the emphasis is on group training and educational goals rather than on the individual child's socio-emotional development" (1992, p. 518).

The Scandinavian approach to early care and education focuses primarily on the immediate needs of the child for supportive interactions and engaging activities and emphasizes the development of motivation and capacity for learning rather than the acquisition of primary knowledge. This orientation to quality early care and education is somewhat unique in its attempt to evaluate quality from the perspective of the child by emphasizing the child's happiness and other short-term social outcomes.

School Preparation

Some countries place governmental responsibility for early care and education in departments of education, which reflects their view that quality early care and education contribute to academic learning. Many European countries favor universal access to preschool education beginning at age two or three and lasting until the start of primary school. A prime example is France, which provides the most extensive preschool coverage of any country for children ages three to five. An emphasis on cognitive development promotes school readiness as one of the prime objectives of the early care and education system, especially because the first grade is notoriously difficult (Bergmann, 1993). Indeed, research shows that those children who do not attend preschool are at a serious disadvantage for successful completion of first grade. Because the objective of early care and education is educational preparedness, quality is measured in terms of success in school.

Teaching children about French culture is another important quality indicator in early care and education and is seen as a way to educate and integrate children, in particular immigrant children, into mainstream French society. As Barbara Bergmann writes, "There is . . . a high consciousness in France of the continuity of the French nation, that the children are the future of the nation, that care for its children has a high claim on the nation's resources" (1993, p. 342).

Some developing countries also believe that education is a key component of quality early care and education. In some cases, early care and education is simply a watered-down version of the primary school system, representing the influence of western values and research that stress the importance of early education. Chada describes the situation in Zimbabwe: "Perceptions of early childhood education and care as a downward extension of primary education and as a child-minding system outside the framework of human resources development strategies were quite common among parents and even the early childhood educators prior to independence, and these conceptions still linger in the minds of many people in the field" (1993, p. 614).

In societies in which formal education is valued, the temptation is often to educate children without understanding the unique way in which younger children learn and develop. It is not uncommon in some countries to find large groups of young children sitting in a barren classroom reciting numbers written on a chalkboard, with no other activities or stimulation available. Given the tremendous competition in primary school in some countries, parents push their children to acquire academic knowledge at a young age to the exclusion of other age-appropriate activities. Once again, the emphasis on education follows from a tendency to stress the child's potential as an adult, so quality is viewed in terms of long-term, societal goals.

Quality as a Homelike Environment

In stark contrast to the countries that have an orientation that emphasizes outcomes—be they health and safety, socioemotional development, or school preparation—some countries or regions emphasize the "homelike" nature of the early care and education setting as the most important proxy for quality. Often in societies in which traditional gender roles prevail, home-based arrangements are preferred over center-based care. In the United Kingdom, for example, family day care—in which a small group of children are cared for in a provider's home—is seen to be closer to the ideal of maternal care.

The homelike environments of family day care are also preferred in some developing countries that are experiencing rapid industrialization and its attendant dislocation of families from their normal rural routines and culture. Anderson writes, "For those sensitive to the significance of 'ecological' frames in child development, home settings, even in very poor shanty dwellings, have clear advantages over the typical public day care center. In these homes, tables and beds, floors and walls are covered with the gear of the domestic and work lives of several family members of different ages" (1993, p. 426).

Quality as Community Orientation

Early care and education systems in a number of both developing and industrialized countries stress a community orientation to concepts of quality, as Phillips calls for the United States to do in this volume. Rather than restricting notions of quality to the inputs or outcomes of programs, this perspective explicitly acknowledges that quality resides in the broader community in which the programs are embedded. This orientation to quality is expressed in a range of ways, including early care and education programs that are consistent with the culture of the particular community, that fulfill the larger role of a community center, and that cultivate parental involvement.

Kenya and Zimbabwe have set up several model early care and education programs that illustrate this idea of embedding local beliefs in programs. The Zimbabwe government, in conjunction with the United Nations Children's Fund, sponsors a National Early Childhood Education and Care program that sets minimum standards on structural inputs such as space and health requirements but allows the communities to tailor programs beyond these structural requirements. Chada writes that "the family- and community-oriented approach that characterizes the policies and the program is an attempt to link our cultural values and beliefs with the policies and the early childhood education and care program in Zimbabwe" (1993, p. 623). In Kenya, the National Center for Early Childhood Education works in conjunction with district Centers for Early Childhood Education to encourage parents, teachers, and communities to establish a curriculum that fits within local contexts (Kipkorir, 1993).

A major issue in many developing countries is rapid industrialization, and early care and education programs can help support the community through change. These programs are an innovative way to provide a range of services in poor, rural areas. Often, the early care and education program becomes a multiservice center that is a focal point for the community. Industrialized countries such as France and Germany also provide examples of early care and education programs serving as multiservice centers. In France, centralized programs are increasingly used for early care and education, community services, and as meeting places for parents. In Germany, early care and education proponents are trying to create neighborhood early care and education centers that provide a meeting place for the community and that are attuned to the local needs of children, families, and caregivers.

Some countries also have come up with innovative approaches to involving parents in programs. Active parental involvement is critical to continued operation of Nicaragua's child development centers. Parents are expected to contribute to the construction or supply of goods for the programs and generally to help with the upkeep of the center. Torres explains that "given the extremely limited financial resources of the state, the survival of each child development center must be ensured through the contribution by the community of material and human resources" (1993, p. 383).

Quality as Coherence and Continuity

Often, those countries that have strong and universal child and family policies have the most successful early care and education systems, because the programs are well conceived, funded, and coordinated. The motivation for extensive family policies can be a combination of social and economic priorities. In Sweden, for example, early care and education programs are part of the larger system of government support for families—providing continuous support for families with young children. Early care and education is an integral part of labor market strategies that form the core of Swedish economic development (Ruggie, 1984). The government actively seeks to shape the labor market and social relations and views women as potential workers, whereas in places like the United Kingdom, women are seen as mothers first and foremost. Kamerman and Kahn (1981) write that "the Swedes are convinced that it is beneficial for women, their husbands, and their children if women work, and Swedish policies are designed to encourage this" (p. 52).

Early care and education enables women to be an integral part of the labor force and plays a prominent role in Swedish employment policies. For instance, working parents are allowed up to eighteen months of job-protected leave after the birth of a new child. The policy is also designed to address gender inequities by enabling fathers to take parental leave. In addition, employment policies include family and medical leave and several paid "contact" days throughout the year, which allow parents to visit their child in early care and education. Finally, parents of small children also have the option of working fewer than six hours a day if they choose. Employment, labor strategies, and early care and education all fit together in a cohesive and logical way to offer support for families with children.

Quality as a Process of Consensus Building

Definitions of quality are clearly not agreed on internationally, or even by everyone in a country or community. Pence writes that "within, as well as between cultures, consensus on 'quality indicators' is difficult to achieve. Roles, relationships, class, and culture, all drive separate agendas and shape different values. Given this inherent lack of agreement on 'quality,' perhaps the process of involvement should take precedent over the product of definition" (1992, p. 5). Processes to identify and prioritize objectives in early care and education have not yet occurred on a large scale, but there is evidence that ongoing discussion of such objectives can contribute to better care for children. In this volume, Phillips calls for a focus on the process of defining quality in the United States. New Zealand has recently initiated a chartering system, which institutionalizes the process of defining quality. Local communities apply for a charter to start an early care and education system. Although they must abide by national standards on staff-to-child ratios, group size, and caregiver training, they have the freedom to construct a system that meets the unique needs of particular communities. Determining these needs involves a consensus-building process among parents, policy makers, and professionals as an essential step toward submitting a charter for approval. The various stakeholders are forced to grapple with questions about what they think constitutes quality early care and education and what goals and priorities they have for an early care and education system. Though New Zealand's chartering system is still fairly new, it illustrates the importance of the process of defining quality as an element of achieving quality (A. Smith, personal communication, July 1993).

The First Nations (an aboriginal community) in Canada provides another example of the process of defining quality in early care and education. Due in part to its federalist system, Canada has many of the same beliefs regarding the limited role of government found in other English-speaking countries, combined with a strong tradition of cultural and ethnic diversity throughout the different regions. First Nations is building community consensus on what kind of early care and education system will achieve a good fit with its values and cultural beliefs and is defining the policies that will enable this system to evolve. First Nations has articulated a system that highlights the importance of its community and culture and is less individualized than early care and education programs found in most Western countries. In an environment in which quality in early care and education is intentionally explored from several different viewpoints, although disagreement is inevitable, the process raises the profile of early care and education, heightens awareness of various viewpoints, and distills goals and priorities (A. Pence, personal communication, July 1993).

Factors Affecting Conceptions of Quality

Quality is a relative term, which can vary according to socioeconomic and cultural factors, perspective of the stakeholder, age of the child, and beliefs about the role of government. The ways in which each of these factors influences definitions of quality are considered below.

Stakeholders

Every country's early care and education system serves multiple groups within society—children, parents, employers, and, in the broadest sense, the public at large. Moss (1988) refers to the variety of stakeholders in early care and education, each of whom holds a different conception of quality. The child's perspective, especially that of an infant or toddler, is not always evident or reliable and must be inferred by adults. Katz (1992) calls the child's experience of early care and education the bottom-up perspective on quality. As Larner reviews in this volume, not as much is known about the parental-adult perspective, which Katz calls the top-down perspective, perhaps reflecting the lack of awareness and involvement of these stakeholders. "Probably more is known about parental preferences and satisfaction on washing powder than on early care and education arrangements" (Moss, 1988, p. 202).

There is evidence that parents tend to accept what is available and subsequently decide they are satisfied with it. Broberg and Hwang explain:

One can speculate that one way adults can cope with the often incompatible demands put on them as parents and as gainfully employed persons is to adjust their perception of what constitutes children's basic needs. . . . In societies (subcultures) where very early out-of-home care is becoming increasingly common, this means that parents will have a tendency to overemphasize infants' needs for nonparental stimulation, the educational value of early socialization with other adults and peers, and children's need to become independent of their parents very early in life. Contrastingly, in societies or subcultures where the importance of the maternal role is stressed and mothers are reluctant to work outside the home when their children are young, children should be seen as more dependent and in less need of nonparental stimulation during their early years. [1992, p. 516]

Katz (1992) also refers to the "societal perspective" of quality, which is the public or community opinion of early care and education. She says that the professionals, the practitioners of early care and education, have the "inside perspective on quality," which takes into account their working conditions and staff-parent relationships. Only recently has any attempt been made to examine interrelations among these differing vantage points on quality. The National Child Care Staffing Study (Whitebook, Howes, & Phillips, 1989), for example, revealed that quality from the provider's perspective is closely related to quality assessed by structural inputs and children's development.

Socioeconomic and Cultural Factors

Research shows that early care and education preferences are often related to socioeconomic status and culture. When publicly provided early care and education is only for at-risk children, the service is disproportionately provided to ethnic minorities or lower-income groups. However, in countries where there is more universal access to publicly provided early care and education, these same groups are less well represented in formal programs. Kamerman and Kahn explain, "The less-educated and the foreign are not so sure of the responsiveness of the system and of their capacity to use it" (1981, p. 137).

Child's Age

In most countries, usually one government agency administers early care and education for children under three and another agency for children over three, a trend that has important implications for quality. Many countries base early care and education services for children under three in health departments, whereas early care and education for children over three is based in education or social services (although Sweden and Finland base early care and education services for all ages in their social welfare departments, and Spain is moving to consolidate all of its early care and education services under educational auspices). This phenomenon reflects age-linked conceptions of quality care. Early care and education for older children is seen as an educational endeavor, whereas programs for younger children are viewed as promoting general health.

Quality as a Right Versus a Privilege

Perspectives on quality are affected by whether a country believes that early care and education is a right for all children or a privilege. Whether or not it is viewed as a right is embedded in social values regarding appropriate policy responses by government to families with young children. In other words, is early care and education a public or a private responsibility?

Early care and education in most Western European countries, at least for children aged three to five, is considered to be a right that the public should support for all families. Because it is perceived as a right for all, rather than just as a privilege or an intervention for those with lower incomes, there is more discussion regarding and higher expectations for quality. In countries where early care and education is considered to be a privilege and a private responsibility, society views the only public role as providing programs for a small group of socially marginalized individuals; quality discussions figure less prominently in the national debate (see endnote). "Basic to this view is a commitment to a libertarian economic ideology combined with a traditional moral conservatism, which opposes societal infringement on the private domain" (Broberg & Hwang, 1992, p. 513).

Countries that see early care and education as a private responsibility tend to value maintaining parental choice in programs. The countries are often free-market societies that emphasize autonomy and the privacy of the family. Teghtsoonian writes about the early care and education debate in Canada: "Federal minimum standards . . . would limit parents' options in selecting care for their children, and contain an implicit criticism of parental ability to make appropriate judgments regarding the adequacy of such care" (1992, p. 217). She discusses how government involvement and centralized standards are seen as encroaching on parental rights, illustrating that early care and education quality is viewed strictly from the perspective of the parents rather than the child. Family day care can be appealing in these countries as "it d[oes] not break too sharply with traditional child-rearing patterns. It is also a 'small business' approach which is appealing in the context of a private sector, market economy" (Cochran, 1993, p. 641).

Countries in which early care and education is considered a privilege for some and a necessity only for the at risk tend to develop two-tiered systems. At-risk children receive publicly provided custodial care, whereas better-off children attend private programs, where they receive extracustodial care, often with an educational orientation as in the United Kingdom (Ruggie, 1984). In countries where early care and education is an inherent right, access to quality programs tends to be universal, and program quality is much more consistent across income boundaries.

Conclusion

In the United States, the quality of early care and education, fundamentally viewed as each parent's choice and responsibility, does not tend to be a subject of significant national attention or debate. Quality tends to be defined narrowly, in terms of structural inputs and outcomes such as school readiness. Supply and cost issues often masquerade as quality issues. Our nation's diversity suggests that perhaps efforts to shape the quality of early care and education programs at the local level, as in New Zealand and Canada, would provide not only heightened awareness through the process of defining quality early care and education but also a better fit with the variety of values in the United States. Achieving quality is a formidable challenge but all the more reason to expand the debate. It is our hope that this chapter will stimulate such discussion.

Note
1. Early-intervention programs in the United States, such as Head Start, are an anomaly. Those who are served are of lower socioeconomic status, but considerable attention is paid to quality concerns, such as how best to provide for a child's future academic success later in school. In contrast, early care and education programs that are provided as part of welfare programs do not tend to concern themselves with quality issues.

References

Anderson, J. (1993). Peru. In M. Cochran (Ed.), *International handbook of child care policies and programs* (pp. 415–430). Westport, Conn.: Greenwood Press.

Bergmann, B. (1993). The French child welfare system: An excellent system we could adapt and afford. In W. J. Wilson (Ed.), *Sociology and the public agenda* (pp. 341–350). Thousand Oaks, Calif.: Sage.

Broberg, A. G., & Hwang, C. P. (1992). The shaping of child care policies. In M. E. Lamb, K. J. Sternberg, C. P. Hwang, & A. G. Broberg (Eds.), *Child care in context: Cross-cultural perspectives* (pp. 509–521). Hillsdale, N.J.: Erlbaum.

Chada, R.N.E. (1993). Zimbabwe. In M. Cochran (Ed.), *International handbook of child care policies and programs* (pp. 605–626). Westport, Conn.: Greenwood Press.

Cochran, M. (1993). Public child care, culture, and society: Crosscutting themes. In M. Cochran (Ed.), *International handbook of child care policies and programs*. Westport, Conn.: Greenwood Press.

Kamerman, S. B., & Kahn, A. J. (1981). *Child care, family benefits, and working parents: A study in comparative policy.* New York: Columbia University Press.

Katz, L. (1992). *Multiple perspectives on the quality of early childhood programs.* Paper presented at the second European Conference on Quality of Early Childhood Education. Worcester, England.

Kipkorir, L. I. (1993). Kenya. In M. Cochran (Ed.), *International handbook of child care policies and programs.* Westport, Conn.: Greenwood Press.

Marx, E., & Richardson, G. (1989). *A welcome for every child: How France achieves quality in child care—practical ideas for the United States.* Report of the Child Care Study Panel of the French-American Foundation.

Moss, P. (1988). *Childcare and equality of opportunity.* Brussels: European Commission Childcare Network.

Pence, A. (1992). *Quality care: Thoughts on R/rulers.* Paper presented at a workshop on defining and assessing quality, Seville, Spain.

Ruggie, M. (1984). *The state and working women: A comparative study of Britain and Sweden.* Princeton, N.J.: Princeton University Press.

Teghtsoonian, K. (1992). Institutions and ideology: Sources of opposition to federal regulation of child care services in Canada and the United States. *Governance: An International Journal of Policy and Administration, 5*(2), 197–223.

Tolbert, K., & others. (1993). Mexico. In M. Cochran (Ed.), *International handbook of child care policies and programs* (pp. 353–376). Westport, Conn.: Greenwood Press.

Torres, A. (1993). Nicaragua. In M. Cochran (Ed.), *International handbook of child care policies and programs* (pp. 377–390). Westport, Conn.: Greenwood Press.

Whitebook, M., Howes, C., & Phillips, D. (1989). *Who cares? Child care teachers and the quality of care in America: Final report of the national child care staffing study.* Oakland, Calif.: Child Care Employee Project.

Chapter Five

Multicultural Perspectives on Quality

Nancy E. Cohen
Delia Pompa

Introduction

The last chapter explored differences in definitions of quality in
cultures across the globe. In this chapter, we target definitions
of quality in cultures throughout the United States. We ask: Should
quality in early care and education be defined the same way for all
young children and families, or should definitions vary with children's and families' cultural backgrounds? Within our culturally
diverse country, racial, ethnic, and other background differences
among young children, their parents, and early care and education practitioners pose challenging issues for quality. Cultural diversity means that the hopes and expectations that adults have for
young children, as well as how they interact with young children—
from comforting to disciplining to teaching—differ, sometimes
dramatically.

Note: The research for this chapter included interviews with a group of experts
in early childhood education and diversity—Barbara Bowman, Dwayne Cromp-
ton, Yolanda Garcia, Luis Laosa, Rebecca New, Alice Paul, and Carol B. Phillips.
Carol B. Phillips and Deborah Phillips identified these experts, conceived of the
interview questions, and gave feedback on drafts of this chapter. Eugene Garcia,
Muriel Hamilton-Lee, Sharon Lynn Kagan, and Mary Larner shared insights and
also gave feedback on earlier drafts. The authors wish to thank each person for
her or his unique and thoughtful contribution.

Although the fundamental question of the nature of quality for children and families of different backgrounds has surfaced repeatedly over the years in the early care and education field, it has perhaps never been as central to quality discussions as it is today. The country's racial diversity is most evident among children under the age of six (Center for the Study of Social Policy, 1992), and early care and education programs are increasingly viewed as critical to improving academic performance in schools and to developing a productive society. To make early care and education programs successful, definitions of quality must be appropriate for young children from a range of backgrounds.

In this chapter, we consider multicultural perspectives on quality in early care and education, exploring whether there should be universal quality criteria that apply to all children, or whether quality criteria should vary for children of different cultures. We first examine teacher practices (the means of early care and education) and then child outcomes (the ends). Then, we consider how differences in parents' and teachers' culturally based preferences about means and ends (practices and outcomes) can be addressed. We go on to discuss the implications for preparing teachers and for including diverse voices more effectively in discussions about the nature of quality. We conclude with suggestions for practice and policy. This chapter presents a synthesis of the views of the authors, of a series of experts in the fields of early care and education and diversity who were interviewed in preparation for this chapter, and of the relevant literature.

Conceptions of Quality

Part of the challenge of discussing multiculturalism and quality is specifying what is meant by quality. In this chapter, we consider two key components of quality from the perspective of cultural diversity—the quality of early childhood teacher practices and the learning environment (the means of early care and education), and the quality of outcomes for children resulting from early care and education programs (the ends).

We define *teacher practices* as the methods or approaches teachers use to assist children, including the ways they relate to children, their expectations of children, and the languages they use. The

National Association for the Education of Young Children's (NAEYC) Statement of Developmentally Appropriate Practice (Bredekamp, 1987) is an example of one conception of quality teacher practice. Teacher practices include key aspects of the learning environment that teachers help determine, including how children are grouped for activities, how the day is structured, and how materials are used and arranged.

We use the term *child outcomes* to refer to the skills, knowledge, and competence children possess when they make the transition from early care and education programs to schools. The Goal One Technical Planning Group of the National Education Goals Panel outlines the following areas in which outcomes for young children should be determined, to assess if they are ready to learn when they enter school—physical well-being and motor development, social and emotional development, approaches toward learning, language usage, and cognition and general knowledge (Kagan, Moore, & Bredekamp, 1995).

These two components of quality—teacher practices and child outcomes, or the means and the ends—have crucial implications for children in a multicultural society, and especially for those from minority backgrounds. For example, the match or mismatch of early childhood teacher practices with parent practices can help prepare children to succeed—or not—in the home and school. Another example is that the expectations of children and the outcomes they will achieve have historically been lower for minority children, perhaps reflecting the belief that they do not have the same abilities or that they are not as motivated to learn.

What Is Culture?

Another part of the challenge of discussing multicultural perspectives on quality is the meaning of culture. In the context of this chapter, culture is defined as "the organized body of 'rules' about how individuals in a population communicate with one another, think about themselves and their environments, and behave toward one another and toward objects" (Laosa, 1979, p. 264). Culture is not manifest just in holidays or foods but has a deep and profound impact on how people view themselves, others, and how the world works (Derman-Sparks & the ABC Task Force, 1989).

Culture is not the same as racial and ethnic group, community of residence, language spoken at home, or socioeconomic level, although these elements of people's backgrounds can be factors in and salient influences on people's behaviors and their culture. Culture is manifest in the practices used to teach and care for young children, which can vary among countries, within single countries, within cultures, and even in the life of a single child. Cultures vary in how adults hold, diaper, feed, speak to, and interact with children (Gonzalez-Mena, 1993).

It is also important to note, however, that socioeconomic level and education seem to play a particularly important role within culture. Family income and parental—in particular maternal—education levels may explain more of the differences in approaches to interacting with children than such factors as race or ethnicity (Laosa, 1979, 1982). Finally, any consideration of culture should stress that individuals' cultural backgrounds can be difficult to specify and that family and individual variation can be great.

Quality and Teacher Practices

The experts interviewed for this chapter and much of the literature suggest that the ways in which teachers teach and care for young children—their practices—cannot and should not be defined universally for all young children in the United States. One respondent suggested three factors that quality practice should take into account—the relatively universal stages of human development, children's cultural contexts, and the individual needs of children based on their histories. This paradigm is an expansion of the NAEYC's Statement of Developmentally Appropriate Practice (Bredekamp, 1987).[1] Under this revised paradigm, no practice is good for all children; quality practices vary from culture to culture and from child to child.

Continuity in Parent and Teacher Practices

Many of the respondents and the literature emphasize the importance of cultural continuity between practices in the home and school in facilitating children's learning (Cardenas & Cardenas,

1977; Laosa, 1979; Tharp, 1989). Parent and teacher practices differ to varying degrees, but the literature suggests that particularly when parent and teacher income levels or education levels vary, their practices with children are also likely to vary significantly (Laosa, 1979, 1982; Phillips & Crowell, 1994).

Where parent and teacher practices differ, as long as parent practices are not abusive or harmful, teachers of young children need to adapt their own practices to match the home experiences of children, at least when the children first enter programs. As one respondent puts it, teachers need to meet children "where they are." Tharp (1989) identifies four areas in which compatibility between teacher practices and children's home cultures may be particularly important for young children:

- Social organization—for example, some children work better as part of a group, and others work better individually.
- Sociolinguistics—for example, some children are comfortable with silence, and others are comfortable with interruption.
- Cognition—for example, some children need to hear just part of a story, and others need to hear the whole story before discussion.
- Motivation—for example, some children are motivated by the threat of punishment, and others by fear of shaming their families.

Promoting Biculturalism

A preferred approach to addressing differences in home and school cultures is to help children become bicultural. The respondents and the literature stress the need for children to be bicultural if they are going to be successful in their home cultures as well as in school, and ultimately, in American society (Phillips, 1994). Biculturalism allows children to have successful experiences in their families—where one set of values and behaviors prevails, and in school—where another set of values and behaviors may be expected.

Early care and education can and should play an important role in helping children become bicultural. Heath describes how teachers can help children learn the culture of the school (Heath,

1983). Tharp (1989) emphasizes two areas in which early care and education teachers might help children at risk for school failure become bicultural—promoting children's language development and helping children understand instructions and activities by contextualizing them. Not all children learn sufficient language skills or the ability to follow instructions at home, yet they will need these skills to succeed in school. Early childhood teachers who help children become bicultural in these areas help children prepare to succeed in school.

How do teachers both continue the practices to which children are accustomed at home and help children become bicultural? Take the example of poorly educated low-income Hispanic mothers, who tend to rely on modeling rather than conversation to teach their children (Laosa, 1980). In a culturally sensitive approach, early care and education teachers would use modeling when such children enter programs. Slowly, as they continue to use modeling, teachers would introduce and increase the practice of teaching via direct inquiry, particularly using verbal questions and answers. This practice would help increase the children's verbal skills and their ability to follow directions. Both modeling and question-and-answer practices would continue to be used, thus making children bicultural and building their ability to function in the home, neighborhood, and school.

It must be stressed, however, that teachers need to work actively to affirm simultaneously both the culture of the school and the culture of the home (Lubeck, 1994). Phillips suggests an analogy to illustrate this point: "In the same way that we tell children that one whispers in the library and yells on the playground, *without devaluing either whispering or yelling as a human act,* we must address the conflicts that they face in reconciling home and neighborhood experiences and school experiences" (1994, p. 150).

The potential benefits of biculturalism suggest that it might also be a goal for children of the majority culture. For example, bilingualism—one aspect of biculturalism—seems to promote cognitive and social skills (Kagan, Moore, & Bredekamp, 1995), including the ability to discriminate among people and environments and to behave appropriately in different contexts. In truly multicultural programs, all children would develop a broad range of approaches to learning (Tharp, 1989). Children who enter programs with home experiences of learning via verbal questions and answers might be exposed to learning via modeling. In our quickly changing and increasingly global society, success may be based on the ability to adapt to change; being bicultural or multicultural is likely to be helpful to all for life success.

Finally, it is important to note that becoming bicultural is a life-long process. The adaptation children can make to more than one culture while they attend early care and education programs is best seen as a model for a continuing process. Schools must also strive to be more adaptable to the variety of approaches to learning that children bring with them (Laosa, 1979, 1982). Realistically, early care and education can help ease children's transitions to school but will not be able to assure single-handedly that all children will be able to achieve in school. It is worth noting that U.S. schools are seen as also failing to meet the educational needs of many children from the majority culture, further supporting the case for school reform.

Quality and Child Outcomes

The other key component of quality that we consider in this chapter is child outcomes. By child outcomes, we mean the skills, knowledge, and competencies that children develop in early childhood programs. Teacher practices, just discussed, facilitate children's achievement of outcomes.

Across the cultures of the world, there are few completely universal child outcomes or early care and education practices (Bowman & Stott, 1994; Laosa, 1979; New, 1994; Rogoff & Morelli, 1989). Cognitive abilities, competence profiles, emotional display and affect, moral development, gender role differentiation, and conceptions of selfhood vary among cultures (New, 1994). A Vygotskian approach would suggest that all outcomes—cognitive, emotional, and social—are constructed via children's interactions with institutions and other people: "development is inseparable from human social and cultural activities" (Rogoff & Morelli, 1989, p. 345). Perhaps the only basis on which outcomes can be judged as better or worse is the degree to which they prepare children to succeed in a culture. That is the assumption made in this chapter.

The experts who were interviewed for this chapter suggest that outcomes for young children in the United States can and should be the same for children of all cultural backgrounds. They report that the overarching outcome desired by most American parents of varied cultures is for their young children to be able to learn and achieve when they enter school.[2] This goal is also shared by the nation's governors and the president—embodied in the First Education Goal: by the year 2000, all children will start school ready to learn.

The respondents and the literature emphasize that minority parents are as likely to have the goal of their children succeeding in school as are culture-majority parents. Pipes McAdoo argues that a similarity of ethnically diverse families is that they want "to have their children succeed in school" (1993, p. xiii). Universal outcomes are also important for children of all cultures in the United States because they embody a fundamental belief that all children can learn at high levels.

Although there may be agreement among parents and policy makers on the general outcomes that young children should attain, there is much controversy in the early care and education field on this topic, regardless of the cultural backgrounds of children. Early childhood professionals question and debate the desirability and feasibility of specifying outcomes—identifying the particular skills and knowledge, and the levels of these skills and knowledge, that indicate that children are "ready to learn" (Kagan, Rosenkoetter, & Cohen, 1996).

To resolve the varying perspectives of parents, policy makers, and professionals, we suggest that outcomes for young children should be as culturally sensitive as possible, constituting the full range of skills, knowledge, and approaches that are, in fact, outcomes necessary for success. As the Goal One Technical Assistance Group cautions, "Approaches to learning that vary within and between cultures must be respected so we do not encourage a uniform or 'cookie cutter' approach to early childhood education, with the goal of all children coming out the same" (Kagan, Moore, & Bredekamp, 1995, p. 3). For example, though young children may need basic social-conventional knowledge to succeed in school, such as learning alphabetic letters and understanding holidays, they may be able to succeed if they know the letters of the Hawaiian language (rather than of English) or Muslim holidays (rather than Christian holidays); they will eventually need to learn English letters and Christian holidays but can do that once they are in school. Bowman argues that we need to move our thinking about minority children from theories of deficiency to the recognition of cultural competence; such an orientation would accept greater diversity in how children represent their developmental achievements (Bowman, 1994).

Addressing Cultural Differences

In this section, we suggest an approach to addressing—or living with—cultural differences that builds on the analysis of quality teacher practices and child outcomes in the preceding section.

Focusing First on Outcomes

An acknowledged approach for addressing cultural differences is parent-teacher dialogue. It is crucial for parents to know that teachers are committed to having frank and open conversations at all times, and especially when misunderstandings or disagreements arise (Far West Laboratory, 1993). It is particularly important for parent-teacher dialogue on issues of quality to focus first on what the parents and teachers want for children—the desired child outcomes—and only then to consider teacher practices in helping children achieve those outcomes. In many cases, it is possible for parents and teachers from diverse backgrounds to share their hopes and desires and to agree on the outcomes that they want for children—the skills and knowledge that children should develop. Reaching agreement on outcomes—first—can encourage parents and teachers that they can reconcile diverse perspectives on practices. "Once [parent and teacher] understand what the parent wants for his or her child, you can together examine whether or not the practice in question reflects those goals" (Gonzalez-Mena, 1993, p. 37).

Whose Voice Prevails?

In many and perhaps most cases, parent-teacher dialogues about what they want for children will result in agreement. In the event that parents and teachers do not agree, however, the respondents are of mixed opinion concerning whose voices should prevail in defining quality outcomes and practices. Some respondents feel that the final word about quality should rest with parents. Others suggest that a variety of voices should be heard, but that the final decision "is not a voting thing;" the opinion of a small number of people may prevail if it is in the "best interest of children."

We suggest that if parents and teachers cannot agree concerning the outcomes for children, then parents' voices should prevail. In terms of teacher practices to achieve the outcomes, there are several possible ways in which conflicts can be resolved. In a resolution-through-negotiation approach, a satisfactory solution may be found that feels good to both parents and teachers; in ongoing management of the unresolved conflict, parents and teachers carry on a relationship despite differences of opinion: agreeing to disagree is a valid approach that can be satisfactory if it involves mutual respect. In a teacher-education approach, teachers may come to understand the parents' perspective and adapt to their wishes. And in a parent-education approach, parents may come to see the teachers' points of view and add to their own practices or change them (Gonzalez-Mena, 1993).

Perhaps the point to stress is the ongoing nature of discussions when there are cultural differences among the adults who care for young children. The goal should not be reaching agreement once and for all, but rather identifying resolutions that are renegotiated as children grow. The respondents point out that although opening dialogue among diverse groups inevitably leads to differences of opinion, it also allows people to examine their own beliefs. As one respondent puts it, "It's only in interacting with others that we become aware of our differences." Ultimately, dialogue among diverse stakeholders can result in the thoughtful refinement of quality practices and outcomes or in seeking alternate programs that might meet the needs of parents and children more appropriately.

Teacher Qualifications and Preparation

The central importance of appropriate teacher practices to achieving quality in early care and education leads us to the topic of teacher preparation. Teacher qualifications—both training focused on early childhood education and formal education—have been correlated with higher-quality programs in multisite studies of program quality (Hofferth, Brayfield, Deich, & Holcomb, 1991; Whitebook, Howes, & Phillips, 1989). Given the points made thus far—that teacher practices should be culturally sensitive, that child outcomes should be the same for all children, and that cultural difference should be resolved through dialogue—what particular preparation should early care and education personnel have?

The experts who were interviewed, as well as the literature, are in agreement about teacher qualifications. At least some teachers need to share—or at least be sensitive to—children's backgrounds and cultures, *and* teachers need to have formal academic education. The respondents also stress the need for all teachers to have training in cultural competence.

Sharing Children's Cultures

The respondents feel that it is valuable for at least some early care and education teachers to have backgrounds similar to those of at least some of the children with whom they work, because this will increase the likelihood that they will have learned common cultures. Having similar backgrounds includes coming from the same racial or ethnic groups, living in the same neighborhoods, and speaking the same language. All these factors may increase the ability of teachers to comprehend and communicate with children. In order to hire significant numbers of culture-minority teachers, the respondents point out that directors may need to be flexible in evaluating personnel's preparation experiences. Culture-minority teachers are less likely to have formal academic preparation (National Black Child Development Institute, 1993), and directors will need to take into consideration life experiences and informal training.

Teachers' Academic Preparation

Simultaneously, the respondents and the literature stress the critical nature of formal academic education in preparing teachers *and* the need to build a pool of minority teachers with formal academic training. They repeatedly urge the commitment of necessary resources to making formal education accessible to all (National Black Child Development Institute, 1993). As one respondent puts it, "It's not OK to accept the current situation; we must make higher education a viable and realistic end point for low-income ethnic-minority women [and men] in the United States." Requiring staff to be well educated must not preclude hiring people from culture-minority communities.

A number of respondents mention that the lack of culture-minority teachers with formal education qualifications results from "institutional racism," not just in early care and education but also in higher education. The National Black Child Development Institute (1993) recommends establishing a consortium of early childhood teacher-training institutions to coordinate existing efforts and develop new strategies to increase the number of culture-minority graduates. Head Start has made strides toward mitigating institutional racism in early care and education and in higher education with preferential hiring of community members and by promoting the child development associate certificate (CDA) as preparation. Much progress, however, remains to be made in this area.

Training in Cultural Competence

The respondents and the literature clearly state that teachers with different backgrounds from the children with whom they work need training to become competent in the cultures of the children with whom they work (Bowman & Stott, 1994; Laosa, 1979; New, 1994). Several respondents suggest that all teachers need training in cultural competence because of the diversity of the children in programs. Respondents also point out that coming from the same racial background as the children in care does not guarantee that teachers will understand their culture; for example, African American teachers socialized in the majority culture may have trouble relating to the values and behaviors of low-income African American children.

Culturally competent teachers recognize culture-specific behaviors and patterns of interaction. They look for developmental equivalences, identify cultural values rather than using memorized lists of behaviors for each cultural group, have awareness of their own values that they bring to the classroom, and have the facilitation and negotiation skills to address differences among teachers and parents (Bowman & Stott, 1994; Kagan, Moore, & Bredekamp, 1995; Laosa, 1979; Lubeck, 1994; New, 1994).

The respondents and the literature suggest that direct experiences with other cultures is the most effective way to gain self-awareness and cultural competence (Laosa, 1979). Gonzalez-Mena suggests learning about other cultures "on the spot," by "observing yourself and the people you interact with in your program. Become aware of your discomforts and discuss them when appropriate. When you begin to share, you'll learn more than you could learn from any book" (1993, p. 14). The best source of information about a family's preferred approaches and style is the particular family; teachers should speak regularly with families and visit the communities and homes of children.

Given the pluralistic society in which we live, training in cultural competence should be integrated into all teacher preparation, ongoing training, and credentialing programs. As noted, however, such training need not educate teachers in the practices of other cultures; rather, it can teach them how to recognize and distinguish cultural values and behaviors and how to learn about the cultures of the children with whom they work.

The Process of Defining Quality

This chapter is just one attempt to specify what quality should be for children of different cultural backgrounds. The bottom line, however, is that quality has been and will continue to be defined and redefined by varied groups for varied purposes. The *process* of defining quality—and in particular who helps define it—may be as important as the definition reached.

As Larner discusses earlier in this volume, the perspectives of minority parents and providers have been noticeably absent from the dialogue about quality. A number of the experts who were interviewed, as well as the literature, suggest that prevailing theory and practice in early care and education reflect European American middle-class values and that practices and outcomes identified as high quality are not neutral and purely data driven (Gonzalez-Mena, 1993; Mallory & New, 1994). As one respondent puts it,

"Particular people decide the questions to be studied, interpret the data, and come to conclusions."

The obstacles to including diverse voices in defining quality are complex. There may actually be tension within the professional development movement in early care and education about including diverse perspectives. Traditional concepts of professionalism suggest that the field should define its work as a specialty requiring training. To increase the input of diverse voices—particularly those of diverse parents—the field may need to develop an alternative model of professionalism, a model that values and encourages dialogue among people with different views and values.

The experts we interviewed and the literature make a variety of recommendations for increasing the diversity of voices that define quality. Effective dialogues about quality are:

- Open—everyone participates and considers personal change.
- Ongoing—dialogues continue as beliefs and needs evolve.
- Between equals—everyone has critical knowledge and skills.
- Inclusive of decision making—to be included is not just to be present, but to participate, influence, and be influenced (Mallory & New, 1994).
- Welcoming and supportive—people who are not accustomed to attending meetings or discussing quality issues need to be made to feel comfortable, welcome, and encouraged to state what they want for children.
- Encouraging of minority leadership—diverse voices are facilitated when minority family and staff members have significant leadership positions.

Dialogues about quality should take place at multiple levels and in different arenas. At a minimum, diverse voices—parents and teachers—should participate in periodic dialogues about quality for *individual children:* these include the discussions mentioned earlier concerning the outcomes parents and teachers want children to achieve and the progress the children are making toward these ends. *Programs* also need to increase the diversity of voices discussing quality issues by including diverse parents and staff in advisory or governance structures, such as boards of directors, advisory committees, and parent input committees. The process of defining quality may be so important in some places that *community-wide* forums can be held on the topic, which should include diverse stakeholders, such as parents, teachers, community leaders, researchers, business people, and the media.

Conclusion

We began this consideration of multicultural perspectives on quality in early care and education by asking whether there should be universal quality criteria in early care and education that apply to all children or whether quality criteria should vary for children of different cultures. The answer to this question, and the implications for resolving cultural differences, preparing teachers, and discussing and defining quality, form the basis for our following recommendations for teachers, administrators, parents, teacher trainers, and policy makers.

1. *Quality outcomes for children in early care and education programs should be universal—the same for all children of all cultures in the United States.* Parents and policy makers of varied ethnic and racial backgrounds share a belief that children should be ready to learn when they enter school and in other situations that they will encounter in their lives. Universal outcomes are powerful because they move us beyond cultural differences and highlight what we have in common as a nation. The message to policy makers and early childhood professionals is that national, state, and local outcomes identified for young children should be applied to children across cultures.

2. *Quality teacher practices—how early care and education providers help children achieve the universal outcomes—do vary and need to be based on the cultural and developmental needs of individual children.* Early childhood teachers should strive to provide some continuity for children as they enter early care and education programs, continuing the practices and languages used at home. Additional practices and languages can be added that children will need to succeed in school. All children can benefit from being bicultural or multicultural and should be exposed to different styles of learning and languages. The early childhood profession should revise practices and training to help children become bicultural.

3. *Ongoing parent-teacher dialogue is the key to resolving cultural differences.* Dialogues need to begin with discussions of child outcomes—what parents and teachers want for their children—and only then move to discussion of teacher practices. Such dialogues can demonstrate the common desires that most parents and teachers have for children, paving the way for productive discussions of how teachers can help children achieve these outcomes. Teacher training and guidelines for practice should reflect this approach to parent-teacher dialogue.

4. *In our multicultural nation, preparation for early childhood teachers needs to include academic education and training in cultural competence and negotiation skills.* It is crucial that the teachers of young children in this country have academic preparation and that they represent the diversity of children in programs. Special efforts must be made to increase the pool of minority teachers with academic backgrounds.

5. *All teachers need training to become culturally competent.* Teacher trainers, practitioners, and policy makers should take note that teacher-training curricula should be expanded to address cultural competency skills, particularly the abilities to interpret cultural variations of beliefs and behaviors and to learn about cultures.

6. *We must expand the voices discussing and defining quality to include more ethnically and racially diverse stakeholders, including parents.* These dialogues can begin with parents and teachers discussing quality for individual children. They can grow into dialogues with diverse parents, practitioners, administrators, and community leaders discussing quality for individual programs. These efforts can then blossom into dialogues including this group, as well as policy makers, business leaders, and other stakeholders, focusing on the definitions of quality for entire communities. Who it is that defines quality will influence—and is as important as—the ultimate definition.

Notes
1. NAEYC is in the process of building consensus in the field on an updated Statement of Developmentally Appropriate Practice that will address cultural diversity and contextual variation.
2. As discussed by Bush and Phillips in the preceding chapter, not all countries view school readiness as the desired outcome of early care

and education. For example, developing countries often see the goal as child health and safety; Scandinavian countries see the goal as socioemotional and personality development.

References

Bowman, B. T. (1994). The challenge of diversity. *Phi Delta Kappan, 76,* 218–224.

Bowman, B. T., & Stott, F. M. (1994). Understanding development in a cultural context: The challenge for teachers. In B. L. Mallory & R. S. New (Eds.), *Diversity and developmentally appropriate practices: Challenges for early childhood education* (pp. 119–136). New York: Teachers College Press.

Bredekamp, S. (Ed.). (1987). *Developmentally appropriate practice in early childhood programs serving children from birth through age 8: Expanded edition.* Washington, D.C.: National Association for the Education of Young Children.

Cardenas, J., & Cardenas, B. (1977). *The theory of incompatibilities.* San Antonio, Tex.: Intercultural Development Research Association.

Center for the Study of Social Policy. (1992, September). *The challenge of change: What the 1990 census tells us about children.* Washington, D.C.: Center for the Study of Social Policy.

Derman-Sparks, L., & the ABC Task Force. (1989). *Anti-bias curriculum: Tools for empowering young children.* Washington, D.C.: National Association for the Education of Young Children.

Far West Laboratory. (1993). *Essential connections: Ten keys to culturally sensitive child care.* Sacramento, Calif.: California Department of Education.

Gonzalez-Mena, J. (1993). *Multicultural issues in child care.* Mountain View, Calif.: Mayfield.

Heath, S. B. (1983). *Ways with words: Language, life, and work in communities and classrooms.* Cambridge, England: Cambridge University Press.

Hofferth, S. L., Brayfield, A., Deich, S. G., & Holcomb, P. (1991). *The national child care survey 1990.* Washington, D.C.: Urban Institute.

Kagan, S. L., Moore, E., & Bredekamp, S. (Eds.). (1995). *Reconsidering children's early development and learning: Toward shared beliefs and vocabulary.* Washington, D.C.: National Education Goals Panel.

Kagan, S. L., Rosenkoetter, S., & Cohen, N. E. (1996). *Considering child-based outcomes for young children: Definitions, desirability, and feasibility.* New Haven, Conn.: Bush Center in Child Development and Social Policy, Yale University.

Laosa, L. M. (1979). Social competence in childhood: Toward a developmental, socioculturally relativistic paradigm. In M. W. Kent & J. E. Rolf (Eds.)., *Primary prevention of psychopathology. Vol 3. Social competence in children* (pp. 253–279). Hanover, N.H.: University Press of New England.

Laosa, L. M. (1980). Maternal teaching strategies in Chicano and Anglo-American families: The influence of culture and education on maternal behavior. *Child Development, 51,* 759–765.

Laosa, L. M. (1982). School, occupation, culture, and family: The impact of parental schooling on the parent-child relationship. *Journal of Educational Psychology, 74,* 791–827.

Lubeck, S. (1994). The politics of developmentally appropriate practice: Exploring issues of culture, class, and curriculum. In B. L. Mallory & R. S. New (Eds.), *Diversity and developmentally appropriate practices: Challenges for early childhood education* (pp. 17–43). New York: Teachers College Press.

Mallory, B. L., & New, R. S. (Eds.). (1994). *Diversity and developmentally appropriate practices: Challenges for early childhood education.* New York: Teachers College Press.

National Black Child Development Institute. (1993). *Paths to African American leadership positions in early childhood education: Constraints and opportunities.* Washington, D.C.: National Black Child Development Institute.

New, R. S. (1994). Culture, child development, and developmentally appropriate practices: Teachers as collaborative researchers. In B. L. Mallory & R. S. New (Eds.), *Diversity and developmentally appropriate practices: Challenges for early childhood education* (pp. 65–83). New York: Teachers College Press.

Phillips, C. B. (1994). The movement of African-American children through sociocultural contexts: A case of conflict resolution. In B. L. Mallory & R. S. New (Eds.), *Diversity and developmentally appropriate practices: Challenges for early childhood education* (pp. 137–154). New York: Teachers College Press.

Phillips, D., & Crowell, N. A. (Eds.). (1994). *Cultural diversity and early education: Report of a workshop.* Washington, D.C.: National Academy Press.

Pipes McAdoo, H. (Ed.). (1993). *Family ethnicity: Strength in diversity.* Thousand Oaks, Calif.: Sage.

Rogoff, B., & Morelli, G. (1989). Perspectives on children's development from cultural psychology. *American Psychologist, 44,* 343–348.

Tharp, R. G. (1989). Psychocultural variables and constants: Effects on teaching and learning in schools. *American Psychologist, 44,* 349–359.

Whitebook, M., Howes, C., & Phillips, D. (1989). *Who cares? Child care teachers and the quality of care in America: Final report of the national child care staffing study.* Oakland, Calif.: Child Care Employee Project.

Part Two

The Infrastructure
The Case for a Quality System

Chapter Six

Licensing
Lessons from Other Occupations
Anne Mitchell

Introduction

There is ample evidence that early care and education practitioners who have attained higher levels of education, who have been educated specifically about working with children of the ages of those in their care, and who are well compensated, are better teachers; that is, they deliver higher-quality care, which leads to better outcomes for children. Ensuring that those who work with young children have these critical qualifications is essential to advancing the quality of early care and education programs and improving child outcomes. Professionalizing early care and education is a means to improve quality through a focus on practitioners.

To advance and support professional development in the early care and education field, this chapter examines the entry standards, preparation systems, and individual credentialing practices of various occupations, seeking lessons from these other occupations that might be applied in the early care and education field. The chapter opens with a brief picture of early care and education as a profession, considers the status of preparation and credentialing in a series of other occupations in the United States, explores the general implications for early care and education, and then focuses on the licensing of individuals as one measure that may be of particular benefit to the early care and education field.

Methodology

The U.S. Department of Labor's *Occupational Outlook Handbook,* published every two years, describes in detail about 250 occupations that represent about 90 percent of all U.S. jobs. Each description covers the nature of the work, working conditions, employment outlook through the next decade, training requirements for entry and advancement, and earnings based on the most recent data from current population surveys. There are about a dozen major categories of occupations—executive, administrative, and managerial occupations; professional specialty occupations; technicians and related support occupations; marketing and sales occupations; service occupations; agriculture, forestry, fishing, and related occupations; mechanics, installation, and repair occupations; construction trades and extractive occupations; production occupations; and transportation and material-moving occupations (U.S. Department of Labor, 1993).

For the study on which this chapter is based, occupations across the spectrum of professional, service, sales, technical, and construction trades were selected to cover a wide range of occupational categories that have some relationship to early care and education. Basic information on each of the selected occupations was compiled from Department of Labor handbooks and supplementary written materials. These were augmented by a series of telephone interviews with the major professional or trade organizations associated with each occupation and with their accrediting bodies and credentialing organizations. A total of twenty-eight interviews were conducted during 1994.

Terminology

Throughout this chapter, the terms license, certificate, and credential are used repeatedly. It is important to remember that each has a specific meaning, which may be a bit different from how they are commonly used (and confused). A *license* is official permission granted by a competent authority, usually the state, to engage in a business or activity that would otherwise be illegal. Many occupations require that an individual acquire a license in order to practice in the occupation. License is also the correct term for the permission a child care center must get in order to operate legally. In this chapter, license almost always refers to the licensing of individuals. A *certificate* is a document certifying that an individual has mastered the knowledge of a field and has met the requirements, usually of a professional organization. An example of a certificate in early care and education is the Child Development Associate (CDA), although it is commonly called a credential. A *credential* is a broad term covering all types of certificates, licenses, academic degrees, and other qualifying documents.

Early Care and Education as a Profession

Early care and education is an occupational field that encompasses a wide range of work with young children and their families. Early childhood is usually defined as the period of children's lives from birth through about age eight. Teachers who work with young children in preschools, nursery schools, Head Start centers, child care centers, kindergarten, and the primary grades are all in the early care and education field. Also included are family child care providers who work with small groups of children in their own homes and nannies who work with children from one family in the children's home. Roles include working directly with children (teacher, family child care provider), working primarily with parents (child care referral counselor), or administering and managing programs (center director).

Defined by Others

The occupation of early care and education is defined by sources outside the field, such as state regulations for child care centers. Child care regulations focus mainly on the facility in which programs occur and only minimally, if at all, on the qualifications of the individuals who do the work. The regulation of public schooling, on the other hand, focuses more heavily on the individual who does the work—the teacher—through teacher certification standards and less on the facilities themselves, which are addressed by state building codes. The U.S. Department of Labor categorizes kindergarten and elementary teachers as *professional specialty occupations* and preschool workers and private household workers as *service occupations.*

Defined by the Field

The National Association for the Education of Young Children, with significant commentary and input from the field, developed its Conceptual Framework for Early Childhood Professional Development between 1989 and 1993. The framework seeks to unify the diversity of practitioners and settings. The field is characterized as a set of interrelated occupations distinguished by role, setting, and the ages of children involved, as well as by levels of practice from entry to mastery, defining progressive qualifications for the various occupations. The relationship among the various occupations and levels of practice is conceptualized as a latticework or a set of interconnected pathways, rather than a ladder, of career advancement (Johnson & McCracken, 1994). In related work, the Center for Career Development in Early Care and Education, Wheelock College, has been evolving models of career development systems, mainly through its work with states, that seek to create an integrated system of preparation and continuing development for the diversity of job roles, ages of children, and settings that characterize the field (Morgan & McGimsey, 1993; Azer, 1993).

The field's concept of itself as an occupation is rooted in two fundamental principles. First, the occupations that constitute the field all have as their foundation the same body of knowledge, and competent practice in the field requires familiarity with the full range of this body of knowledge.

Second, it is desirable to have multiple entry points to the various occupations that constitute the early care and education field and to have multiple connected pathways among the occupations. Thus, individuals can easily enter occupations in the field and move within and among the different roles and settings. Those who have prepared for roles in the field may obviously enter, but so may those individuals who show aptitude for the work and have relevant experience but no prior formal preparation. This does not imply that the field has no entry standards, but rather that open entry and mobility require that there be easy access to training and education for all who choose to enter. High-quality in-service training and supportive supervision by well-prepared and more experienced teachers are also necessary to ensure that all entrants can function effectively.

Concern about the deteriorating quality of children's experiences in early care and education, coupled with the clear relationship among the preparation of those who work with children, the quality of programs, and the outcomes for children have spurred increasingly serious efforts to address the issues of professionalism in this field.

From Occupation to Profession

The early care and education field grapples with the occupational terms *profession* and *career*. Is early care and education a profession, many professions, or not a profession at all? Profession is defined as an endeavor requiring specialized knowledge or mastery of a body of knowledge and meeting agreed-on standards of practice. The occupations that form the early care and education field do share some characteristics of a profession. For example, there is consensus about what constitutes the core body of knowledge necessary for good early care and education practice. Accreditation schemes exist for both centers and family child care homes. There is a competency-based credential for some of the roles in the field—the Child Development Associate (CDA)—which is widely recognized, but not widely implemented outside of Head Start.[1] The existence of program accreditation and credentials for individuals is evidence of common standards of practice. Early care and education is unlike other professions, however, which generally require individuals to meet standards before commencing practice. The field's standards are voluntary for programs and for individuals. Only teachers of young children in elementary schools are required to have an individual credential—a license to teach. Perhaps career, meaning an occupation undertaken as a permanent calling, is an apt term for describing early care and education, implying both commitment to the work and longevity. Early care and education is a an occupational field in the early stages of its development, with much still to be learned.

Preparation and Credentialing in Selected Occupations

The occupations studied span the professional, technical, and service sectors and were chosen to match the functional, demographic, and occupational characteristics of early care and education. Professions that are characterized as dealing with people—so-called "helping" professions—were included (social work and nursing), as well as those whose focus is not working directly with people (architecture and electrical engineering). Licensed practical nursing, a technical occupation related to the profession of nursing, was selected to examine how levels of an occupation are related in terms of preparation and advancement. Among occupations that are not considered professions, both those that focus on people (travel agents, cosmetologists/beauticians) and those that do not (electricians) were considered.

Occupations were chosen that vary in both size and median salary as compared to early care and education. Early care and education is a fairly large occupation with extremely divergent salaries. There are about one million preschool–child care workers and about one and a half million kindergarten and elementary school teachers. In comparison, there are about two million registered nurses in the United States and about 425,000 electrical engineers, but only about 100,000 architects. The median annual salary is about $10,000 for preschool–child care work, whereas public school teachers have median salaries of about $32,000. Among the occupations studied, engineers earn the most ($55,000 median salary), nurses are in the midrange ($30,000 median salary), and cosmetologists earn the least ($14,000) but still surpass preschool–child care workers (U.S. Department of Labor, 1993).

Table 6.1 summarizes the basic characteristics of entry and advancement in each of the eight occupations studied. Analogous information for the field of early care and education is included in the table for ease of comparison. As one looks across the eight occupations summarized, a number of interesting patterns emerge.

Similarities

There are striking similarities among these eight occupations. Every one of them has an association whose members are the individuals that practice in the occupation (in the case of electricians, it is the union). The purpose of these associations is the advancement of the profession or occupation. In line with this purpose, nearly all of the occupational organizations offer advanced levels of certification above those required for entry into the occupation. Further, with the sole exception of travel agents, all of these occupations have a system of individual licensure governed by a state board, use a standard examination as part of the licensing process in all (or most) states, and have a body that accredits the schools that prepare individuals for the occupation. Given the wide range of occupational types examined, these fundamental similarities are astounding.

Differences

There are also interesting differences among the eight occupations, which distinguish the professional occupations from the non-professional ones. Those occupations that the Department of Labor classifies as professions—architects, engineers, social workers, and registered nurses—have preparation systems that are exclusively within institutions of higher education. Preparation requires completion of a degree at the bachelor's or master's level, (although nurses have the option of an associate degree instead). In contrast, the occupations that are not considered professions—licensed practical nurses, travel agents, and cosmetologists—are prepared through systems that include a wider variety of preparation institutions, such as trade and vocational schools as well as colleges. When colleges are involved, they are usually two-year colleges. Technical (licensed practical nurses) and service occupations (cosmetology) have much shorter preparation periods than the professions, rarely longer than one year, and in the case of travel agents, no preparation is required at all.

Electricians are an interesting counterexample to this pattern. Though not considered a profession, they must complete lengthy preparation (a four-year apprenticeship) but have little or no involvement with vocational or educational institutions because the training incorporated in the apprenticeship is organized by the union. Although licensed electricians are not classified as professionals, they share some characteristics of a profession—lengthy preparation, an examination, state licensure, and a clear continuing education system. The electricians' union is key in creating and maintaining this professionlike preparation and licensure system.

Table 6.1. Entry Requirements and Additional Credentials for Eight Selected Occupations and Early Care and Education.

	Education required	Experience required	National exam	Credential granted	Additional credentials available	Professional Organization
Architect	1–3 years beyond college	3 years beyond degree	yes	registered architect	no	American Institute of Architecture
Electrical Engineer	BS degree	4 years beyond degree	yes	professional engineer	yes, various specialty areas	Society of Electrical Engineers
Social Worker	BA degree or MSW degree	generally 2 years	yes	licensed social worker	ABCSW (for BAs), ACSW (for MSWs), and DCSW (for clinical)	National Association of Social Workers
Registered Nurse	AA degree, BS degree, or MS degree	within program	yes	registered nurse	certified generalist (for BS degree); certified specialist (for MS degree)	American Nursing Association and nursing specialty organizations
Licensed Practical Nurse	state-approved 1-year program	within program	yes	licensed practical nurse	yes, from 2-year colleges offering programs	National Federation of Licensed Practical Nurses

Travel Agent	none	none	no	N/A	Certified Travel Counselor	Institute of Certified Travel Agents
Cosmetologist	8th grade and state-approved program	none	no, each state has exam	licensed cosmetologist	no	National Cosmetology Association
Electrician	high school degree	5-year apprenticeship	yes	licensed electrician	Master electrician	National Joint Apprenticeship and Training Committee
Early care and Education: Preschool & child care worker	varies by state	varies by state	no	none required, except in NYC, FL, & MA for teachers in centers	Child Development Associate (CDA) & Child Care Professional (CCP)	National Council for Early Childhood Professional Recognition & National Child Care Association
Early care and Education: Kindergarten & primary teacher	BA degree	within program	yes, or state exam	certified teacher	Early childhood/ Generalist	National Board for Professional Teaching Standards

Whereas all of the occupations considered rely partially on a standardized written test as part of the licensure process, only cosmetologists and electricians must demonstrate their knowledge and skills as part of their licensure examination during the process. Licensure for the professions relies solely on written examinations (registered nurses), examinations in combination with internships (architects), or examinations plus accumulated experience in a supervised setting (engineers and social workers). Performance assessment in the licensing of professionals in the education field has become a hot topic; a number of states have instituted or are considering establishing performance-based systems of licensure for public school teachers (Wise & Darling-Hammond, 1987; National Council for Accreditation of Teacher Education, 1994). Competency-based credentialing is familiar to the early care and education field, which has many years of experience with the CDA, a competency-based certificate granted by the profession.

Individual Licensure

One of the more striking common characteristics among these eight occupations is that (except for travel agents) individuals are required to have a license in order to practice the occupation. Architects, registered nurses, licensed practical nurses, cosmetologists (and public school teachers for that matter), must be licensed in every state. The principal engineer in a firm and any engineer practicing independently must be licensed in all states. Most states require that electricians be licensed if they are the principal of a firm or are practicing independently. All states require at least some social workers to have a license, with various exceptions granted depending on the state.

There are two major reasons that individuals are required to have licenses. One rationale for individual licensure is to protect the health, safety, and welfare of the *public,* especially in situations in which the public is unlikely to be able to judge for itself the competence of a product or service. The regulation of public accommodations, such as restaurants and the premises of child care centers, is done for much the same reasons. This rationale accounts for the licensing of architects, engineers, and electricians. A second rationale for licensing is to protect the health and safety of *individuals*. Those who deliver services directly to people—who practice on people—are licensed to protect individual health and safety. This accounts for the licensing of registered nurses, practical nurses, cosmetologists, and social workers (and public school teachers).

The other major factor affecting individual licensure is independence. When an individual practices independently, rather than under the supervision of others, greater assurance of competence is presumed necessary to protect the general public and individuals. This is the main reason for the licensure of social workers, and the rules for engineers, electricians, and architects, in which cases licenses are required for the principal of a firm and for anyone practicing independently.

Comparisons

Having discussed the essential characteristics of other occupations, the chapter now considers early care and education in comparison with these other occupations.

First, it is important to recognize that early care and education is not one occupation but apparently is at least two distinct ones. Notwithstanding the firm belief of early childhood educators that the knowledge base required to teach young children is the same for children of a particular age across settings, the occupational characteristics of the preschool–child care sector are distinct from the occupational characteristics of the public school (kindergarten–primary) sector.

The structure of preschool–child care occupations looks most like travel agents. No license is required of individuals, with the exceptions of the certification systems in place in Massachusetts, New York City, and Florida. There are no national or state examinations. Generally, quite minimal training and experience are required, and these requirements vary widely among the states. There are voluntary credentials—the child development associate (CDA) and the certified childcare professional (National Child Care Association, 1992)—offered by professional organizations. Rather than one major professional organization, however, there are numerous professional organizations, which focus on segments of the field. The organization that accredits preparation programs, the National Council for Accreditation of Teacher Education (NCATE), only addresses programs in four-year colleges and universities.

The early care and education occupations of kindergarten and elementary teaching share many of the characteristics of the professions. To teach in public schools, an individual is required to be licensed (although this is usually called a certificate). There is a body that accredits the schools that prepare teachers (NCATE), and there is a national exam (National Teachers Examination). There are professional organizations (American Federation of Teachers and the National Education Association) whose missions are the advancement of the profession and the support of teachers and that act as unions for teachers in many states. An advanced level of certification in early childhood will soon be available from the National Board for Professional Teaching Standards. Although this advanced certificate will be available to early childhood educators working in settings other than public schools, as a practical matter, public school teachers will be more likely to apply for it. The major difference between public school teachers and other professions is that most teachers are not licensed by independent state boards but through state departments of education. However, there is a trend toward establishing a board system of individual licensure for teaching. In about a dozen states, for example, Minnesota, there are independent teaching boards licensing public school teachers (National Council for Accreditation of Teacher Education, 1994).

Issues from Other Occupations to Consider

Numerous issues for the early care and education field arise from considering the characteristics of preparation and entry into other occupations. This chapter attempts to raise some issues for thoughtful debate and discussion, not to suggest immediate solutions or changes.

Organizational Missions and Relationships

Every occupation has at least one related professional organization, whose members are those who practice the occupation and whose mission is to advance the profession or occupation. Nurses have the American Nursing Association, architects have the American Institute of Architecture, and as noted earlier, the public school–early care and education occupations have similar organizations, one of which is a union (American Federation of Teachers).

Interestingly, as noted earlier, there is no one professional organization that unites the preschool–child care occupations across all roles and settings. Instead, there are a number of what might be called role-related professional organizations, two organizations of agencies, and one multifaceted organization that primarily represents the interests of young children in addition to those of its adult members (National Association for the Education of Young Children). The role-related or sector-specific organizations are the National Association for Family Child Care, the National Head Start Association, the National School Age Care Alliance, the National Child Care Association, the National Association of Early Childhood Specialists in State Departments of Education, and the Family Resource Coalition. This list could also include the National Association for Regulatory Administration to which child care licensers belong, and one very new organization, USA Child Care, that represents the interests of child care and seeks center directors as members. The primary characteristic of all of these organizations is that the vast majority of their members are the people who work in these particular sectors or roles. Their organizational missions are to support their members in their roles, provide peer support, and otherwise represent their members' concerns.

Although the plethora of professional organizations in early care and education distinguishes the field from other occupations, there is at least one similarity. A common characteristic of professional organizations in other occupations is to offer advanced certificates to members. Two of the many early care and education organizations currently offer certificates (National Association for Family Child Care and the National Child Care Association), and another is planning to do so in the near future (National School Age Care Alliance). There is discussion in the Head Start community about establishing a competency-based credential for the variety of roles in Head Start beyond those covered by the CDA; for example, health coordinator, family–social services worker, and parent involvement coordinator. Though this would not be a credential offered by a professional organization, it is an important development.

Another organization that might be considered role related, but whose members are agencies, is the National Association of Child Care Resource and Referral Agencies. It behaves like a professional organization, representing the interests of its member agencies as well as the individuals who work in child care resource and referral agencies. The National Association of Child Care Resource and Referral Agencies has considered offering accreditation for agencies but has not as yet considered individual credentials.

How professional organizations relate to one another and the differences in their goals are important to understand, as attempts are made to advance early care and education as a profession. The relationships between the two licensed practical nursing organizations (and their differences in purpose) as well as the relationships among the many engineering societies are instructive. One of the licensed practical nursing organizations (National Federation of Licensed Practical Nurses) is exclusively for licensed practical nurses, whereas the other (National Association for Professional Nurse Education and Service) is devoted to the general field of practical nursing, drawing in doctors, practical nursing instructors, and others interested in the practice of licensed practical nursing. This is somewhat similar to the distinctions that currently exist between the sector-specific organizations in early care and education and the National Association for the Education of Young Children. Take, for example, the National Association for Family Child Care and the National Association for the Education of Young Children. The National Association for Family Child Care is specifically devoted to family child care and made up almost exclusively of family child care providers (somewhat like the National Federation of Licensed Practical Nurses). The National Association for the Education of Young Children is a broader organization focused on the education of young children in all settings, whose members are drawn from a wide range of roles and settings, including child care teachers, directors of early care and education provider agencies, state administrators, and faculty of higher education institutions (somewhat like the National Association for Professional Nurse Education and Service). Although the National Association for the

Education of Young Children is genuinely interested in and supportive of family child care and family child care providers, it is not exclusively devoted to them and their advancement.

In the field of engineering, the various types of engineers (electrical, mechanical, chemical, and so forth) have their own societies. In addition, there is an umbrella organization (Association of Engineering Societies) that conducts research, promotes the field of engineering generally, and engages in other activities designed to advance the entire engineering field. The Association of Engineering Societies is guided by and financed through the various engineering societies. If this model were to be applied to the early care and education field, the role-specific organizations would be analogous to the engineering societies, and the National Association for the Education of Young Children would be analogous to the Association of Engineering Societies. Currently in early care and education, there are no ongoing, formal cooperative relationships among the various sector-specific organizations and the National Association for the Education of Young Children, although a few cooperative interorganizational projects have occurred, such as developing joint position statements. Interactions among organizations in early care and education are characterized by episodic cooperation amid an atmosphere of mild competition (for attention, funding, members). To become an umbrella group like the Association of Engineering Societies, the National Association for the Education of Young Children's governance structure would require substantial change. Currently, all National Association for the Education of Young Children members are individuals. The organization has a layperson governing board, and a network of affiliates.

Occupational organizations in other fields appear to play important roles in advancing their professions by lobbying for laws and regulations governing their professions, promoting continuing education, and offering advanced certificates of practice. Clearly, somewhat similar organizations already exist in the early care and education field; more (or fewer) may be needed. Further, umbrella organizations appear to be an efficient way to work on common issues in a field with many branches. The early care and education field might benefit from inventing (or adapting) an umbrella organization that could bring together individuals and organizations with common concerns in the field. Key questions for the early care and education field are: What kind of organizational structures would benefit the field most? Is the model of engineering organizational relationships adaptable to early care and education? If so, should the role and purpose of the National Association for the Education of Young Children be rethought? Do we need new organizations? One cautionary note concerns the differences in average salaries between early care and education and other fields. Engineers can afford to support more organizations than licensed practical nurses can. In this respect, early care and education is similar to licensed practical nursing.

Levels of Education in Related Professions

The helping professions (social work and nursing) seem to have struggles concerning professionalism among practitioners in various roles as well as differences of opinion about the levels of education and the preparation required to perform in different roles. Considering that early care and education has the same problems, perhaps this is a characteristic of professions that focus on people, and it may be instructive for early care and education to consider the experiences of social work and nursing concerning professionalism and preparation.

The clear tensions between licensed practical nurses and registered nurses over professionalism and status echo the tensions in early care and education between those who work with children under age five—preschool–child care workers—and those who work with children in school-based prekindergarten, kindergarten, and primary grades—public school teachers. The public image is that teachers in public schools are professionals who need at least four-year degrees. The public image of child care workers is a mixture of teachers (in center-based programs), who need some educational preparation, and home-based providers, who do not need any preparation beyond, perhaps, parenting experience. Parents consistently report that training is not high on the list of qualities they seek in a good child care situation, and somewhat contradictorily also report that they believe child care is educational for their young children (Mitchell, Cooperstein, & Larner, 1992).

Licensed practical nurses seem to have professional image problems similar to child care workers. However, licensed practical nursing is an established profession with licensure and a national examination, professional organizations, and certifications beyond the entry level. The nursing profession as a whole builds on a range of levels of educational preparation, with licensed practical nurses needing one or two years of preparation, and registered nurses needing either an associate degree or a bachelor's degree. The hierarchy of roles is clear in nursing: licensed practical nurses are supervised by registered nurses working in the same setting. This hierarchy does not apply to early care and education. Public school teachers do not supervise child care workers; they work in different settings, one public and the other mainly private. This may suggest that child care workers need the same or similar licensing as public school teachers do.

Although social work is considered one occupation, not two as in the case of licensed practical nurses and registered nurses, similar tensions are manifest within the social work profession between bachelor's level social workers and master's level social workers. Even though the National Association for Social Work offers certification for the bachelor of social work and the master of social work, as well as at the doctorate level, the master of social work is the profession's preferred level for practicing social workers. In a few state licensure laws, definitions of social work practice begin with a licensed social work associate with a high school education or a social work technician with an associate degree (American Association of State Social Work Boards, 1993). In both nursing and social work, levels of practice are defined both by educational attainment and an examination.

Perhaps the early care and education field would benefit from defining these kinds of progressive levels and considering how to codify them as individual licenses. Early care and education occupations are envisioned as an interconnected set of pathways on which movement can be lateral (moving to the same role in another setting), vertical (advancing to a higher role in the same setting type), or lateral progressive (moving to a new role in a new setting). To support this intricate vision with individual licenses for each role and setting might not be feasible because of the large number of licenses that would be created.

Further, if agreement could be reached on a set of licenses, the process of enacting them in every state is daunting. The success of the National Association of Social Workers' campaign during the 1980s to enact social work licensing laws in every state is certainly a notable effort that may offer a model. However, it is important to note that many of these laws have significant exemptions, allowing many unlicensed individuals to practice social work (American Association of State Social Work Boards, 1993); only sixteen states have no exemptions. For example, twenty-nine states exempt students working under supervision; twenty-two exempt government employees; and eight exempt employees of nonprofit organizations. Further, in eighteen states, individuals may practice as social workers without acquiring licenses as long as they do not call themselves licensed social workers (American Association of State Social Work Boards, 1993). This situation is not unlike the states' child care facility-licensing laws, some of which include significant exemptions of centers operated by churches or public schools, as well as exemptions for a large proportion of family child care providers. Changing these exemptions and upgrading child care regulation has generally proved to be difficult, although not impossible. An important point to remember is that early care and education would likely need an organization that parallels the National Association of Social Workers to organize such a campaign across all the states.

Rationales for Individual Licensure

Perhaps the most significant difference between early care and education and other occupations is individual licensure as the entry requirement for practice. Moving toward individual licensure may be the right step for early care and education. Licensure in other occupations is related to public health and safety protection, work that involves direct practice with individuals, situations in which a principal is responsible for the work of others, and situations in which individuals practice independently. Individual licensure may be most reasonable when more than one of these factors is present. All early care and education workers practice directly with individuals—children and to some extent parents. Many early care and education practitioners are responsible for the work of others (center directors), and many practice independently (family child care providers). Should each of these roles require a license? Would a director's license cover all those who practice in the "firm," as is the case for engineers and architects?

Licensure is also related to consumer protection in situations in which consumers are unable to judge for themselves. In some sense, early care and education is regarded by the public as close to parenting, which consumers are presumed to know how to do, thus undercutting arguments for individual licensure on the basis of lack of knowledge. Note, however, that one definition of a profession is an activity or field of endeavor undertaken for gain or livelihood that is often engaged in by amateurs. Although the care and education of groups of children has some connections with parenting, it also has many distinctions: hosting birthday parties or weekend sleepovers with one's own children and their friends is different from being responsible for a group of diverse children all day, every day. Perhaps the fact that early care and education requires skills beyond parenting, especially when done for financial gain, is an argument for establishing some entry requirements and perhaps even licenses.

Occupational Sectors Within a Field

One possibility to consider is that early care and education is not one, but many, occupations. For example, health is a broad field that encompasses many occupations, some professional (doctors, nurses) and some not (nursing aides). Trying to fit all the occupations that currently constitute the field of early care and education into one profession (or occupation) may not be reasonable. The key questions may be: How should the sectors be defined? How can it be determined which are professions? The Department of Labor has made one choice, based on current practices, which is unsatisfactory to most in the field: kindergarten and elementary teaching is professional, whereas preschool child care is service work. Although some interpret it as the care-versus-education split, it may be more closely related to differences in setting—public schools versus other settings. Alternatively, early care and education may be two distinct occupations—center based and home based. Another possibility is independent practice (family child care providers) versus supervised practice (teachers who are supervised). Yet another option is to differentiate among distinct role-setting age combinations (teachers in infant care centers, family child care providers with preschoolers, directors of school age programs in schools).

An individual license for center-based early care and education teachers of children under five could be modeled on the social work system, including a variety of levels up to the doctorate. A smooth path to teacher licensing could be made for those teachers who wish to enter the public school arena. The nursing field offers another model in which licensed practical nurses can become registered nurses without starting over in their training. The early care and education teacher would be analogous to the licensed practical nurse and the public school kindergarten-primary teacher to the registered nurse. Perhaps an associate degree would be sufficient educational preparation for the license to work with children under five, with additional education acquired later on in one's career to reach the level required for the public school teaching license.

However, the early care and education field has not uniformly required any form of licensure or certification for individuals. The basic questions to ask are: Why is there no required individual licensure in early care and education, and should there be?

Open Entry

Coupling open entry into the early care and education field with easy access to training is a strongly held principle for many in the field. The critical factor is easy access to training. In current practice, there are minimal training requirements, little motivation to pursue training, and insufficient access to training. None of the occupations considered, except travel agents, allow such open entry. Some other occupations have entry points that precede the licensed level of practice and also keep the various levels of practice distinct. Engineering has engineering technologists; social work has social work assistants; nursing has nurses' aides. Perhaps if early care and education clarified the entry qualifications for the differentiated roles in the field, it could achieve better occupational definition and could still allow entry to certain roles that might be deemed apprenticeships, internships, or otherwise practiced under supervision. Another option might be to allow open access to a wider variety of roles but require (and support) movement toward acquisition of a license within a specified period of time.

Establishing entry requirements such as licensure and the upgrading of qualifications by a profession (as has happened in both teaching and nursing) is closely related to wages. If there are nonexistent or minimal entry standards, then there is by definition an unlimited supply of workers and no incentive to increase low wages. Entry standards serve to limit the supply of workers deemed to be qualified and thus act as an indirect catalyst to raise wages. Obviously, entry requirements can also be used as a tool of discrimination to exclude certain groups from a profession. For example, access to jobs as firefighters and police officers was routinely denied to women on the basis of physical entry requirements, many of which were shown to be unrelated to job performance. One of the toughest problems in early care and education is low compensation (wages and benefits). All of the occupations considered here have both better entry-level salaries and much better median salaries than early care and education. Even beauticians make more than child care workers. Individual licensure may well be the reason.

The Nexus of Individual Licensure

The apparent success of individual licensing in other occupations may not be due to licensing itself but to the set of related factors that characterize occupations: licenses are required by law to practice an occupation; boards set the standards for the license; schools prepare people for the occupation; standards set by the boards influence the offerings of the schools; and professional organizations offer advanced credentials. Facility regulations (not discussed in this chapter) reinforce the individual licensing laws in other occupations by requiring certain numbers of properly licensed persons in various work conditions (for example, hospital regulations specify minimum numbers of nursing personnel based on patient load or bed density). Finally, the hiring practices of employers have to comply with the laws and regulations governing the industry.

These factors are obviously interdependent and collectively influence the development and advancement of an occupation. This may be the most powerful lesson the early care and education field can learn from other occupations and one that should provoke much more discussion. Do early care and education practitioners want to create the set of factors that characterize other occupations? Which factors are present and which are lacking? If the field chose to move in this direction, how should it proceed?

Conclusion

If early care and education followed the approaches and patterns of other occupations, our field might look quite different than it does at present. Over time, the majority of individuals who work with young children in all types of settings would be licensed. A national professional organization whose members are those who work with young children would work through its state affiliates to establish licensing laws in every state, or a coalition of sectoral organizations would jointly mount such a campaign. The state licensure laws would establish independent boards to grant licenses and would use nationally developed performance assessments as part of the licensing process. The National Council for Accreditation of Teacher Education (or a similar organization) would accredit not only four-year colleges but all levels of preparation programs according to national standards. National professional organization(s) would offer numerous advanced certificates for specializations within the field. The result might well be significantly better quality daily experiences and outcomes for children. The stature of early care and education as an occupation and its compensation might rise as well.

Before we embark on such a bold journey, there are undoubtedly other issues to be explored and considerations to be addressed that go beyond the scope of this chapter. As a first step, it is important that those in the early care and education field think critically about the issues raised herein and discuss them widely and thoughtfully.

Note

1. The sole exception is the state of Florida, which requires that there be one adult with a CDA or its equivalent for every twenty children in a child care center.

References

American Association of State Social Work Boards. (1993). *Social work laws and board regulations: A state comparison summary.* Culpeper, Va.: American Association of State Social Work Boards.

Azer, S. L. (1993). *Promising practices in teacher education.* Boston: Center for Career Development in Early Care and Education, Wheelock College.

Johnson, J., & McCracken, J. B. (Eds.). (1994). *The early childhood career lattice: Perspectives on professional development.* Washington, D.C.: National Association for the Education of Young Children.

Mitchell, A., Cooperstein, E., & Larner, M. (1992). *Child care choices, consumer education and low-income families.* New York: National Center for Children in Poverty.

Morgan, G., & McGimsey, B. (1993). *States' policies on qualifications for roles in early care and education: A working paper.* Boston: Center for Career Development in Early Care and Education, Wheelock College.

National Child Care Association. (1992). *Child care professional credentialing program for the early childhood education specialist.* Atlanta: National Child Care Association.

National Council for Accreditation of Teacher Education. (1994). *Conditions and procedures for State/NCATE partnerships.* Washington, D.C.: National Council for Accreditation of Teacher Education.

U.S. Department of Labor. (1993). *Occupational outlook handbook, 1992–93 edition.* Washington, D.C.: U.S. Department of Labor, Bureau of Labor Statistics.

Wise, A. E., Darling-Hammond, L., with Berry, B., & Klein, S. P. (1987). *Licensing teachers: Design for a teaching profession.* Santa Monica, Calif.: Rand Corporation.

Chapter Seven

Training and Professional Development
International Approaches
Eliza Pritchard

Introduction

With the demand for early care and education continuing to grow in the United States, straining the disconnected system of early childhood services that exists, the tension in the field between increasing the quantity of services and improving their quality remains grave. This tension is particularly apparent when one considers the training of U.S. early childhood workers. In the United States, professional development for early childhood educators—a powerful tool for improving the quality of services in a field—has until recently been largely overlooked in the struggle to meet demand. What has been the result? Professional development in the nation's early care and education field has taken the form of a training nonsystem, characterized by inconsistent training requirements across states and program types, disconnected training programs, and limited opportunities for professional advancement (Morgan & others, 1993). As early child care workers are confronted with increasing responsibility for the learning and devel-

Note: The author would like to acknowledge the generosity and helpful comments of Moncrieff Cochran, Sheila Kamerman, and Rosemary Renwick, who reviewed earlier drafts of this chapter.

opment of America's young children, the nation demands little or no preparation of early care and education personnel and provides them with few incentives to enhance their teaching and caregiving skills.

Providers, academics, and policy makers alike have identified the inadequacies of professional development in American early care and education and have envisioned solutions (Copple, 1990; Morgan & others, 1993); yet, the challenge remains significant, calling for further attention and broadened debate. An area of inquiry left largely unexplored is that of international approaches to professional development in early care and education. Though the training of early childhood workers is a challenge worldwide, several early childhood–professional development systems abroad have emerged as sophisticated models that are useful to consider in the United States.

This chapter initiates such consideration. Specifically, the chapter explores the regulation and delivery of early care and education training in other countries and discusses implications for the United States as it moves forward to establish a quality system of early childhood professional development. Discussion throughout the chapter focuses on professional development in seven industrialized countries—Finland, France, Japan, New Zealand, Norway, Sweden, and the United Kingdom. Based on secondary sources, this chapter and its conclusions should be regarded as exploratory, providing a preliminary framework for understanding professional development internationally and making comparisons with the United States.

Regulation of Early Care and Education Training

Given the poor quality of the current system of training regulation in the United States, international approaches to the regulation of early care and education professional development deserve consideration. Throughout the United States, the regulation of training for early care and education staff is inadequate and inconsistent at best and nonexistent at worst. Standards for the professional development of early childhood personnel are determined on a state-by-state basis and are tied either to the licensing of child care facilities or to public school certification.

When facilities are exempt from licensing—as are many church-run centers, family child care homes, part-day private nursery schools, and school-based programs across the states (Morgan & others, 1993)—early care and education personnel (except those in public schools) are also exempt from requirements for professional preparation. For facilities subject to licensing standards, only sixteen states require that early care and education providers receive specialized, preservice training. This training is minimal in most states, with many demanding less than twelve credit hours in early childhood education, and only two states requiring college level certificates as a minimum qualification for nonpublic school–early childhood teachers (Morgan & others, 1993).

The regulation of early care and education training in other industrialized nations tends to be more centralized and stringent than in the United States. Centralized administration of training and high standards for staff preparation are crucial components of early childhood professional development in each of the nations discussed.

Centralized Administration of Training

In contrast to the United States, each of the industrialized nations reviewed in this chapter has developed centralized administration of early care and education training. Although centralization may be feasible in some of these countries due largely to their small sizes, their relative geographic homogeneity, or their traditions of centralization in other human service areas—none of which characterizes the United States—the benefits of central administration in establishing coherent early childhood professional development are useful to consider.

In other industrialized countries, centralized administration of training is usually housed at the national level in either departments of education or in departments of health and social services. Central administration typically involves setting national training standards, determining the content of training for various staff positions, specifying staffing patterns, monitoring training-delivery institutions to ensure that the content and quality of courses remain adequate, and setting up a system to enforce training standards—usually at the state or county level.

Benefits in Several Countries

France addresses many of these regulatory tasks through centralized administration. Reflecting Western Europe's trend of establishing an extensive national infrastructure to support children and families (Kamerman & Kahn, 1991), France has developed a relatively large sector of publicly supported, licensed early care and education programs, serving 29 percent of children under three and 98 percent of children aged three to five (Combes, 1993). The administration of training for early care and education staff in France is based at the national level, with day care (birth to three) training standards set by the Ministry of Health and Social Affairs, and *école maternelle* (three to five) preparation requirements specified by the Ministry of Education. France's national training standards for day care personnel require health-oriented preparation focusing on child development, developmental theory, and practice. Central requirements for *école maternelle* teachers involve training in theory, school subjects, administrative and social knowledge, and teaching practice (Pascal, Bertram, & Heaslip, 1991).

Finland provides a second example of a nation with a centralized training system in early care and education. Finland's 1973 Day Care Law—administered nationally through the Ministry for Social Welfare and Health—sets training standards for day care (birth to seven) and family child care (birth to three) in both public and private settings. For day care centers, the national law requires that staffing patterns include a combination of child nurses, social pedagogues (personnel with social service training), and preschool teachers, depending on the composition of the group under care (Ojala, 1989). Administration of training and professional development for Finland's preschool teachers falls under the national Ministry of Education.

The examples of France and Finland demonstrate several benefits of centralized administration of early care and education training. First, the specification of uniform, national training standards minimizes regional variation in the quality of teaching and caregiving in each country. Service provision throughout the countries becomes more equitable and continuous, making transfers from early childhood programs in different regions minimally disruptive for children, families, and teachers. Second, as illustrated in the case of Finland, when staffing patterns are specified through centralized administration, teachers and caregivers with different backgrounds can be linked in a coherent professional framework. Third, national specification of the content of early care and education training, as in France, can assure quality and continuity across training-delivery institutions.

Care-Versus-Education Split

Centralized administration of early childhood professional development has its drawbacks as well. In France, Finland, and other countries, centrally controlled training tends to be split for teachers working with children of different ages. The professional development of day care teachers—who work with children under age three—is typically overseen by national departments of health and social services, whereas the training of preschool teachers—who work with children over age three—is most often controlled by national departments of education. Professional development for day care personnel tends to be vocationally oriented and health focused. In contrast, preschool teacher training is frequently carried out at the college or graduate level with a strong focus on pedagogy. Thus, day care centers are staffed primarily by pediatric assistants, child nurses, and social pedagogues, whereas preschools are dominated by teachers.

The terms vary from country to country, yet the trend is the same. This segregation of day care and preschool staff into separate professional development tracks—focusing on health versus pedagogy or care versus education—does not reflect children's comprehensive needs and contributes to the division within the early care and education profession. Historical reasons exist for the care-versus-education divide, including the need to focus on health when caring for very young children who are vulnerable to malnutrition and disease (Richardson & Marx, 1989). In the absence of such pressing health issues in most industrialized countries, however, the professional development of all early childhood teachers can be enhanced by an integrated, cross-age conception of the goals of early care and education.

Preliminary steps toward this age-integrated approach have been taken in some centralized training systems. In Finland, for example, though preschool and day care teachers pass through different training systems, which vary in focus and administration, they are brought together in day care centers via nationally specified staffing patterns. Requiring a mix of staff trained in health and social services alongside preschool teachers with more background in pedagogy, Finland's staffing patterns help meld care with education and provide children in day care centers with a multidisciplinary staff capable of addressing their comprehensive needs.

Trend Toward Decentralization

A second drawback to centralized administration of training is a lack of flexibility. Under fully centralized training systems, students, local regulators, and training institutions have limited input into early childhood professional development. When training is controlled centrally, courses and administrative procedures usually cannot be tailored to local needs and preferences.

Recognizing these problems, most industrialized countries have begun to decentralize parts of their early care and education training systems.[1] In Sweden, for example—where training standards and program content are specified nationally through the Board of Health and Welfare—decentralization has been introduced in the area of curriculum development. The board has replaced detailed and closely regulated curricula for early care and education training courses with more general study plans, focusing broadly on the purpose, content, and structure of early care and education training. Individual training institutions—in conjunction with committees composed of teachers, students, and early care and education workers—are now responsible for the details of training curricula (Pascal, Bertram, & Heaslip, 1991). This shift toward more local responsibility for training development serves to tailor training courses to local needs and to increase the involvement and investment of local institutions and community members.

High Preparation Standards

In the industrialized countries that this chapter examines, centralized training systems require early care and education personnel to meet high preparation standards. Such rigorous standards in other countries are closely linked to nationally specified ratios and staffing patterns, as well as to the status and compensation of early childhood workers.

Levels of Training Required

In France, the minimum preparation standard for preschool teaching surpasses the requirements of most other industrialized nations. *École maternelle* teachers in France are trained in the same institutions and classes as elementary and secondary school teachers, all of whom are required to have a three-year university degree and two years of professional teacher training at the master's level (Pascal, Bertram, & Heaslip, 1991). Slightly less rigorous standards in Finland, Japan, Sweden, and the United Kingdom all require at least two years of specialized, college level training before individuals can begin work as official early childhood teachers. In Finnish preschools, teachers must have at least three years of training at a teacher-training college (Ojala, 1989). In Japan, all teachers in early care and education are required to complete two years of college education in subjects including child development and health (Lassegard, 1993). Sweden's early childhood teachers must complete two and a half years of college education in order to enter the workforce with the required certificates in infant and nursery education (Gunnarsson, 1993). Finally, early care and education teachers in the United Kingdom are required to complete four years of college level training to gain Qualified Teacher Status (Pascal, Bertram, & Heaslip, 1991).

In countries where there is a split in the administration of day care and preschool training, minimum training standards for day care staff (usually not called teachers) are more vocationally oriented, yet still demanding and specialized in comparison with United States requirements. In Finland, for example, day care personnel must complete at least one year of post–high school nurse training to become child nurses or four years of social service training to become social pedagogues (Ojala, 1989). Similarly, France's day care workers are required to complete pediatric-assistant training, which is equivalent to two years of college (Combes, 1993).

In other countries, early care and education training standards require little of preschool teachers and day care staff but high levels of preparation for supervisors and directors. In New Zealand, supervisors in all day care centers and kindergartens are required by the Department of Education to complete nationally recognized training in either primary teaching or nursing (Smith & Swain, 1988).[2] In Norway, the training requirement for lead teachers and directors is three years of early childhood teacher training at an educational college (Bo, 1993).

In spite of these high preparation standards for early care and education staff, most of these countries exempt family child care personnel from professional development requirements, as does the United States. Even in countries where family child care providers are licensed, publicly supported, and brought under government supervision in public family child care networks, little staff training or preparation is required. In Norway, for example, the main guidance provided to licensed, public family child care providers consists of short-term courses offered periodically in scattered cities and supervised by network directors who are trained early childhood teachers (Bo, 1993).

Several exceptions to this trend of exemption exist, however. In the United Kingdom, family child care providers are required to register with their local social services departments, and as a part of this process, they must participate in preregistration training programs (Cohen, 1993). In Finland, the Day Care Law requires that family child care providers complete a 16-hour first aid class and a 250-hour training course approved by the National Board of Vocational Education (Ojala, 1989).

Ratios and Staffing Patterns

In conjunction with elevated training standards, several industrialized nations allow higher child-staff ratios than does the United States. Ratios considered optimal in the United States are three infants to one adult, six toddlers to one adult, and ten four- and five-year-olds to one adult (Bredekamp, 1987). In contrast, nationally specified child-staff ratios for French day care centers are five to one for children not yet able to walk, and eight to one for children under three who can walk. In French *écoles maternelles,* the required child-staff proportion is twenty-eight to one (Richardson & Marx, 1989). Similarly, Japan's child-staff ratios for day care centers are set at six to one for infants and toddlers, and thirty to one for children over age four (Shwalb, Shwalb, Sukemune, & Tatsumoto, 1992).

Without consideration of context, such ratios appear potentially detrimental to children, possibly depriving them of close, individual interaction with adults. Often, however, high child-staff ratios in other nations are linked to elevated preparation standards and variegated staffing patterns that promote positive child-staff interactions and thereby enhance the quality of services children receive. In Japan, for example, teachers caring for relatively large groups of children in day care centers have at least two years of college level preparation. Similarly, staffing patterns required in French *écoles maternelles* include master's level teachers as well as untrained teacher aides and a lunch and nap time staff. These additional staff members provide overall classroom support and allow each *école maternelle* teacher a two-hour break at midday (Richardson & Marx, 1989). In sum, ratios in other countries are not crafted in isolation from other elements of early care and education programs. In many of the nations examined, national standards for ratios, staffing patterns, and the training of personnel are closely linked.

Status and Compensation

Standards for professional development in early care and education are also closely linked to the status and compensation of early childhood workers. Surprisingly, in spite of high staff preparation standards, the status and salaries of early care and education personnel in most industrialized nations are low in comparison with similar occupations (Bo, 1993; Gunnarsson, 1993; Smith & Swain, 1988). The United Kingdom and France are two exceptions, with preschool teachers in both countries receiving status and compensation equivalent to that of teachers in elementary and secondary education (Pascal, Bertram, & Heaslip, 1991). In both nations, such elevated status and wages have been achieved by raising preschool training requirements to equal those of elementary and secondary school teachers.

Without a centralized system of professional development and the use of cost-effective measures—such as high child-staff ratios in classrooms—it would be difficult to raise the status and compensation of early childhood workers in these nations. It should also be noted that France and the United Kingdom have increased the status and compensation of teachers in only one type of early education—preschool. In addition, both countries may have sacrificed a degree of specialization in the early care and education field by combining professional development for all teachers, whether at the early childhood, elementary, or secondary level. These limitations aside, the examples of France and the United Kingdom emphasize the interconnections between training standards and other crucial components of professional development, including status and compensation.

Overall, the regulation of early care and education training in many industrialized nations has led to the development of relatively sophisticated systems of professional preparation. Combining centralized administration of training, elevated training standards, flexibility in ratios and staffing patterns, and in some cases enhanced status and compensation, foreign approaches to training regulation provide fresh ideas for planners and policy makers in the United States.

Delivery of Early Care and Education Training

The impact of training regulation in the early care and education field depends largely on the accessibility and quality of the training opportunities that prospective teachers and caregivers encounter. The United States's patchwork approach to the regulation of professional development is matched by a fragmented, inadequate training-delivery system. In navigating this system, early childhood educators find they have limited access to the professional development opportunities they seek. Early care and education training delivery in the United States is marked by a shortage of specialized training courses, especially for early childhood providers with higher levels of education and experience (Kagan, 1990). Training programs and courses that do exist are delivered through a variety of community organizations, as well as public and private two- and four-year colleges. Few of these institutions have developed articulation agreements to facilitate the transfer of credit. Moreover, funds for training programs—emanating from disconnected sources at the federal, state, and local levels—are minimal. As a result, most in the early care and education field, already undercompensated, are forced to pay for their own professional development (Morgan & others, 1993). In sum, given the training-delivery system that currently exists, it is difficult for early care and education providers in the United States to access, piece together, and afford a coherent program of study that will enhance their work in the field.

Not surprisingly, more rigorous regulation of early care and education training in other industrialized countries is coupled with more coherent and accessible training delivery. In the countries discussed in this chapter, national training standards tend to be backed by extensive systems of public vocational and higher education that offer nationally monitored programs of study in early childhood education. Although such centralization of training delivery is unlikely in the United States, several foreign nations have addressed issues of training accessibility—including availability, coherence, and affordability—through innovative strategies that are useful to consider in any context.

Availability of Training

Recent developments in the United Kingdom illustrate the possibility of expanding training opportunities by increasing the number of paths to teaching in the early care and education field. Under previous regulations, the United Kingdom set two training requirements for staff in public day nurseries and nursery schools. The minimum requirement was two years of post–age sixteen vocational training to become a nursery nurse. Nursery nurses worked alongside qualified teachers who were required to complete four years of college level teacher training to receive Qualified Teacher Status (Pascal, Bertram, & Heaslip, 1991). Recently, however, alternative paths to meeting the requirements for Qualified Teacher Status have been developed: first, students with a minimum of two years of college who are over the age of twenty-six can begin teaching without a period of professional training and can study part-time under the guidance of a local authority in order to receive Qualified Teacher Status; second, another route allows college graduates who have not studied pedagogy to teach part-time while completing a two-year postgraduate course leading to Qualified Teacher Status (Pascal, Bertram, & Heaslip, 1991).

In developing alternative routes to Qualified Teacher Status, the United Kingdom has enhanced the availability of relevant training and potentially has increased the number of qualified early care and education teachers. The nation has done so without significantly restructuring its established training-delivery system. In the face of limited resources, the diversification of routes into the early childhood profession can be a useful first step in increasing the availability of early childhood training opportunities.

Coherence of Training Opportunities

Promising efforts to address training coherence in other nations focus on coordinating multiple, fragmented routes into the profession. Though it is important to maintain multiple paths to early childhood teaching—especially when the availability of training opportunities is limited as discussed above—such open access is compromised when training routes are isolated and unconnected, when credit cannot be transferred from one type of training to another, and when educational experiences cannot build on one another. Sweden and Japan both have addressed these problems and have established coherence between their multiple training paths.

In Sweden, various routes into the profession have been coordinated through the establishment of a common training base for teachers and caregivers in all types of early care and education. The system works as follows: both day care centers and preschools in Sweden are staffed by some combination of preschool teachers, who are required to obtain a certificate in nursery and infant education, and nursery nurses, who are required to complete nursing training. Nursing training consists of a two-year, post–age-sixteen secondary school nursing program. Beyond that, there are three alternative routes to the certificate in nursing and infant education held by preschool teachers; each route is based on an individual's previous training and experience. The first is two and a half years of college level training for caregivers without previous children's nurse education; the second, two years of training for students who have completed children's nurse training; and the third, one and a quarter years of training for students with children's nurse training plus four years of work experience in preschool or day care programs (Pascal, Bertram, & Heaslip, 1991). The coherence of this system stems from the fact that each of the routes into day care and preschool teaching has the common base of nursing training, which is regarded as valid preparation across different types of care and can always be built on if a teacher wants to train further for a different staff position.

Also addressing the coherence of professional development, Japan has recently worked to connect two segregated training paths. Regulated early care and education in Japan consists mainly of *yochien*, care for three- to six-year-olds, which is supervised by the Ministry of Education, and *hoikuen*, care for children from birth to age six, which is regulated by the Ministry of Health and Welfare. Although previously training requirements for both types of care were quite different, making it difficult for *hoikuen*-trained teachers to find jobs in *yochien*, certification requirements have since been better aligned. Now most *hoikuen* instructors are trained to work in *yochien* as well. This has been achieved by generalizing the training for both types of care to consist of two years of college education in various subjects including child development, health, and music (Lassegard, 1993).

Affordability of Training

Though the costs of early childhood professional development abroad may not be high for individuals—due to more extensive systems of publicly supported vocational and higher education than in the United States—several nations have instituted notable systems of financial support and incentives for individuals pursuing early care and education training.

In New Zealand, though funding for early childhood professional development has recently changed due to Ministry of Education reforms (Ministry of Education, 1994), a former system of financial support provided training grants to early care and education teachers. As of 1987, the grants were distributed on a weekly basis to part-time and full-time early childhood personnel. In U.S. equivalents, the compensation was $14.47 for trained supervisors, $13.07 for trained staff, and $4.35 for staff in training. Yearly totals of the grant funds received by early childhood workers were significant, with trained supervisors, for example, receiving $7,500 over twelve months of work (Smith & Swain, 1988). In addition to providing funds to offset the costs of training, this system offered incentives for career advancement by linking increased dollars to higher levels of education.

In France, training for *école maternelle* staff has been made affordable through support from the national Ministry of Education. The ministry provides free education and a stipend during the training period to teachers who agree to spend five years working in *écoles maternelles* after completing their preparation. As a result, a large number of qualified applicants have been attracted to preschool teacher-training programs, and the retention rate of qualified personnel in *écoles maternelles* has increased (Richardson & Marx, 1989). Although France's strategy is limited because it applies to staff in only one type of early childhood program, it addresses the problems of staff recruitment and retention effectively.

Such innovative approaches to training delivery are crucial to consider in any effort to enhance the accessibility of professional development opportunities in early care and education. A delivery system in which an array of training is readily available, coherent, and affordable forms the backbone of professional development. Without such a delivery system, regulation becomes ineffective; motivated early care and education providers have little incentive to meet high standards.

Implications for the United States

The seven nations discussed in this chapter—Finland, France, Japan, New Zealand, Norway, Sweden, and the United Kingdom—have addressed many important issues related to professional development in early care and education. Although these countries differ significantly from each other and from the United States, their efforts to prepare teachers and caregivers for employment in the early childhood field display common themes that may be useful in guiding work in this country.

The first theme is centralized administration. Given the decentralized nature of government in the United States, the concept of centralized administration in any domain or field may seem implausible. Yet, in order to attach more coherence, consistency, and rigor to early care and education professional development in the United States, questions related to centralization are important to address. At what level—state or federal—might centralized administration of training be most effective in the United States? If centralization occurs at the state level, what state agencies or departments should be responsible for enhancing and overseeing early childhood professional development? How can linkages be made with state certification for teaching in elementary and secondary education to avoid institutionalizing two separate systems for child care and public education—that is, a care-versus-education split? Would it be beneficial to link state–professional development systems nationwide through model guidelines and certification exams at the national level? The nature of administration in an improved early care and education–professional development system is a recurring theme that our nation must confront.

A second theme emerging from other industrialized countries is high preparation standards for early care and education staff. The time has come for the early childhood field in the United States to reconcile its worthy tradition of open entry into the profession with the need for a well-prepared, credentialed workforce. In confronting this need, early care and education providers, planners, and policy makers must recognize the implications that elevated training standards might have for staff-child ratios, staffing patterns, and status and compensation within the field. High training standards should not be considered in isolation; rather, the benefits and changes they may occasion should be envisioned as an important part of all professional development–related decisions. If higher training standards are required for lead teachers, what types of staffing patterns might serve to maximize the potential of assistant teachers and aides who have not yet met these standards? Could fewer teachers work effectively with more children if staff were better prepared? If early childhood teaching standards were aligned with standards for public school teachers, what would be the implications for the status and compensation of early care and education personnel?

Still other questions need to be raised around a third theme of professional development in industrialized nations abroad—accessible training opportunities. Though early care and education training in the United States is delivered through a mixed-sector system that is perhaps more unwieldy than the educational landscapes in other countries, international efforts to increase the accessibility of training may be adaptable to the U.S. context. For example, if various states in the nation set high training requirements for early care and education teachers, the availability of necessary training opportunities could be maximized by specifying a number of training-equivalency options, as has been done in the United Kingdom. The United States might also explore the possibilities of promoting training coherence via a common, recognized training base and credential for all early care and education workers, or of minimizing the costs of training through a national service plan similar to the system in France. In short, the United States should take its cue from other industrialized nations to make professional development in early care and education feasible for all and to support training delivery as the functional gear that sets in motion the vision of a well-prepared and esteemed early childhood workforce.

Notes

1. Certain developing countries—not discussed in this chapter due to their limited relevance to the United States—have also focused on decentralizing the administration of early care and education training. Kenya's approach is especially interesting, involving a national effort to develop in-service training models at the local level in collaboration with trainers, teachers, parents, and local leaders. Kenya's effort provides an example of centralized control "brought to the grassroots level" (Kipkorir, 1993, p. 347).
2. Given recent changes in New Zealand's administration of early childhood education, a new *qualifications framework* for staff in a range of early care and education programs is being developed (Ministry of Education, 1994).

References

Bo, I. (1993). Norway. In M. Cochran (Ed.), *International handbook of child care policies and programs* (pp. 391–414). Westport, Conn.: Greenwood Press.

Bredekamp, S. (Ed.). (1987). *Developmentally appropriate practice in early childhood programs serving children from birth through age 8: Expanded edition.* Washington, D.C.: National Association for the Education of Young Children.

Cohen, B. (1993). The United Kingdom. In M. Cochran (Ed.), *International handbook of child care policies and programs* (pp. 515–534). Westport, Conn.: Greenwood Press.

Combes, J. (1993). France. In M. Cochran (Ed.), *International handbook of child care policies and programs* (pp. 187–210). Westport, Conn.: Greenwood Press.

Copple, C. (1990). *Quality matters: Improving the professional development of the early childhood work force.* Washington, D.C.: National Institute for Early Childhood Professional Development.

Gunnarsson, L. (1993). Sweden. In M. Cochran (Ed.), *International handbook of child care policies and programs* (pp. 491–514). Westport, Conn.: Greenwood Press.

Kagan, S. L. (1990). A profession growing up: Painting our think. In C. Copple (Ed.), *Quality matters: Improving the professional development of the early childhood work force* (pp. 17–27). Washington, D.C.: National Institute for Early Childhood Professional Development.

Kamerman, S. B., & Kahn, A. J. (1991). A U.S. policy challenge. In S. B. Kamerman & A. J. Kahn (Eds.), *Child care, parental leave, and the under 3's: Policy innovation in Europe* (pp. 1–22). Westport, Conn.: Auburn House.

Kipkorir, L. I. (1993). Kenya. In M. Cochran (Ed.), *International handbook of child care policies and programs* (pp. 333–352). Westport, Conn.: Greenwood Press.

Lassegard, E. (1993). Japan. In M. Cochran (Ed.), *International handbook of child care policies and programs* (pp. 313–332). Westport, Conn.: Greenwood Press.

Ministry of Education. (1994). *Better beginnings: Early childhood education in New Zealand.* Wellington, New Zealand: Ministry of Education.

Morgan, G., & others. (1993). *Making a career of it: The state of the states report on career development in early care and education.* Boston: Center for Career Development in Early Care and Education, Wheelock College.

Ojala, M. (1989). Early childhood training, care, and education in Finland. In P. P. Olmsted & D. P. Weikhart (Eds.), *How nations serve young children: Profiles of child care and education in 14 countries.* Ypsilanti, Mich.: High/Scope Press.

Pascal, C., Bertram, T., & Heaslip, P. (1991, September). *Comparative directory of initial training for early years teachers.* Worcester, England: Association of Teacher Education in Europe, Early Years Working Group.

Richardson, G., & Marx, E. (1989). *A welcome for every child: How France achieves quality in child care—practical ideas for the United States.* New York: French-American Foundation.

Shwalb, D. W., Shwalb, B. J., Sukemune, S., & Tatsumoto, S. (1992). Japanese nonmaternal care. In M. E. Lamb, K. J. Sternberg, C. Hwang, & A. G. Broberg (Eds.), *Child care in context: Cross-cultural perspectives* (pp. 331–353). Hillsdale, N.J.: Erlbaum.

Smith, A. B., & Swain, D. A. (1988). *Childcare in New Zealand: People, programs, politics.* Wellington, New Zealand: Allen & Unwin/Port Nicholson Press.

Chapter Eight

Regulation

Alternative Approaches from Other Fields

Katherine L. Scurria

Recent history has precipitated a crisis of public confidence in the value of regulation, as changes in prevailing political ideology have affected both the substance and the procedure of regulation as a government tool. This crisis of confidence, in conjunction with the rise of cost-benefit analyses used to determine public policy, has generated an increasingly popular and widespread school of thought, which suggests that government need not do away with regulations altogether but can obtain its regulatory goals more effectively by using incentive-based methods (such as self-regulation through training and professional organizations, consumer education, and ombudsmen) rather than "command-and-control" methods (such as fining or closing programs with violations).

Note: Discussion at two meetings on regulation of early care and education was the impetus for this chapter. The meeting participants included, for the Washington, D.C., meeting, March 1993—Helen Bank, Children's Defense Fund; Harriet Fields, National Citizen's Coalition for Nursing Home Reform; William Gormley, Graduate School of Public Policy, Georgetown University; Paulene Koch, Delaware Department of Services for Children, Youth and Their Families; and Ruth Ruttenberg, Ruth Ruttenberg and Associates, Inc.; and for the San Francisco meeting, April 1993—Eugene Bardach, University of California at Berkeley; David Dodds, Community Care Licensing Division, California Department of Social Services; Erica Grubb, Attorney; Nettie Hoge, Consumers Union; Pat McGinnis, California Advocates for Nursing Home Reform; David Roe, Environmental Defense Fund; and Carol Stevenson, Child Care Law Center.

According to this school of thought, traditional forms of regulation have proven ineffective, as has marketplace regulation. Arguments supporting a laissez-faire market approach do not account for market imperfections that result from limited purchasing power and poor constituent information about the goods to be purchased. Thus, in an absolute laissez-faire marketplace, consumers are forced to choose inadequate programs if alternatives do not exist or if they lack the resources to choose otherwise. Proponents of incentive-based regulations argue that if the government eradicated traditional preconceptions about regulation and used incentives, it would be possible to obtain more quality for less cost. Providers would self-enforce standards because it would be in their economic best interest to do so.

In the context of the prevailing crisis of confidence in government regulations, this chapter delineates the primary points of contention that hinder effective regulation in the field of early care and education; examines factors that make regulation of an industry acceptable to both the public and policy makers; and explores an array of incentive-based regulatory mechanisms used in other fields, which are potentially more effective than the current command-and-control regulatory scheme in early care and education.

Obstacles to Effective Regulation

Six contentious issues have developed over the history of early care and education and now stand as formidable obstacles to effective regulation of the field. They are (1) whether the government should regulate this industry; (2) if so, at what level of government the responsibility for regulating should reside; (3) the scope of state and local regulations; (4) whether certain types of providers should be exempt from regulation; (5) who should bear the cost of regulation; and (6) the lack of consensus within the field.

Whether to Regulate

Ideologically, the nation harbors strong feelings that family matters are private and should be free from government interference. The thought of early care and education as an industry to be regulated is repugnant to those who view early care and education as solely a family matter. Practically, government regulation of the field is complex because out-of-home early care and education is simultaneously considered a family matter, a market commodity, and a public good. Making it even more complicated for government to regulate, this "industry" includes early care and education centers serving scores of families, family child care providers with small numbers of children, and in-home nannies.

For economic reasons, many for-profit providers of early care and education oppose regulation. They emphasize that regulations increase costs, thereby decreasing the supply of care, and that regulation drives providers underground, which creates unfair competition. For-profit providers argue that the marketplace is a better regulator than the government because in an unchecked marketplace, providers can compete on a level playing field (National Child Care Association, 1993).

What Level of Government Should Regulate

States currently maintain the primary responsibility for both licensing and inspection, sharing regulatory power with local governments, which enforce fire, building, land use, and health codes that vary dramatically from locale to locale. Advocates for a coherent and substantive federal role in early care and education cite the need for federal leadership to counter both the extreme variability of state regulations and the unregulated programs in which children risk injury. Those who oppose a federal role argue that because it is important for local jurisdictions to be able to tailor early care and education regulations to meet local needs and because of the cost implications of a federal regulatory program, a substantive federal role would do more harm than good (Phillips, Lande, & Goldberg, 1990).

Scope of State and Local Regulations

At the state level, there are baseline requirements that many early care and education programs must meet in order to operate legally. Most states exempt certain providers from regulation, including some family child care providers, church-based programs, school-based programs, and part-day programs, although some states still require these entities to register with the state. Programs that fail to be licensed or registered in a state with such requirements are operating underground.

Regulations at the local level often exert significant influence on supply and can be inappropriately stringent. Although many zoning laws and building codes were never intended to preclude day care, because they were developed for other purposes, such as zoning laws to keep funeral homes out of residential neighborhoods, these local regulations make it difficult for providers to operate and discourage some from obtaining licenses (Gormley, 1992).

Whether Some Programs Should Be Exempt

The crisis of confidence in regulations is intensified in early care and education because current regulations are not enforced, and many providers are exempt from regulation altogether. Many entities operate underground without meeting state and local requirements. They are able to do so because enforcement agencies are inadequately funded, assess only mild penalties for infractions, and exert only minimal oversight. Depending on the state, church and public school programs, part-day programs, and family child care homes with smaller numbers of children may be exempt. The issue of exemption goes far beyond confidence in regulation, however, and extends to problems of equity, access, and cost.

Who Should Bear the Cost of Regulation

Economics is a central issue in the regulation of any industry because regulation imposes artificial limits on the levels of production and costs of goods and services. In most industries, the cost of regulation is passed on to consumers through higher prices. When a violation of regulatory requirements is detected, consumer advocates generally examine a company's solvency to evaluate how much penalty it can bear. Early care and education providers, however, often have empty pockets and cannot pass along increased costs because most consumers of early care and education cannot afford to pay them. If mandated requirements cost providers too much, they either move underground or go out of business.

Regulation of early care and education is particularly difficult because the field is underfunded, and there is no universal or sustained third-party payer.

Lack of Consensus Within the Field

Although academics and professional associations generally agree on what constitutes quality early care and education, the early care and education community at large, including providers and administrators of programs, is not in agreement on what elements of quality should be regulated, stringently enforced, voluntarily encouraged, or left entirely to market forces. There are differences of opinion among providers under different auspices, including Head Start, family child care, for-profit centers, nonprofit centers, schools, and churches. Common ground exists among many of these players in their shared view that there is an uneven playing field due to exemptions and that parents can benefit from consumer education to recognize and demand quality through parental choice. Providers differ, however, in their beliefs about which providers should be regulated, which aspects of care should be regulated, and at what levels—federal, state, or local—these variables should be regulated.

Lessons from Other Fields: Creating Acceptance of Regulation

Lessons from other fields have demonstrated that, regardless of the industry, certain elements must be in place to generate an effective regulatory policy. John Mendeloff (1979) has described the requirements of this process: a rationale for government intervention must be articulated; there must be a political decision to intervene that results in legislation; and chosen methods of intervention and enforcement must be developed. The remainder of this chapter addresses those requirements, looking at how other fields have met them successfully and how early care and education might learn from such experiences.

Necessity of Having Clear Goals

The first lesson learned from examining other fields is that advocates of regulatory policy must explain why government should intervene and must articulate clearly the goal of that intervention. Legislation governing drunk driving, consumer products, workplace safety, environmental protection, and nursing homes occurred as a result of clear articulation of a rationale for intervention (Jacobs, 1989; Silber, 1983; Wilson, 1980; National Citizens' Coalition for Nursing Home Reform, 1992).

The goals of regulation must be conceived of before deciding on the rationale for government involvement and the particular regulatory tools that will most effectively carry out the mandate. This has proven important in the design of environmental and workplace regulation, in which cases regulations that were initially overly broad attempted to control more factors than necessary, resulting in higher costs, decreased productivity, private sector resentment, and businesses falling short of unnecessarily burdensome enforcement requirements (E. Bardach, personal communication, April 1993).

The comparative advantage of regulations may be greater for some aspects of early care and education, such as health and safety, than for other aspects, such as academic instruction of very young children or types of activities conducted. Trade-offs between regulatory stringency and cost-supply must be considered before regulations are put in place, and a decision must be made about what needs to be controlled in each type of program to reach the regulatory goal. Traditional command-and-control regulations and incentive-based regulations are not mutually exclusive tools for achieving the goals of regulation, however. In fact, the two strategies together have the potential to operate more effectively than either one alone (Cheit, 1990).

In early care and education, the goal of regulation can be both prevention of harm and encouragement of optimal child development: mandatory regulations could provide protection against harm, and regulatory incentives could work to increase quality. A similar two-tiered approach is used in the nursing home industry, in which regulations represent minimum-quality standards, and accreditation is awarded to providers that offer even higher quality. In early care and education, anything that fails to meet minimum standards would harm children, so the licensing agency could close down any programs that violated these basic requirements.

Incentives could be designed as a second tier for providers to meet higher standards that promote optimal child development, but the only punitive action taken against programs that do not meet them would be market based. Under the nursing home reform law, the incentive for providers to complete the training and meet the outcome measures necessary for accreditation is listed in a government registry available to consumers.

Necessity of a Consumer Protection Rationale

Advocates of regulatory policy must be able to answer the question of why government should be involved in the industry marketplace at all. In light of what has proven successful in other fields, the overarching rationale behind mandatory baseline regulations for early care and education should be consumer protection from health and safety risks. This rationale was central to arguments for regulating nursing homes to protect the health and welfare of patients and residents, for regulating the environment to protect the public from health risks, and for regulating workplace safety to protect the health and safety of employees. Characterizing the issue as one of consumer protection requires clear articulation about exactly what regulations are protecting consumers from, what can be regulated, and how to define adequacy.

Using Tax Dollars Wisely

An additional rationale that has proven quite powerful in gaining public acceptance of government regulation of an industry is that such regulation will make government intervention more efficient and the use of tax dollars more effective. The articulated goal of environmental regulatory policy has been to use market-based mechanisms to achieve greater pollution control for less money. Since passage of the Clean Air Act, both government officials and environmental groups have emphasized this rationale to support the shift from command-and-control to incentive-based regulations.

Cost-benefit analysis has become an increasingly popular way to choose between regulation and freedom of the marketplace among those who consider regulatory goals admirable but regulations inefficient. Arguing the cost-effectiveness of early care and education regulations would likely prove far more persuasive in garnering support for regulation than would arguing for protected status for early care and education on a moral basis. The net benefit–maximization principle holds that proposed regulation of an industry, as well as each individual regulation, must undergo a cost-benefit analysis and should only be adopted if the benefits outweigh the costs.

Early care and education advocates therefore have the formidable task of defining measurements of the costs and benefits involved. The problem is that even if society could agree on what constitutes quality early care and education, discerning the benefits of quality programs to children and society can be a political question. Measuring the costs of *not* regulating early care and education remains an equally political issue.

Catastrophic Events as a Catalyst for Change

A catastrophe vividly illustrates the need for government to take action to address risk, bringing the issue to life much more effectively than the most carefully argued rationale. Studies of other industries reveal that government intervention almost always follows a catastrophic event that results in a successful lawsuit. For example, regulatory responses followed disasters concerning cars, grain elevators, planes, wood stoves, and gas space heaters (Cheit, 1990). Even though nursing home advocates spent the 1970s building a consensus around regulations, and unions did the same for worker safety, it took deaths in both cases to galvanize public support for regulation.

Catastrophic events occurring in unregulated early care and education have in fact received substantial publicity. Because of their interest to the American public, these events have been sensationalized and brought considerable attention to regulatory and credentialing issues in the field. To date, in early care and education, a widely publicized catastrophe has not yet proven sufficient to bring about full federal support for regulation of the industry, though some states have used catastrophic events to propel the effort to gain more stringent child care regulation.

Role of Expert Knowledge

Experience in other fields has demonstrated that in order for a catastrophe in conjunction with a successful lawsuit to bring about adoption of a regulatory policy, it must appear that expert knowledge and intervention could have prevented the catastrophe (Bardach & Kagan, 1982). Regulations are deemed necessary only in cases in which the accidents demonstrate that due to consumers' limited information or understanding, there is a need for experts to monitor the industry on their behalf.

The importance of the perceived need for experts is exemplified by the creation of the Food and Drug Administration, the Occupational Safety & Health Association (OSHA), and the Environmental Protection Agency (Cheit, 1990). Safe food preparation involves knowledge of chemicals and expertise in making scientific diagnoses of bacteria; maintaining worker safety requires knowledge of exposure effects to various substances and fumes; and determining acceptable limits of environmental pollution requires the ability to calculate the damage of pollution. Few citizens presume to have the scientific knowledge and skills to make the determinations necessary to regulate these fields.

The public's ambiguity about the need for a specialist or an expert to determine the adequacy of early care and education has plagued the field for decades. The need for a specialist with information regarding the availability of programs has become more accepted with the growth of resource and referral agencies, but the need for an expert who has substantive knowledge about quality child development practices remains controversial.

Need for Coalition Building

For the early care and education field to wield real political power to promote effective regulation and other reforms, proponents should not only organize the parents who use programs but also should work to involve the public at large in an effective coalition. Through a grassroots consumer movement of advocates, providers, professional associations, the Health Care Financing Administration, and key congressional committee members, comprehensive nursing home reform laws were passed as part of the Omnibus Budget Reconciliation Act of 1987. A consensus around the legislation was created among parties interested in nursing homes, including providers, consumers, advocates, academics, trade associations, government administrators, and regulators. The early care and education community could conduct outreach to those with similar interests, including advocates of welfare reform that mandates work requirements, health care reform, education reform, and increased business productivity to make explicit the advantage to these causes of quality early care and education.

Use of Incentives

The challenge for those who support higher quality is to find regulatory mechanisms that can accomplish this goal without reducing supply or increasing cost so much that a new crisis is generated. Incentive-based regulations in other industries have been shown to do just that. Because incentive-based regulations are designed to respond to the unique intricacies of each field, incentive mechanisms cannot be used as cookie cutters from one field to another. Nevertheless, lessons that are useful for early care and education can be drawn from fields with successful incentive-based regulations.

Incentive-based regulations use money, goods, or information as tools to encourage self-policing of an industry. The basic idea is best illustrated with certain examples. The use of *marketable rights* in the environmental field allows Company A to sell its right to a legal pollution level to Company B, if Company A keeps its pollution to an even lower level. Thus, the total amount of pollution emitted into the atmosphere remains at the determined regulatory level, and individual companies have a financial incentive to pollute less (Roe, 1989). In another example, the bottle laws that charge consumers for bottles when they buy the product and then refund the consumer only when the bottle is returned for recycling have created a new market incentive for recycling containers and demonstrate the success of this incentive-based regulatory tool (Reagan, 1987).

Incentive-based regulatory tools that have proven effective in other fields include self-regulation through training and professional organizations, consumer education through information dissemination, codified rights and ombudsmen, third-party enforcement and whistle-blowing legislation, and negotiation under private right of action. Each of these tools can provide an incentive to parents or providers to achieve regulatory goals. These tools, and their potential applicability to early care and education, are explored below.

Training and Professional Organizations

The need for enforcement of early care and education regulations could decrease with increased training of providers. These providers would learn optimum practices; their knowledge of how to provide care for young children and their awareness of regulatory expectations would improve their compliance with regulations. Further, the offer of training could serve as an incentive to bring providers who currently operate underground into the regulated system. Since the Older Americans Act legislated mandatory training and competency evaluation for providers of care, those in the elder care field have found training to be highly effective in achieving regulatory goals. A state association helps pay for training, and the industry utilizes many volunteers (H. Fields, personal communication, March 1993). Such mandatory training and credentialing could serve as valuable precedent for the early childhood field.

Consumer Education Through Information Dissemination

Early care and education services present a complex, infrequent-purchase situation: consumers tend to have much less information about these goods or services than about more frequently purchased items. They lack the information that can be learned from prior purchases to make well-educated decisions and choices (Magat & Viscusi, 1992). The more costly it is to acquire information and the less information there is available that is relevant to the purchase, the more likely it is that the consumer will have insufficient information to make an informed choice. It has been proposed that legislation be enacted to address the problems associated with infrequent but important purchases (Magat & Viscusi, 1992).

Information provision tools allow people to prepare for risk and do not evoke a confrontational response. In early care and education, the government could provide or require that information be provided to parent consumers. Informing parents of existing options, of what quality programs look like, and of what they can do to improve quality of care could be a powerful tool for achieving the regulatory goals of early care and education.

Codified Rights and Ombudsmen

In addressing the needs of families with a relative in an elder care facility, the Older Americans Act delineated specific residents' rights, including the right to physical safety, the right to information, the right to visitation, the right to nondiscrimination in transfer or discharge, and the right to access to a long-term care ombudsman (National Citizens' Coalition for Nursing Home Reform, 1992). To enforce these rights, the law established family councils within care facilities and created an ombudsman in each center. Ombudsmen have proven quite useful as an incentive for providers to take families' concerns seriously, because ombudsmen have access to media, make on-site visits, and are legislatively authorized to advocate for residents who cannot take care of themselves.

The potential of these mechanisms to advance the regulatory goals of early care and education warrants close examination due to the similarities in family situations and the wide praise these tools have received as being among the most inventive in the regulatory arena. The Head Start experience of policy councils provides a precedent within the field for this type of mechanism to maintain high standards of program quality.

Third-Party Enforcement and Whistle-Blowing Legislation

Though novel information mechanisms and incentives have improved rates of compliance in a number of industries, adding some bite to regulatory policy has further increased the effectiveness of these tools. Legislation in several areas has granted a private right of action to citizens to bring suit against a government agency or against a private provider of services for failing to comply with regulatory mandates. This grant is meant to broaden the scope of enforcement, both so citizens who have suffered as a result of noncompliance can file suit and to deter noncompliance by using the threat of multiple lawsuits.

In addressing worker safety issues, OSHA granted a right of action to employees, established monetary penalties to be levied by government inspectors, and instituted whistle-blowing protection for workers who report employer violations of the statute. Such legislation was passed because workers are clearly in the best position to see violations but also are clearly at great risk of company retaliation. Courts have attempted to ensure the protection of the rights of workers who report violations to the authorities.

Granting a private right of action to consumers could greatly improve enforcement of early care and education regulations. A private right of action to enforce regulations would offer a powerful method of last resort and would provide a deterrent to potential violators. Other states could follow California's lead and adopt whistle-blowing legislation to protect early care and education workers, so they can report program violations. In addition, many existing generic whistle-blowing laws could be construed to protect early care and education workers.

Negotiation

Companies' and employers' fears of having to pay substantial litigation awards have resulted in a powerful tool for workers and consumers to take to the negotiating table, a tool the early care and education field might use to achieve its own regulatory goals. Under the Clean Air Act, for example, though a citizen now can file an action in federal court, it is the events that occur before going to court that have proven to bring about the most effective results, because companies often prefer to negotiate in private rather than to litigate. In these negotiated settlements, companies can agree to implement operational procedures that are more protective of the environment in lieu of paying financial penalties, which ultimately can be more beneficial for the environment than the results of lawsuits and government enforcement alone.

Negotiation has proven to be an effective, low-cost regulatory tool that brings providers and government agencies to the table. Taking negotiation a step further to prevention, before any violation has been found, workplace safety laws call for the government to offer a consultation program to employers on how they can become better at compliance. Those who do well can become star programs exempted from regulatory checks for a certain period. Further, if violations are discovered, companies can negotiate to have penalty fees reduced by the amount of money they invest in training for their workers (R. Ruttenberg, personal communication, 1993). These preventive measures operate ultimately to increase compliance.

Given the current population needs, the government has a vested interest in encouraging the supply of early care and education. Negotiation with existing providers to address program quality could prove particularly valuable in determining which policies and procedures are effective and appropriate to expand the number of providers in the field.

Conclusion

Although analogies can be made, it is important to remain realistic in applying lessons from other fields to early care and education. The lack of economic resources of the early care and education field may be an obstacle to many regulatory tools that have proven successful in other fields. Further, any regulatory requirement must always be weighed against the concern of pricing people out of the market when the supply of care is so low and demand continues to grow.

As Magat and Viscusi make clear in their discussion of complex and infrequent purchases: "Information alone, no matter how well presented and understood, may not be able to overcome the barriers presented by lack of income or cash flow. In such cases additional features, such as loans and subsidies, then need to be added to the program to make it effective" (1992, p. 160).

Requiring loans and subsidies in the face of shrinking federal investment in early care and education is a formidable challenge. Consumer education, ombudsmen, and codification of rights all appear to be most readily applicable to the early care and education field, but these activities also require ongoing funding. Ultimately, solving the regulatory and quality problems in early care and education is largely dependent on solving funding problems.

In addition to financial concerns, the limited temporal and complex human dynamics of early care and education issues further inhibits decisive governmental action. Unlike workplace safety and elder care, early care and education is generally a time-limited concern for families. Incentives for parents to improve the system, as opposed just to getting through the early care and education years, are minimal. Further, parents often view their early care providers as partners in child rearing on whose services they feel extremely dependent. This dependency creates a strong consumer-based disincentive for any regulatory action that might run the risk of overregulation.

Nevertheless, several measures have the potential to improve the quality of care for the nation's youngest citizens:

- Providing information to parents through government agencies or resource and referral agencies regarding measures of quality programs, available options, and steps to create more options
- Building coalitions with advocates of welfare reform, health care reform, education reform, and increased business productivity to create acceptance of regulation of the early care and education industry
- Opening communication between providers and policy makers to create an industry atmosphere that will encourage more providers to enter the field and to create incentives for providers to achieve regulatory goals
- Improving training and peer support through professional organizations
- Articulating the goal of codified mandatory regulation as consumer protection and effective use of tax dollars
- Lobbying legislators at every level to delineate and codify baseline rights for consumers of early care and education and to provide for on-site ombudsmen, whistle-blowing protection, and a private right of action to aid in enforcement of those rights

If the early care and education field can overcome its internal differences and work together to build on its shared common ground, it will gain political power and strengthen its ability to achieve its regulatory goals.

References

Bardach, E., & Kagan, R. A. (1982). *Going by the book: The problem of regulatory unreasonableness.* Philadelphia: Temple University Press.

Cheit, R. E. (1990). *Setting safety standards: Regulation in the public and private sectors.* Berkeley: University of California Press.

Gormley, W. T. (1992). Food fights: Regulatory enforcement in a federal system. *Public Administration Review, 52*(3), 271–280.

Jacobs, J. B. (1989). *Drunk driving: An American dilemma.* Chicago: University of Chicago Press.

Magat, W. A., & Viscusi, W. K. (1992). *Informational approaches to regulation.* Cambridge, Mass.: MIT Press.

Mendeloff, J. M. (1979). *Regulating safety: An economic and political analysis of occupational safety and health policy.* Cambridge, Mass.: MIT Press.

National Citizens' Coalition for Nursing Home Reform. (1992, January). Residents' rights and quality of life. In *Nursing home reform law: The basics.* Washington, D.C.: National Citizens' Coalition for Nursing Home Reform.

Phillips, D., Lande, J., & Goldberg, M. (1990). The state of child care regulation: A comparative analysis. *Early Childhood Research Quarterly, 5,* 151–179.

Reagan, M. D. (1987). *Regulation: The politics of policy.* New York: Little, Brown.

Roe, D. (1989). An incentive-conscious approach to toxic chemical controls. *Economic Development Quarterly, 3*(3), 179–187.

Silber, N. I. (1983). *Test and protest: The influence of the consumers union.* New York: Holmes & Meier.

Wilson, J. Q. (Ed). (1980). *The politics of regulation.* New York: Basic Books.

Chapter Nine

Governance

Child Care, Federalism, and Public Policy

William T. Gormley, Jr.

The allocation of child care tasks to different levels of government, like the allocation of tasks between the public and private sectors, is both difficult and important. Intergovernmental relations in the United States have become much more complex since the days when *dual federalism* suggested a simple division of labor between the federal government and the states. Today, it is seldom obvious that a particular function should be placed exclusively in the hands of one level of government. The doctrine of *cooperative federalism* suggests the need for governments to share responsibility for various domestic policies but does not pinpoint who should do what.

Yet, we pay a price if we assign responsibilities to the wrong level of government. A given level of government may underprovide vital services. Another level of government may be more generous but less efficient or less responsive. A particular level of government may slight the needs of the poor and other disadvantaged citizens. Another level of government may fail to develop programs that are politically sustainable. Some functions may not be performed at all. Others may be performed without regard to the full range of values at stake—for example, availability, affordability, and quality.

In this chapter, I attempt to sort out some basic roles for different levels of government (federal, state, and local) to play in addressing child care problems. First, I consider how two other federal systems (Canada and Germany) allocate fundamental child care tasks. Second, I consider how the United States assigns tasks in two cognate fields (health care and education). Third, I apply the theoretical perspectives of two prominent scholars (Rivlin, 1992; Peterson, 1995) to the allocation of child care tasks. Finally, I develop my own alternative to these perspectives. A key theme is the need for primary responsibility, with each level of government carving out a distinct niche for itself. Cooperative federalism's emphasis on shared responsibilities makes perfect sense, but sharing should not be haphazard, ad hoc, or confusing.

Other Federal Systems

Among federal systems, Canada and Germany are particularly interesting for comparative purposes. Like the United States, both are prosperous countries with robust economies. Like the United States, both are democratic republics with strong commitments to federalism. Germany's Constitution resembles that of the United States, which served as a template for postwar Germany, and Canada's cultural heterogeneity and vast geographic sweep parallel similar characteristics in the United States. Also, in Canada, as in the United States, a majority of women work outside the home, which is not yet the case in Germany (Kahn & Kamerman, 1994).

In Canada, primary responsibility for formulating and implementing child care policies resides with the provincial governments. They develop and enforce child care regulatory standards that apply to group day care centers and, in some provinces, family day care homes as well. They also decide who will receive child care subsidies and what those subsidies will be. Finally, provinces, to varying degrees, provide financial support to develop and maintain a child care infrastructure, through start-up grants, salary enhancement grants, professional development grants, and other approaches.

The primary role of the national government in Canada is to provide financial assistance to the needy, through a cost-sharing arrangement with the provincial governments. The national government also provides funding for fifteen weeks of maternity leave and ten weeks of parental leave at 57 percent of wages up to a ceiling (Friendly, 1994). A family allowance, available to all Canadian families with young children, was abolished in 1992. The role of local governments is fairly limited, but some local governments are active. For example, the city of Vancouver plays a significant role in planning, advocacy, and capital funding, and the city of Toronto provides subsidies to nonprofit day care centers and encourages the location of day care centers in new commercial developments (Friendly, 1994). In some provinces, such as Ontario and Quebec, municipalities may operate day care centers. Nationwide, however, only 11 percent of all day care centers in Canada are run by local governments or school boards (Friendly, 1994).

In Germany, as in Canada, the state governments, or *Länder*, have the primary responsibility for formulating and implementing child care policies. They establish standards for group day care centers (or *Kindergärten*), and they enforce standards, in collaboration with the churches and local government officials. The *Länder* also decide what percentage of preschool children will be guaranteed access to a *Kindergärten* space at state-subsidized facilities and how substantial those subsidies will be.

The role of the German national government in child care policy is fairly circumscribed (Jaeckel, 1987). However, the national government does guarantee partially paid maternal leave that helps mothers of infants care for their children at home. For ten weeks after the birth of a child, a mother is eligible for paid leave at a rate of 100 percent of wages. Thereafter, a mother may elect to stay at home for two years, while receiving approximately 20 percent of the average female wage (Kamerman & Kahn, 1995).

The national government also provides a family allowance that makes it easier for parents to pay for the many costs of raising children, including child care costs. And the national government collects the taxes that fuel the child care activities of the *Länder* and the churches within the respective states.

Local governments in Germany are actively involved in regulating, subsidizing, and providing child care services. Approximately one-third of all *Kindergärten* are actually run by local governments (Gormley & Peters, 1992). These facilities play a special role in caring for needy children. Local government officials help regulate *Kindergärten*, in conjunction with state government officials. Finally, local governments assess the need for new child care facilities and construct new facilities after conferring with parents in the affected neighborhoods. The significant role played by local governments in child care is consistent with the German concept of *Subsidiarität,* which stipulates that problems should be resolved at the lowest possible organizational level (Pettinger, 1993).

Clearly, the Germans have done a better job than the Canadians in carving out a strong, distinctive role for local governments in providing child care services. Germany's local governments can play this role because, like state governments, they receive a guaranteed percentage of federal revenue. Germany also has a more centralized and a more generous parental leave policy than Canada. Although Germany's child care system has its failings—most notably, a shortage of full-time child care in many states—the division of labor and the provision of benefits help ensure that child care is available and affordable. As for quality, that is left up to the states, as in Canada. However, all the German *Länder* have opted for relatively strict education and training requirements (Gormley & Peters, 1992). In contrast, education and training requirements are much more varied—and often inadequate—in Canada (Friendly, 1994).

Education and Health Policy

How does the United States allocate tasks in cognate fields, such as education and health? Elementary education makes for a good analogy, because it involves the provision of services to young children and because it involves supervision for most of the day but not around-the-clock care. Nursing homes, which involve continuous care, are less analogous in this respect. On the other hand, nursing home policy does affect highly vulnerable persons, who are often incapable of looking after themselves or speaking out on their own behalf. Thus, both policy areas may be instructive.

The most striking feature of education policy in the United States is the relatively modest role played by the federal government. Although we have had a U.S. Department of Education since 1979, the department's budget pales in comparison with total education spending by all levels of government. Specifically, federal assistance accounts for only 6 percent of all education spending by local school districts (Sanchez, 1995). Financially, education is largely a state and local function.

Standard-setting and enforcement are also, for the most part, state and local responsibilities. Although Congress explicitly embraced six National Education Goals in 1993 (Goals 2000), the goals are quite broad and are designed to encourage state and local achievement, not to mandate federal rules. In short, Goals 2000 employs exhortatory, not coercive, control techniques. The federal government does place restrictions on how state and local governments may spend federal money. However, those restrictions apply primarily to eligibility determination, as in the case of Title I funding, aimed at disadvantaged students. The bottom line is that federally funded education programs typically leave state and local governments with considerable or total discretion concerning their staff, their activities, and their physical plant.

Health policy, more than education policy, involves shared responsibilities, exemplifying the classical ideal of cooperative federalism. This is particularly true of Medicaid, which provides financial support to nursing homes, among other functions. In fiscal year 1995, the federal government's spending on Medicaid accounted for 57 percent of all governmental Medicaid expenditures (U.S. House of Representatives, 1994). State governments contributed the remaining 43 percent. Federal cost sharing for nursing homes accounts for approximately one-fourth of all federal spending under Medicaid (U.S. House of Representatives, 1994) and is handled through the same cost-sharing formula as other Medicaid expenditures. In relative terms, the federal government's role in supporting nursing homes is much greater than its role in supporting public schools.

The regulation of nursing homes is also a shared responsibility. In 1967, shortly after establishing the Medicaid program, Congress instructed the then Department of Health, Education, and Welfare to develop regulations for skilled nursing facilities. Since that time, the federal Department of Health and Human Services has promulgated standards for all nursing homes, which the states must adopt and enforce if they wish to retain Medicaid funding. To monitor state implementation of federal standards, the federal government arranges federal inspections of a sample of facilities participating in federal programs. To this extent, federal inspectors oversee the work of state inspectors. As of 1994, the Department of Health and Human Services has authorized states to impose a variety of sanctions, including fines, to facilitate compliance with federal standards (Rich, 1994). However, it is up to each state to decide whether to impose a fine and what the amount will be (Citizens for Better Care, 1995).

The actual content of federal regulations, though detailed in certain areas, leaves the states considerable discretion (Vladeck, 1980). Thus, the federal government specifies that three meals a day will be served but does not require fresh fruit or vegetables. The federal government requires that there be at least one licensed professional on-site at all times but does not require specific ratios of nurses per patient. The federal government requires nurses' aides to have seventy-five hours of training but leaves other training requirements up to the states (Holder, 1991). The federal government also defers to the states on such matters as sanitary codes and personnel licensing. On balance, the federal government stresses safety more than quality of care, though quality has received greater attention in recent years (I. Freeman, personal communication, September 1993).

A review of education policy and nursing home policy in the United States presents two sharply different images—a highly decentralized educational system, in which state and local governments are the key players, and a more centralized nursing home system, in which state governments and the federal government are the key players. Together, the two cases suggest a rough positive relationship between federal funding and federal regulations (both are higher in the case of nursing homes). This raises a question for child care: If the federal government provides more funding for our child care system, *should* it promulgate more regulations as well? A related question is empirical: If the federal government provides more funding, *will* it promulgate more regulations? Child care legislation passed by Congress in 1990, which provided significant new funding without significant new regulations, suggests that funding and regulations can be decoupled. But the question of whether the federal government should provide more funding or more regulation is not as easily answered. To do so, it is necessary to take a broader normative view of intergovernmental relations.

Reallocating Tasks

In recent years, two prominent social scientists have developed explicit blueprints for reallocating tasks to different levels of government. Alice Rivlin, an economist, has presented a strategic vision for reassigning both spending and taxing functions. Paul Peterson, a political scientist, has offered a normative theory for reallocating tasks or functions. Each of these perspectives has something to contribute to debates over child care in a federal system.

Rivlin (1992) begins with an indisputable point: each level of government should specialize in those activities that it is best equipped to perform. Building on this premise, Rivlin argues that the federal government should assume full responsibility for the financing of our health care system. Only the federal government, she believes, can guarantee both universal health insurance and effective cost controls. At the same time, the federal government would devolve responsibility for a variety of economic and social programs to the states. These programs would include elementary and secondary education, job training, economic and community development, housing, most transportation programs, and most social service programs, including child care. According to Rivlin, states have both the inclination and the capacity to design such programs with the needs of particular locales and citizens in mind. Among major programs, only environmental protection and Aid to Families with Dependent Children (AFDC) would remain shared responsibilities. To finance devolution, Rivlin calls for a value-added tax, which taxes goods and services at each stage of production, or some other tax to be shared by all fifty states. To simplify political and logistical tasks, the federal government might even collect the tax on behalf of the states. Whatever the collection mechanism, common shared taxes, in Rivlin's opinion, "would reduce border concerns and could enhance the revenues of poorer states" (1992, p. 118).

Clearly, Rivlin's formula for reallocating tasks would shift substantial power to the states. In this respect, her perspective resembles the thinking of Republican governors and members of Congress more than that of her Democratic colleagues in the Clinton administration and on Capitol Hill. However, a key difference is that Rivlin wants to ensure that tax revenue is available to both rich and poor states to finance important social services. Common shared taxes would accomplish that goal.

In *The Price of Federalism* (1995), Peterson also makes a case for allocating tasks based on the distinctive strengths and weaknesses of each level of government. Building on previous work (Peterson, Rabe, & Wong, 1986), he distinguishes between *developmental* and *redistributive* policies. The former include policies that promote economic development, the physical infrastructure that communities need, and those social programs that benefit all citizens, such as education and public safety. The latter include social policies that transfer income from the haves to the have-nots, including the poor, the sick, and other disadvantaged groups. AFDC and Medicaid exemplify the second category.

According to Peterson, the federal government has no business funding developmental programs, which state and local governments have ample incentives to pursue. Indeed, he points out that the increasing mobility of capital and labor makes state and local governments highly sensitive to economic development opportunities and anxious to compete and to innovate in these areas. In contrast, state and local governments are reluctant to care for the needy, especially because they run the risk of becoming welfare magnets as their generosity to the poor increases. Over the years, the national government has demonstrated a stronger commitment to redistributive policies than state and local governments. According to Peterson, only the national government can provide a safety net to protect all citizens from illness, poverty, and other basic threats to their well-being.

In contrast to Rivlin, Peterson is skeptical of sweeping devolution proposals. Although he and Rivlin agree that economic development programs should be funded and administered by state and local governments, he prefers a stronger role for the federal government in funding and administering social programs that benefit disadvantaged citizens. Although Peterson does not explicitly discuss child care, he does call for a national system of family allowances, comparable to that found in most European countries. He also explicitly recommends national health insurance and a national welfare system.

Certainly, Peterson's theory suggests that child care programs aimed at the poor should be funded by the federal government. The implications of his theory for other child care functions depend in part on whether child care is viewed as having more in common with education policy (best handled by the states) or welfare policy (best handled by the federal government). Many child care programs, such as Head Start, are not easily pigeonholed into policy cubicles; however, one gets the impression that Peterson prefers a relatively strong role for the federal government whenever policies are aimed at disadvantaged children.

Framework Merits and Flaws

Each of the scholarly frameworks has its merits. The Rivlin framework is bold and comprehensive. If taken seriously, it would result in a radical restructuring of our federal system. The Peterson framework is more incrementalist but politically astute in that it recognizes the limitations of state and local governments. Thus, each framework has something to offer. On the other hand, neither framework is fully satisfactory.

Rivlin, who describes herself as an optimist, is in fact overly optimistic about both state fiscal capacity and state priority setting. She envisions a world in which the federal government collects substantial new taxes on behalf of the states or in which states band together to collect new taxes to share among themselves. Neither scenario seems likely. Why should the federal government incur political risks to facilitate state spending when it is experiencing grave difficulties balancing its own budget? Why should Oregon and Idaho go out on a limb to nurse California back to fiscal health? The politics of the moment, like politics most of the time, is decidedly zero-sum, contrary to Rivlin's hopes. And without substantial new revenues, states simply cannot afford to assume responsibility for child care, foster care, child nutrition, remedial education, and other social service programs.

The other problem with Rivlin's argument is that it assumes that states will actually place a high priority on social services programs and disadvantaged constituencies if new revenue comes their way. Yet, when states have received substantial new funds with few strings attached, as in the case of general revenue sharing, they have been more attentive to powerful constituencies than to the disadvantaged (Van Horn, 1979; Gormley, 1989). Though the past is not a certain guide to the future, the evidence suggests that states must be coaxed and encouraged to assist disadvantaged constituencies.

The main problem with Peterson's framework is that it presupposes a durable coalition in support of federal redistributive programs. Yet, the Reagan years and the Contract with America underscore just how fragile that coalition can be. For this reason, Skocpol (1995) recommends that redistributive programs be camouflaged by combining them with popular programs that benefit all or most citizens. She calls this strategy *targeting within universalism*. Skocpol's advice runs directly counter to some of Peterson's prescriptions. Whereas he would have the federal government hoist the redistributive banner and lead the charge to assist the poor, she believes that such an approach is dangerous politically. Instead, she would have the federal government unfurl the colors of a neutral party, thereby avoiding attack over an extended period of time.

An Alternative Framework

A key premise behind both the Rivlin and Peterson frameworks is that cooperative federalism has become an unmanageable jumble. If all functions in all domestic policy areas are shared, who is in charge? And who can be held accountable? As Rivlin and Peterson rightly suggest, we need to do a better job of sorting out functions and assigning them to the level of government that is best equipped to handle them efficiently and effectively.

In child care, a useful starting point is the familiar troika of values—availability, affordability, and quality. Each level of government should accept the lead responsibility for promoting one of the three core values. At the same time, each level of government should play a subsidiary role in promoting the other core values. Such an arrangement promotes accountability without turning it into a fetish. It combines streamlining with sharing. It prevents governments from spreading themselves too thin but also ensures a certain awareness of trade-offs at each level.

What, then, should each level of government do? By virtue of its relatively strong commitment to redistribution, the federal government is best equipped to promote the goal of *affordability*. By virtue of their relatively strong capacity for responsiveness, local governments are best equipped to promote the goal of *availability*. By virtue of their relatively strong capacity for innovative experiments, state governments are best equipped to promote the goal of *quality*.

The case for a strong federal role in promoting affordability has already been made by Peterson. Because the poor require greater financial support than those in other social strata, the emphasis of the federal government's financial support should be on providing child care subsidies to disadvantaged parents and their children, as in the case of Head Start, the JOBS program, and programs aimed at the working poor. However, the federal government should also assist the middle class—especially parents of infants, who often require not just financial support but also societal encouragement to reconcile the competing needs of work and family. In practical terms, this might be done by offering paid parental leave to working parents of children under the age of one (Gormley, 1995).

Local governments lack the financial resources and the political incentives to provide substantial subsidies to poor parents. But they are uniquely situated to assess the child care needs of their own residents, which may differ substantially from those in other communities. Thus, local governments should conduct needs assessments, launch planning initiatives, specify market failures, and identify market niches for new entrepreneurial activities. They should also ensure that parents know where they can obtain information about the availability of particular kinds of child care facilities, including child care facilities of high quality. And they should encourage increased supply, by relaxing physical facility requirements when they are unreasonable or unduly cumbersome and by offering inducements to firms that agree to build on-site child care facilities.

The singular virtue of state governments is that they strike a balance between competence and responsiveness. When issues are sufficiently technical to require some level of expertise but sufficiently conflictual to require differential responses, state governments can satisfy both concerns. That is one reason that we have turned to the states to tackle abortion, capital punishment, and other delicate issues. State governments can formulate child care rules that take both universal truths and local conditions into account. They can confront trade-offs between availability and quality with both research findings and popular sentiments in mind. This suggests that they should take the lead in regulating child care facilities. In addition, they should take the lead in designing a child care infrastructure that reflects the distinctive strengths and weaknesses of their institutions—the robustness of the school system, the generosity of the private sector, the vitality of community organizations, and other factors specific to the state. If state governments can develop effective transportation and communications infrastructures, they can develop an effective child care infrastructure as well, especially if they receive federal encouragement and support.

The allocation of tasks described above differs significantly from the distribution of tasks currently found in cognate fields. In elementary and secondary education, the United States has developed a highly asymmetrical intergovernmental system, in which the federal government's role is quite limited. The system is bottom heavy, with local and state governments playing the dominant roles in both decision making and funding. Thus, in education policy, affordability depends primarily on state and local spending; quality depends primarily on state and local standards; and availability depends primarily on local decisions. The role of the federal government is largely supplemental.

As for nursing home policy making, that constitutes a highly integrated system of shared responsibilities for virtually every function. The federal government and the states spend substantial amounts of money to make nursing homes affordable. The federal government and the states adopt and enforce standards to promote quality. The role of local governments is increasingly negligible.[1] If shared responsibility between the federal government and the states is a virtue, our nursing home system is highly virtuous. But there is a good deal of redundancy built into the system, especially on the regulatory side, and accountability for successes and failures is difficult to pin down.

Neither Germany nor Canada has national child care standards. The United States, though, has a history of national standards in similar areas. It does have national standards for nursing homes, which establish a quality floor that states are free to exceed. Should the United States adopt national standards for child care facilities as well? I have argued against such a policy, on the grounds that states are capable of striking a reasonable balance between quality and other goals, such as affordability and availability. Also, though there is consensus on the factors that contribute to quality, there is no consensus on how those factors can best be intermixed. For example, a well-trained staff can to some extent compensate for relatively high child-to-staff ratios, as several European countries have discovered. Who is to say, therefore, that every state must maintain low child-to-staff ratios, regardless of staff education and training requirements? The relative merits of pre-service and in-service training, children's play and children's education, expensive play equipment and visits to neighborhood parks, frequent inspections and lengthy inspections, are also debatable. If different states can have different student-to-teacher ratios at elementary schools, why not different child-to-staff ratios at day care centers? If states can have different teacher education requirements for elementary schools, why not different staff education requirements for day care centers? The role of the federal government should be to encourage quality, not to mandate it. This can be done by supporting demonstration projects and by setting aside funds for quality, as has been done in the Child Care and Development Block Grant.

For the federal government to encourage quality but not mandate it would seem to be inconsistent with Peterson's admonition that the federal government should concentrate on aid to the poor, who are likely to be neglected by other levels of government. But the federal government does have a role to play in infrastructure support, whether the infrastructure in question is a transportation network, a communications network, or a child care network. The case for federal infrastructure support is not the need for political camouflage but the need to ensure that children from all social strata have access to child care that is safe, supportive, and enriching. That can be done through national regulations, or it can be done through subsidies. A key advantage of the subsidy approach is that it does not extinguish state experiments; federal subsidies should stimulate state investments in children and not displace them. Federal infrastructure support for child care should include a matching-funds requirement, just as federal interstate-highway support included a matching-funds requirement. If Peterson is correct, the states are likely to take advantage of federal subsidies that support the middle class, unless the state match required is unusually high. The federal government should be generous in providing infrastructure support for child care, but it should require states to be generous as well.

Conclusion

Child care policy making in the United States is largely the province of the federal government and the state governments, with local governments playing a relatively minor role. In this respect, the division of labor for child care resembles that for nursing homes more than that for elementary and secondary education, in which cases local governments play a much stronger role. However, child care policy making, with relatively discrete spheres of influence, differs significantly from nursing home policy making, in which case funding and regulatory functions are more intermixed. As argued above, this is probably advantageous for child care policy making, because relatively discrete spheres of influence for different levels of government promote accountability.

The system is not perfect, however. For one thing, local governments are struggling to carve out a constructive role to play. At the moment, the most widespread child care function performed by local governments is to inspect day care centers and family day care homes to ensure compliance with local building codes and zoning requirements. These activities, which overlap considerably with state regulatory functions, are redundant in some instances, dysfunctional in others. When, for example, local governments make it difficult or impossible for family day care homes to thrive in residential neighborhoods, they undermine availability (Gormley, 1990). Local governments could play a more constructive role by following the lead of Toronto, Vancouver, and other Canadian cities, which promote availability through planning, funding, and, in some instances, actual provision of child care services. In deciding when to provide services, local governments could also learn from the German experience. German municipalities frequently build and operate their own day care centers, but only after determining that nonprofit organizations (usually churches) are neither willing nor able to do so themselves.

Funding arrangements in the United States are also flawed. Although the federal government provides the lion's share of government child care subsidies for the poor, those subsidies do not come close to meeting the demand for child care services. Moreover, the federal government does nothing to encourage state infrastructure support for the citizenry as a whole. The Child Care and Development Block Grant's quality set-aside could stimulate additional state spending, with a modest matching requirement (for example, 20 percent). If Peterson is correct, the states would not balk at an inexpensive opportunity to secure federal funds to benefit the middle class, among other constituencies.

A more radical shift of funding responsibilities to the states would, however, be unwise. The states lack the financial wherewithal and the political incentives to provide generous child care support to the poor. Even the working poor, who enjoy greater political support than the truly disadvantaged, have often been unsuccessful in pressing claims for state funding for child care services. For example, in fiscal 1994, states failed to spend 21 percent of the federal dollars available to them through the At-Risk Child Care Program, which seeks to benefit the working poor.[2] In the final analysis, the federal government must retain primary responsibility for meeting the child care needs of poor parents. Matching-funds requirements can then ensure that the states play a significant supportive role.

Notes

1. When new nursing homes were being built at a rapid rate, local governments or regional groupings of local governments sometimes played a significant role in planning decisions. However, that role diminished or ended when states discouraged or prohibited the construction of new nursing homes. In Minnesota, for example, local officials used to recommend approval or disapproval of new nursing homes to the state Department of Health. Following a 1983 moratorium on new nursing home construction, that function was eliminated (I. Freeman, personal communication, August 1995).

2. I have calculated this percentage from figures supplied by the U.S. Department of Health and Human Services (1995).

References

Citizens for Better Care. (1995, June 10). *Bulletin.* Detroit.

Friendly, M. (1994). *Child care policy in Canada: Putting the pieces together.* Don Mills, Ontario, Canada: Addison-Wesley.

Gormley, W. T. (1989). *Taming the bureaucracy: Muscles, prayers, and other strategies.* Princeton, N.J.: Princeton University Press.

Gormley, W. T. (1990, Fall). Regulating Mister Rogers' neighborhood: The dilemmas of day care regulation. *The Brookings Review, 8*(4), 21–28.

Gormley, W. T. (1995). *Everybody's children:.Child care as a public problem.* Washington, D.C.: Brookings Institution.

Gormley, W. T., & Peters, G. B. (1992). National styles of regulation: Child care in three countries. *Policy Sciences, 25,* 381–399.

Holder, E. (1991). Meeting the expectations of OBRA. *Journal of Aging and Social Policy, 3,* 13–20.

Jaeckel, M. (1987). *National report on the situation of childcare in the Federal Republic of Germany for the Childcare Network of the Office for the Equality of Women of the European Commission.* Munich: Deutsches Jugendinstitut.

Kahn, A. J., & Kamerman, S. B. (1994). *Social policy and the under-3s: Six country case studies.* New York: Columbia University School of Social Work.

Kamerman, S. B., & Kahn, A. J. (1995). *Starting right: How America neglects its youngest children and what we can do about it.* New York: Oxford University Press.

Peterson, P. E. (1995). *The price of federalism.* Washington, D.C.: Brookings Institution.

Peterson, P. E., Rabe, B., & Wong, K. (1986). *When federalism works.* Washington, D.C.: Brookings Institution.

Pettinger, R. (1993). Germany. In M. Cochran (Ed.), *International handbook of child care policies and programs* (pp. 211–230). Westport, Conn.: Greenwood Press.

Rich, S. (1994, November 11). Nursing home standards set to take effect. *Washington Post.*

Rivlin, A. (1992). *Reviving the American dream: The economy, the states, and the federal government.* Washington, D.C.: Brookings Institution.

Sanchez, R. (1995, June 22). Direction, not dollars, drives debate over department. *Washington Post.*

Skocpol, T. (1995). *Social policy in the U.S.: Future possibilities in historical perspective.* Princeton, N.J.: Princeton University Press.

U.S. Department of Health and Human Services, Administration for Children and Families, Office of Financial Management. (1995, July 31).

AFDC at risk expenditure adjustments. Washington, D.C.: U.S. Government Printing Office.

U.S. House of Representatives, Committee on Ways and Means. (1994). *The green book, 1994.* Washington, D.C.: U.S. Government Printing Office.

Van Horn, C. (1979). *Policy implementation in the federal system.* Lexington, Mass: Heath.

Vladeck, B. (1980). *Unloving care: The nursing home tragedy.* New York: Basic Books.

Chapter Ten

Funding and Financing

Moving Toward a More Universal System

Martin H. Gerry

Introduction

This chapter explores future funding and financing options for early childhood services in general, and for the provision of a more universal system of early care and education in particular. The term early childhood services, as used throughout this chapter, means benefits or services intended either to support directly the physical, intellectual, social, or emotional development of children (ages birth through five years) or to enhance the ability of children's families to provide such support. Early care and education is one type of early childhood service: it is nonparental care, and its purpose is to provide developmentally stimulating experiences for young children or to enable parents to attend work, training, or school.

First, in this chapter, operating assumptions and policies that shape and constrain current early childhood service financing arrangements are discussed. Then, several alternative approaches to future public financing of a comprehensive structure of quality early care and education programs are presented, together with recommendations on how to proceed.

Trends in Governmental Support for Children's Services

The genius of the U.S. social and economic systems has been their fundamental reliance on the independence, productivity, and social responsibility of our citizens, families, and local communities. American families have traditionally borne the primary responsibility for the development of their children. In times when unusual stress or need has overwhelmed the capacities of families, extended families and informal networks of community institutions, religious organizations, and local associations—autonomous from state control—have played the central role in providing support to the family.

Prior to the passage of the Social Security Act in 1935, the role of the federal government in supporting the development of young children was a minimal one (Olasky, 1992). The roles of local and state governments in child development were restricted to providing free and public education, protecting child health through quarantine and immunization, and ensuring the welfare of children who were orphaned, neglected, or delinquent. Social and economic policy operated synergistically—with private economic growth benefiting from prudent public investments in the capital infrastructure, public schools, and higher education institutions; and private economic prosperity in turn leading to full public treasuries even at comparatively low rates of personal taxation.

In the 1960s and 1970s, however, hundreds of new federal and state categorical grant programs were created to address a broad range of educational, health, and social problems perceived to be impairing the healthy development of certain groups of children. By the end of the 1980s, as the U.S. economy began to slow, the full political and economic implications of this strategy became clear: the principal costs of these new government programs were being borne by large numbers of U.S. taxpayers who could perceive in this major investment few, if any, benefits for themselves.

Today, government has assumed an unprecedented responsibility for directly financing and administering a large number of programs that provide a wide range of benefits designed to promote the healthy development of young children. In fiscal year 1992, for example, 26 percent of total annual expenditures for early care and education (including Head Start and other preschool programs) came from government directly or through tax credits, and 74 percent came from out-of-pocket expenditures by families (U.S. Department of Commerce, 1993).

Since the midterm elections of 1994, Congress has been working aggressively both to reduce the levels of federal government
expenditures across virtually all categorical programs and to decentralize their administration, chiefly by shifting control to state governments. Rhetoric has suggested that by devolving many of these
decentralized programs to the states through the block grant strategy, they would gain much greater flexibility. In practice, however,
it appears that many of the old strings may simply have been
replaced by new ones tuned to a more conservative pitch.

Current Public Funding, Financing Assumptions, and Policies

Public funding for early childhood services is currently provided
through a large number of separate, chiefly categorical programs,
which are administered and implemented by both public and private agencies and organizations. In some early childhood service
categories, expenditures from nonpublic funds—such as family resources, charitable contributions, and business contributions—provide some or much of the financing. The largest source of financing
for child health services, however, is private health insurers.

In exploring the future financing options for early care and
education services, it may be helpful to examine two important policy approaches and the assumptions that underlie them—the categorical nature and the crisis orientation of most early childhood
service programs, and the disempowerment of families to which
they contribute.

Categorical, Crisis-Oriented Programs

Most publicly funded early childhood services are categorical in
nature. In a categorical approach, access to needed services is not
universal, but is conditioned on the presence or absence of a particular secondary characteristic of the child or family, such as
poverty, disability, or even enrollment in another categorical program. The central feature of every categorical program is an all-or-
nothing approach to access. This uniquely American policy
approach appears predicated on an almost obsessive desire to separate deserving children and families from others who are perceived as less deserving (Gerry & Paulsen, 1995).

The approach taken by most western European countries is quite different. Their primary assumptions are that all young children and families who need a service should have access to it and that families should contribute to the financing of services consistent with their economic resources. The result is a structure that ensures all young children and families universal access to a broad array of early childhood services (including early care and education), with gradually increased family cost based on ability to pay. Poverty is treated as a relative and highly variable condition that affects financial contribution rather than participation (Gerry & Paulsen, 1995).

The application of categorical eligibility standards in the United States leads to large numbers of children and families with severe needs for service being found ineligible as well as to extraordinary equity problems on the thresholds of eligibility. For example, eligibility for Medicaid and for Aid to Families with Dependent Children (AFDC) extends to just about half of children now living in families with incomes below 80 percent of the poverty level.

Perversely, the categorical approach also works to punish rather than to reward program success. Often, the only feasible way to increase program support under a categorical system is to demonstrate that children and families are continuing to have problems, which, in effect, is demonstrating that the programs serving them are not effective. Communities that serve at-risk children poorly are rewarded with increased funding, whereas communities that serve the same type of children well are penalized with decreased funding.

The categorical approach also severely restricts the use of funds. For example, despite the fact that parental literacy is generally acknowledged to be an excellent predictor of child development, only a few categorical grant programs permit funds to be used to provide short-term early care and education so that single parents can learn to read.

Many of the funding streams for important early childhood services also suffer from a crisis orientation. Most are triggered only when children's problems or family dysfunction has progressed to the point that family stability is threatened: funds are available only in response to clearly diagnosed problems, usually problems that have gone unattended for some time (Farrow & Joe, 1992). Restrictions make it virtually impossible to finance a comprehensive structure of early childhood services in which the core values are heavily oriented toward prevention and healthy development.

Family Disempowerment

The financing structures of many early childhood service programs also work at cross-purposes with what should be a central social policy objective—strengthening the abilities and increasing the opportunities for families to solve all or most of their own problems without fostering the need for ongoing government intervention. Empowerment refers to the process of extending the influence of individuals and communities over the conditions and outcomes that matter to them, including the healthy development of young children (Fawcett & others, 1995).

The financing approaches of most early childhood services for lower-income families are disempowering. Whereas economically advantaged families determine their own service needs, sometimes with outside advice that they solicit, economically disadvantaged families most frequently are dependent on program agencies and service providers to determine what, if any, services they need. These decisions are often influenced heavily by criteria for categorical eligibility and budget constraints rather than by child or family need. Economically advantaged families set their own service priorities and use their purchasing power to reach agreement with service providers on service goals, whereas economically disadvantaged families have their service priorities and goals determined by program agencies and service providers, often with limited input from family members. In certain circumstances, economically advantaged families may specify their desired service locations and schedules through competitive selection of providers, whereas economically disadvantaged families are usually faced with limited service locations, fixed schedules, and a take-it-or-leave-it philosophy. Perhaps most important, economically advantaged families determine service effectiveness and demand direct accountability via their checkbooks, whereas economically disadvantaged families must depend on service providers to determine service effectiveness, with little consultation with the affected families.

If strengthening families is an underlying social policy goal, a financing structure for early childhood services should work to rebuild, reinvigorate, and re-create strong families and diverse neighborhood-based services that empower families in the course of delivering services. The current role of economically advantaged families in service planning, decision making, and evaluation should be the standard for all.

Alternative Funding and Financing Strategies

Public financing for both early childhood services and early care and education needs to be shifted from a group of categorical programs to one universal-access model, similar to the approach taken by most western European countries, in which the primary assumptions are that all children and families who need a service should have access to it and that all families should contribute to the financing of services consistent with their economic resources.

The philosophy of such a new financing structure for early childhood services and early care and education would be one of normalization, in which *all* families would have access to a range of supportive services. The following section considers how the necessary funds could be raised to support a universal structure of early childhood services. First, local and state strategies for generating new funds are examined. Then, federal strategies are explored. Finally, an innovative approach to increasing investment in prevention is considered.

Local and State Strategies

In examining the options for developing a comprehensive plan to finance early childhood services at the local and state levels, three basic avenues should be seriously explored—the use of innovative decategorization strategies, such as pooled and blended funding; the increased leveraging of federal entitlement funds; and the redirection of existing local and state outlays. Each of these approaches, and its limitations for generating significant new funds, is discussed below:

Decategorization: Pooled and Blended Funding

The problems with the current financing approach discussed in the previous section—the all-or-nothing approach to eligibility, the severe restrictions on the use of categorical grant funds, and their frequent crisis orientation—are serious impediments to the flexible financing needed to ensure universal access to a comprehensive range of early childhood services. *Decategorization* is a process that removes these categorical restrictions or makes funds more flexible so that the services and supports can be tailored to meet the individual needs of children and families. Under decategorization, categorical funds are pooled or blended, giving states and localities the flexibility to develop more coherent strategies to integrate early childhood services (Center for the Study of Social Policy, 1991). In a *pooled*-funding strategy, two or more funding sources are used to support the same service consistent with categorical restrictions applicable to each; funding may be integrated for the family, but the funding sources remain separate at the administrative level. In a *blended*-funding strategy, all categorical restrictions are waived so that funds from different categorical funding sources may be integrated both for families and for the purposes of day-to-day administration.

Pending legislation in both houses of Congress may significantly limit the use of decategorization strategies. For example, although in theory the substitution of block grants for currently open-ended categorical entitlements should create substantially increased flexibility in both service eligibility and the use of funds for early childhood services, much of the current block grant legislation contains significant restrictions on the use of these funds at the community level. Moreover, governors—faced with serious triage problems because of the reality that funds are being cut at the same time the new block grants are going into effect—are just as likely as Congress to set their own categorical restrictions on the use of block grant funds when they reach the local level. Contrary to the stated goals of the block grant approach, significant decategorization, pooling, and blending of funds may actually be impeded by the new block-granting efforts.

Increased Leveraging of Federal Entitlement Funds

Financing strategies that maximize the leveraging of federal entitlement funds can make substantially increased amounts of federal dollars available to support early childhood services as well as new initiatives focused on early care and education, without increasing overall service expenditures at the local and state levels.

An essential characteristic of open-ended federal entitlement programs is that localities and states, rather than receiving a fixed grant amount each year, draw down federal funds as needed to meet the actual costs of providing covered services to eligible children and families. However, before federal funds can be drawn down, they usually must be matched with funds from nonfederal (usually state or local) sources. Although ceilings have been established under each of these programs, which now make them less than truly open-ended, few states have come near the point of actually drawing down the maximum amount of federal dollars that are potentially available. The chief limitation on greater access to federal entitlement funds within open-ended programs has been the inability to produce matching funds from nonfederal sources. Pending block-granting legislation in both houses of Congress would also significantly limit the use of current leveraging strategies.

Redirection of Existing Local and State Outlays

Another option for generating new funds for early childhood services is to redirect existing local or state expenditures from other sources. Interested parties can participate in local and state budgetary and allocation decision making to encourage the increased expenditure of funds on young children and their families (Center for the Study of Social Policy, 1991). In a period of extreme budget austerity at the national, state, and local levels of government, however, the prospects of redirecting existing outlays to support a quality system of early care and education are not good.

Three factors make it unlikely that a significant share of current outlays at the local level could be redirected to support a significant portion of the costs of a new early care and education structure.[1] First, taxpayer rebellions have seriously eroded the ability of local property tax revenues to fund adequately the local share of public school operating costs. In addition, even if such a redirection were politically feasible at the local level, most states have enacted maintenance-of-efforts laws, which forbid localities from reducing their current level of outlays for public education. Second, the capital infrastructure of a large number of local communities is in serious disrepair. Because of the direct effects of capital infrastructure on economic development, the likelihood of diverting local outlays from this source is equally improbable. Third, growing concerns with crime and rapidly increasing rates of incarceration in local jails make the likelihood of redirecting public safety outlays virtually nil.

Similarly, several factors make it unlikely that a large share of current outlays at the state level could be redirected to support a significant portion of the costs of a quality early care and education system.[2] First, the serious erosion of local property tax revenues as the primary source of funding for public schools has placed major financial demands on states to provide additional direct support. In addition, even if such investment of funds were politically feasible at the state level, federal maintenance-of-efforts requirements attached to programs such as Title I and the Individuals with Disabilities Education Act keep states from reducing current levels of outlays for public education. Second, state expenditures for Medicaid have undergone the fastest increase of all state budget outlays, and recent events at the federal level suggest that in the near future, states will have to bear a greater share of the overall costs of the Medicaid program. Third, the same factors that make it unlikely that local governments will redirect capital and public safety outlays are just as applicable at the state level. Finally, recent changes in federal student loan programs and the current fiscal crisis being faced by many public higher education institutions make it equally inconceivable that any appreciable state outlays for higher education could be channeled to support a new structure of early care and education programs.

Arguably, state outlays for welfare and social services (approximately $70 billion annually) provide the best possibility for redirecting funds to support a new early care and education structure. In this category, the AFDC program is perhaps the best prospect. AFDC is an open-ended, state-administered program jointly funded by the state and federal governments. It offers income support to dependent children in their own homes by providing cash to needy families that have been deprived of parental support. Operating under broad federal guidelines, states administer or supervise AFDC programs and set standards to determine eligibility and payment. Like Medicaid, the AFDC program is funded under a matching formula that varies according to the state's per capita income: the minimum federal share is 50 percent and the maximum is 83 percent. Overall, states contribute 46 percent of the total dollars expended for income support.

Pending welfare reform legislation should reduce significantly over time the number of families receiving AFDC benefits at any point in time. In theory, as a result of welfare reform, significant numbers of adults now living in AFDC households will become and remain gainfully employed. This shift to employment will create a new and severe demand among current AFDC families for full-day early care and education. One feasible approach for redirecting current state and federal AFDC outlays to support a new structure of early care and education would be to allow parents leaving AFDC for work to retain some or all of their current AFDC benefits in the form of early care and education vouchers. Because employment of chronically unemployed individuals results in a significant revenue gain to both state and federal governments, as well as a reduction in outlays, even the shift of 100 percent of current AFDC benefits into such vouchers would be state and federal budget positive.

Federal Strategies

In examining the federal options for developing a comprehensive plan to fund and finance a quality early care and education system, five basic avenues are explored below—redirecting existing federal outlays, increasing either or both federal individual or corporate income tax, expanding federal payroll taxes and trust funds, creating a new sales or value-added tax, and creating a new trust fund–based savings and loan concept.

Redirecting Federal Outlays

Current annual federal general-fund outlays (not including $244 billion in annual outlays from the Social Security trust funds) for domestic activities (approximately $650 billion) are distributed as follows: health and human services (43 percent), agriculture (10 percent), labor (7 percent), transportation (5 percent), education (5 percent), housing and urban development (4 percent), interior (4 percent), public safety and corrections (2 percent), and all other (20 percent) (U.S. Department of Commerce, 1994).

On balance, it would appear extremely unlikely that a significant share of current and future domestic outlays at the federal level could be redirected to support a significant portion of the costs of funding and financing a quality early care and education system. The perilous financial status of several of the Social Security trust funds also makes them unlikely candidates. Moreover, recent actions by both the Senate and the House of Representatives that rejected extending child care coverage in the context of the welfare reform debate do not bode well for efforts to redirect existing funding into expanded early care and education. Also, current and impending state budget crises make it even more difficult to redirect federal outlays that are state matched.

The only federal program from which a possible redirection of existing resources toward early childhood services might be feasible is Title 1. Title 1 provides approximately $7 billion of federal assistance per year to local school districts to meet the special needs of economically disadvantaged and educationally deprived children. More than 90 percent of all school districts receive Title 1 funds, and three-fourths of all elementary schools and one-third of all secondary schools provide Title 1 services to over five million children annually. A growing portion of Title 1 funds are devoted to the education of preschool children by public schools. Despite the apparent overlap, the demographics of the current service population—the high incidence of poverty and the overrepresentation of children from racial and ethnic minority groups—make any effort to divert Title I funds to the general population of young children difficult.

Increasing Federal Individual and Corporate Income Taxes

In the United States, over half of the federal government's tax revenue comes from income taxes, with the personal income tax accounting for about 45 percent and the corporate income tax for another 10 percent of the total tax revenue (U.S. Department of Commerce, 1994). For fiscal year 1993, the net federal receipts from personal income tax payments were nearly $510 billion, and from corporation income tax payments, nearly $118 billion. Either or both of these sources could be increased to fund a universal structure of early care and education. Under either approach, increases in tax receipts could be accomplished by increasing the marginal rates of taxation or by surcharging actual tax payments.

The principal advantages of using the federal individual income and corporate income tax mechanisms are their relative efficiency and apparent fairness. Both are familiar and relatively easy to administer. Neither would require the creation of significant additional tax collection overhead. The individual income tax is both income sensitive and progressive and has an automatic adjustment for inflation. A combined approach of using both individual and corporate income taxes would result in a smaller additional tax burden on individuals and would distribute equally the tax burden between individuals and businesses, both of whom would benefit directly from the expansion of early care and education services.

The general disadvantages of these taxes are primarily political. Federal income taxes are widely conceded to be the least popular of virtually all tax approaches. In addition, from the standpoint of generational equity, the personal income tax would result in senior citizens bearing a full share of the tax burden for a new structure of early care and education. Business would likely also object to increased corporate income taxes, claiming that the additional tax burden would interfere with global competitiveness and result in decreased employment opportunities. Also, to the extent that corporate profit margins that are reduced by taxes would hold down wages, the tax impact could be shifted onto workers via downward salary adjustments.

Expanding Federal Payroll Taxes and Trust Funds

Social Security is a complex of national programs that began to evolve with the passage of the Social Security Act of 1935 and that are now administered by the Social Security Administration and the Health Care Financing Administration of the Department of Health and Human Services. Within the Social Security system, two large trust funds—the Old-Age, Survivors, and Disability Insurance (OASDI) and the Medicare Hospital Insurance (HI) trust funds—provide direct payments to maintain the income of retired or disabled workers, their dependents, and their survivors. These funds are also used to defray some medical expenses of the long-term disabled and of retirees and their spouses aged sixty-five and older. For fiscal year 1993, payments into the OASDI Trust Fund administered by the Social Security Administration totaled approximately $312 billion, and payments to the HI Trust Fund were approximately $81 billion.

Funding and financing for an expansion of early care and education could be accommodated through an expansion in Social Security payroll taxes, either through expansion of the OASDI trust or the creation of a new, freestanding trust fund. This approach would require an increase in combined annual employer-employee payroll deduction payments and could be accomplished with the current cap on taxed income (at about $60,000 annually) or without a cap (which would make the tax less regressive).

The principal advantages of a payroll tax approach are its familiarity, high efficiency, and certainty. The payroll tax contribution structure is easy to administer and would require no significant additional tax collection overhead to businesses. By its nature, the payroll tax structure is automatically adjusted for inflation and is the least unpopular of all major taxation strategies. In addition, the use of a payroll tax base avoids the political problem of taxing unearned as well as earned income: under the payroll tax option, most senior citizens would be excused from bearing the tax burden for a new structure of early care and education programs. The payroll tax approach also offers major equity advantages because the tax burden is borne equally by families and businesses.

One disadvantage of a payroll tax strategy is the potential for serious opposition from businesses, who may argue that it would cause adverse effects on global competitiveness followed by decreased employment opportunities. In addition, as currently capped, the payroll tax is highly regressive. Also, current Social Security trust funds are experiencing inherent financing problems, which the system will have to confront before the turn of the century. Furthermore, the aging of the American workforce means that the majority of current wage earners do not and will not in the future have young children who would actually benefit directly from the increased availability of early childhood or early care and education services.

Creating a New Sales or Value-Added Taxes

The creation of a new national sales tax or a value-added tax is another potential national funding vehicle to support an expanded structure of early care and education services. A sales tax is imposed on the sale of goods or services. It is computed as a percentage of the total sales price and may be imposed either on the purchaser or on the seller. For fiscal year 1993, the net receipts from state sales taxes were approximately $212 billion (U.S. Department of Commerce, 1994). A national sales tax could impose an across-the-board tax surcharge on current state sales taxes. For example, if a state sales tax is 5 percent, a 10 percent federal surcharge could be added to create a new .5 percent national sales tax in that state. The new federal sales tax would be collected through existing state sales tax structures.

The principal advantages of the sales tax approach is its familiarity, high efficiency, and relative ease of administration. The approach would not involve any significant additional tax collection overhead to businesses. By its nature, a sales tax structure is automatically adjusted for inflation and is among the least unpopular of all major taxation strategies. The major disadvantage of a sales tax strategy is its regressivity: lower-income families, who spend virtually all their income on necessities, pay a much higher percentage of their income in sales taxes than do wealthier citizens. Indeed, some jurisdictions, as a way of alleviating the most regressive features of the sales tax, have excluded clothing, food, and rent from the items taxed.

The valued-added tax (VAT) is the standard form of indirect taxation in most European countries. The VAT is collected at each stage of the production and distribution process, from the sale of the raw material to the final retail transaction. The amount of the tax is based on the value added to goods or services at each particular stage. The overwhelming disadvantages of a VAT strategy are its complexity and total unfamiliarity in this country. If it were already being seriously considered, it might provide a sound financing framework for a universal structure of early care and education. However, as a new, stand-alone financing strategy for early childhood services or early care and education, it seems highly infeasible.

Creating a New Savings and Loan Approach

Another federal financing strategy that could yield the amount of funding needed to support a universal structure of early care and education involves the concept of advance payments to families from the OASDI Trust Fund, the largest fund in the Social Security system. Under this approach, families would be permitted to borrow funds from their OASDI Trust Fund accounts for the limited purposes of making payments to support the enrollment of their young children in early care and education programs. In this scenario, adult family members would have the options of paying this loan back over the remaining working years, delaying the age at which OASDI benefits would be paid out to them, or reducing their OASDI retirement benefit level.

The principal advantages of this funding and financing approach are its focus on family self-sufficiency and its use of a combination off-budget funding strategy. Families would be empowered by being given a range of new options for using the funds that they are required to contribute to a social insurance structure and from which they may never obtain benefits. Disadvantages of the trust fund savings and loan component include the serious possibility that it would be actively opposed by senior citizens, who would view the approach as a serious threat to the financial integrity of the OASDI Trust Fund, as well as the complex overhead implicit in actually administering the loan and repayment concept.

Borrowing from Capital Markets

An as yet untapped funding and reallocation approach, which involves the local, state, and federal governments, that might provide long-term financial support for a universal structure of early childhood services or early care and education would be to borrow from capital markets to invest in preventive services. Communities, adopting the posture of prudent insurers, would first identify "downstream," long-term financial risks associated with school failure and impaired child development. To mitigate these risks, communities would substantially increase investment in prevention activities by negotiating waiver agreements with state and federal governments to ensure the ongoing flow of entitlement funds, as well as by using a range of other approaches to raise the additional funds needed for increased investment in prevention services. Localities could borrow from private capital markets, reallocate local funds, and raise investment funds from foundation and corporate sources. Once preventive services have their impact and reduce the need for remedial services, funds for remedial services could be shifted to provide ongoing support for preventive services (Gerry & Paulsen, 1995).

Recommended Fund Generation Approach

There are a series of policy principles that should guide the selection of an approach to generate new funds for a quality early care and education system:

- The structure of early care and education should guarantee universal access.
- The financing of a universal structure of early care and education should be accomplished through a systematic fund-generating mechanism that is as simple as possible.
- The costs of a universal structure of early care and education should be borne equally by families and businesses.
- The funding structure should ensure a choice by families from among a wide array of early care and education opportunities within the community.
- The amount individual families contribute toward the costs of early care and education should differ based on family income and resources.

Based on these principles, the recommended source of an increased revenue base for supporting the ongoing operations of a new universal structure of early care and education would be a new, uncapped federal payroll tax, which would be borne by workers and businesses equally and administered through the current federal payroll tax system.

As discussed earlier, the likelihood of local and state governments' making significant new contributions to early care and education is minimal. The federal level presents by far the broadest range of new funding and financing alternatives. In addition to the reasons discussed above, the use of the federal tax base is preferable because it ensures uniform application across the nation and avoids some of the equity problems associated with local and state tax structures.

An uncapped federal payroll tax is most consistent with the guiding principles. It would be a simple, systematic fund-generating approach, which would allocate the financial burden equally between wage earners and businesses. A payroll tax would spread family economic contributions beyond the actual years of early care and education, and the amount individual families contribute toward the costs of early care and education would be determined by family income. Politically, given the current inclination of Congress to reduce the deficit and cut taxes, expansion of the system of dedicated trust fund payroll taxes appears to have the best chance of being realized. Although it is never a propitious time to generate new funds, an uncapped payroll tax seems to be the most politically feasible approach and the one that would also be fair, efficient, and effective.

Notes

1. At the local level, taxes on real property are by far the largest source of current tax revenues, although some jurisdictions collect a local sales tax and a few collect an income tax. The balance of local tax revenues are derived from fees related to motor vehicles and other personal property. Nationally, an average of almost 60 percent of local property tax revenues are dedicated to financing the ongoing operation of public elementary and secondary schools. The balance is used for financing basic government services, such as police and fire, and for maintaining the capital infrastructure, including roads, sidewalks, and sewer systems.

2. Current annual state general-fund outlays (approximately $638 billion) are distributed as follows (U.S. Department of Commerce, 1994): public elementary and secondary education (23 percent), Medicaid (21 percent), public safety and corrections (14 percent), transportation (13 percent), welfare and social services (11 percent), higher education (9 percent), and all other (9 percent).

References

Center for the Study of Social Policy (1991). *Building a community agenda: Developing local governance entities.* Washington, D.C.: Center for the Study of Social Policy.

Farrow, F., & Joe, J. (1992, Spring). Financing school-linked, integrated services. *The Future of Children, 2,* 56–67. Menlo Park, Calif.: David and Lucile Packard Foundation.

Fawcett, S., & others. (1995). Using empowerment theory in collaborative partnerships for community health and development. *American Journal of Community Psychology, 23,* 663–697.

Gerry, M., & Paulsen, R. (1995). *Building community-based networks of children's services and family supports.* New York: Aspen Institute.

Olasky, M. (1992). *The tragedy of American compassion.* Washington, D.C.: Regnery.

U.S. Department of Commerce, Bureau of the Census. (1993). *Statistical abstract of the United States, 1992.* Washington, D.C.: U.S. Government Printing Office.

U.S. Department of Commerce, Bureau of Economic Analysis. (1994). *State and local government receipts and expenditures, 1993.* Washington, D.C.: U.S. Government Printing Office.

Chapter Eleven

Quality Infrastructure for Family Child Care

Shelby H. Miller

Introduction

Family child care—care for a small group of children in the provider's home—constitutes a substantial part of all early care and education services available in the United States today. The best estimates are that, of the approximately 8 million children under the age of six in out-of-home care, 700,000 are in regulated family child care homes, and another 1.3 million are in unregulated home-based settings (Willer & others, 1991).

The limited research on family child care suggests that its quality is as variable as that of center-based programs. A recent study of family child care in three communities across the country found that 35 percent of the homes were of inadequate quality, 56 percent were of adequate custodial quality, and just 9 percent were of good quality (Galinsky, Howes, Kontos, & Shinn, 1994). This chapter synthesizes what is known about effective approaches, as well as about some promising approaches, for building infrastructure services to increase the quality of family child care. Infrastructure services include a variety of supportive activities for family child care providers, such as training, technical assistance, funding, and social support. Lessons are drawn from a variety of demonstration projects from the last decade and from some of the best practices in related human services. The chapter ends by considering the implications of this knowledge for improving the quality of family child care across the country.

Family Child Care, Quality, and Infrastructure

The Study of Children in Family Child Care and Relative Care (Galinsky, Howes, Kontos, & Shinn, 1994) was the first, in-depth observational study of family child care in more than a decade. The researchers found that both regulated providers and unregulated providers across ethnic and income lines concurred on the aspects of family child care programs that are important to quality. These include the child's safety, the parent's communication with the provider about the child, and a warm and attentive relationship between the provider and the child. When observing providers at work, researchers found providers' sensitivity to children to be significantly related to the strength and quality of the children's relationships with them. In addition, providers' responsiveness to children was significantly associated with the complexity of children's play—an indicator of cognitive skill. Higher-quality providers had more years of higher education, deeper levels of commitment to taking care of children, and more of a connection to infrastructure services. Specifically, better providers took advantage more frequently of opportunities to learn about children's development and about early care and education, participated in family child care training, and sought out the company of other providers.

Despite the progress made by this study, there is still an overwhelming lack of consensus among service providers, policy makers, and, to some extent, researchers and parents about what constitutes quality in family child care and about what types of infrastructure services are necessary to improve the quality of programs. One reason for this lack of consensus is the absence of a shared vision for a quality early care and education system that includes distinct roles for family child care. A second reason is that most of the programs assessed in the United States, both family child care and centers, are of mediocre to poor quality. Consequently, some may have grown to see this as the norm and not as a problem to be addressed. A third reason for the lack of consensus about quality in family child care and about how to respond to it is the heterogeneity of family child care: some family child care homes look a lot like parental care, and others can barely be distinguished from small centers.

There has been some progress in the last decade. The public's general understanding has grown regarding the requirements that are essential for influencing a child's early development, and about the roles parents, early care and education practitioners, and other significant adults must play in that process. During this time, demonstration projects aimed at improving the quality of family child care have yielded important lessons about how infrastructure services can promote quality in family child care. Some of these projects are reviewed in this chapter.

Innovative Demonstration Projects

A variety of demonstration projects that have built infrastructure services to support quality in family child care have been implemented over the last decade. These efforts have varied extensively and have focused on a number of different dimensions, including initiators and implementers, overarching goals and objectives, outcomes and effects, scale, and strategies. Several particularly innovative projects are described below, and their lessons are considered in the following section. The descriptions are useful because they illustrate the types of infrastructure services from which family child care can benefit.

One of the more comprehensive family child care quality-improvement initiatives has been the Family-to-Family Project in which the Dayton Hudson Foundation, Mervyn's, and Target Stores have invested almost $10 million over a period of seven years to increase the quality of family child care in thirty-two communities across the country. In each community, an organization (often a child care resource and referral agency and sometimes a family child care–provider association or community college) is funded to create a range of infrastructure services tailored to the local provider community, including sponsoring a training course of at least fifteen hours, starting a program to help providers become accredited, creating or strengthening local provider associations, and conducting consumer education activities. Evaluations have found that training does improve the quality of providers' practices and that it actually spawns other supportive services with long-term benefits, including the establishment of provider associations and the formation of teaching and mentoring roles for providers

(Cohen & Modigliani, 1992; Dombro & Modigliani, 1993; Galinsky, Howes, & Kontos, 1995). Evaluators also suggest that the success of Family-to-Family has been attributable, in part, to the active and complementary roles taken by the funding organizations and the local implementers.

Another large-scale quality-improvement initiative, one that has focused on all types of early education and care programs, is the American Business Collaboration for Quality Dependent Care. This effort is coordinated by Work/Family Directions and involves over 150 businesses and public-private sector organizations, which have committed over $25 million to fund a wide array of child and elder care programs in forty-four communities in twenty-five states and the District of Columbia (Dombro, 1994). More than 10 percent of the funding is targeted to improve the quality and supply of family child care. In 1993, over 350 local projects that provided infrastructure services for family child care in twenty-five states and the District of Columbia were funded. Services included recruitment and training, purchasing equipment, assistance in getting accreditation, and promoting the development of provider networks. Evaluation findings on provider retention indicate that there is substantially less provider turnover among those participating in the local projects, suggesting one way in which infrastructure services support the quality of family child care for young children and families.

The National Family Day Care Project was yet another major initiative to enhance family child care in communities, and one of the few to involve volunteers. This four-year demonstration project, which ended in 1992, worked through the National Council of Jewish Women's volunteer membership chapters in twenty states (National Council of Jewish Women Center for the Child, 1992). The volunteers assessed communities' needs for family child care infrastructure services and developed appropriate community service, education, and advocacy efforts in response. These efforts were carried out in collaboration with key leaders and organizations from the public and private sectors. Unlike many other national initiatives, the project concluded with an intensive information dissemination phase to distribute its print and other resources and to assure their long-term availability through other national and state organizations.

The California Child Care Initiative is probably the most sizable and longest-operating statewide program aimed specifically at building a comprehensive set of infrastructure services in communities to increase the supply of licensed, quality family child care. Begun in 1985 by the California Child Care Resource and Referral Network and the BankAmerica Foundation, the initiative operates as a public-private partnership that, to date, has involved over 450 different funders and has amassed almost $7 million to advance its objectives. The initiative works by funding and supporting community-based child care resource and referral agencies to provide infrastructure services, including recruiting and training new family child care providers and offering training to existing providers. Overall, the initiative has generated almost four thousand new licensed family child care homes, making available more than fifteen thousand new child care spaces for children of all ages. Over twenty-five thousand family child care providers have received basic and advanced training. The initiative's approach of building and maintaining a range of infrastructure services for family child care has been adapted throughout Oregon and Michigan, and initiative staff have provided training and technical assistance to bring about its replication in other states.

Coastal Enterprises, a statewide community development corporation in Maine, was among the first organizations to use a joint economic and social development strategy to address the barriers to finding employment experienced by families faced with a lack of early care and education for their children—including family child care. The Child Care Development Project was initiated in 1988 as a partnership between Coastal Enterprises, the Maine State Legislature, and the Ford Foundation. The project has worked to create financial, educational, and social supportive infrastructure services that are appropriate for rural communities. Strategies include a revolving-loan fund to create or stabilize slots for children in family child care homes and centers, as well as training and technical assistance for family child care providers both in early childhood education and care and in running a small business. The training and technical assistance is tailored to the individual needs of providers (Collins, 1990). The loans have created or stabilized 1,400 child care slots. More than 2,200 hours of training and technical assistance have been given to the providers. The original $500,000 revolving-loan fund has leveraged over $4 million from banks, foundations, and other sources, all of which has gone to expanding the supply and improving the quality of child care.

A very different collaboration of private foundations and corporate donors came together as the Child Care Initiative in eastern Massachusetts in the late 1980s. Begun by the United Way of Massachusetts Bay, the initiative was created to improve the practice of staff who work with children from low-income families and children with special needs, as well as to improve the physical facilities in which the programs are offered. The initiative has two unique components—the Child Care Careers Institute and the Child Care Capital Investment Fund. The Child Care Careers Institute has developed innovative training models for all types of early care and education, has trained over four hundred providers, has created a college and university consortium to help standardize and professionalize the early care and education field through accreditation, and has assisted in the development of family child care systems in low-income neighborhoods. The Capital Investment Fund offers technical assistance and low-interest loans to family child care providers and centers to improve the quality of programs. Since 1991, it has helped create three hundred new child care slots and has enhanced the quality of over seven hundred more programs. Further, technical assistance and loans have been provided to almost forty child care organizations, including large centers with networks of family child care providers.

Save the Children's Neighborhood Child Care Network is another local effort aimed at improving the quality and availability of child care for families, especially those with low incomes. The network is special in its focus on the range of training, technical assistance, and other supports it offers to create a supportive infrastructure for family child care. These infrastructure services include intensive training and technical assistance for providers via resource rooms and toy-lending libraries housed at local churches, the Parent Services Project—a family support program offered by clusters of family child care homes, Parents First—a home-based early literacy project, and a book-reading program staffed by volunteers. Funding for the Neighborhood Child Care Network has been provided by foundations, government, and community organizations and churches.

Lessons from Demonstration Projects

A number of lessons can be learned from these national, state, regional, and community-level initiatives concerning infrastructure services that can improve the quality of family child care. These lessons can be organized around these dimensions—sponsors, goals and outcomes, scale, and infrastructure services.

Sponsors

Most of the quality-enhancement approaches reviewed have entailed collaborations of a number of different private and sometimes public funders. The private funders have included corporations; independent, family, and corporate foundations; volunteer organizations; and churches. Often, those in the private sector have led the way, recognizing the importance of quality early care and education of all types, and in particular, the necessity of family child care.

The funders typically have selected community-based intermediary organizations, such as child care resource and referral agencies, community development organizations, and family child care associations, to implement the infrastructure services. An understanding of the importance of these intermediaries to the development, maintenance, and enhancement of infrastructure services for family child care has grown greatly in recent years. Many of the funders have assumed joint responsibility with the local intermediary organizations for the design of the projects, thus merging knowledge gleaned from demonstration projects from across the nation with a deep understanding of particular community conditions.

Goals and Outcomes

In terms of goals, many of these projects are trying to address simultaneously the quantity and the quality of family child care. Although this dual focus is sometimes necessary, it becomes a more complex challenge than just improving the quality of the existing supply of programs. Sometimes these dual goals and related objectives become confused in the implementation of activities. For example, *quantity* indicators, such as the number of children served and the hours of care provided, can become proxies for *quality*.

The lack of a consistent definition for quality family child care was a consistent challenge in assessing the outcomes of the projects reviewed. Program materials and evaluation reports typically describe the interventions implemented and the populations served, but they do not explicitly address the elements or standards of quality desired. Only a few of those who implemented or evaluated the projects used specific proxies to quantify the quality enhancements. Although something is known about the level of quality improvement of a family child care home when it becomes regulated or when the provider earns a child development associate certificate (CDA), little is known about the impact of other quality-improvement efforts. This gap in knowledge points to the need for a continuum of professionally agreed-on quality indicators for family child care to use in assessing the progress of many different types of providers.

Scale

With a few exceptions, the projects have been relatively small in scale, in part because the initiators wanted to demonstrate first that the interventions could be successful on a small scale, and in part because they were constrained by limited resources. Consequently, there is not extensive experience with large-scale implementation, replication, or institutionalization of infrastructure services to improve and support the quality of family child care. Expanding the promising experimental approaches to full scale will be a major challenge for the coming years. More attention needs to be directed to acquiring the financing that will be required to make this happen.

Infrastructure Services

Training was the most heavily relied-on infrastructure service in the quality-enhancement initiatives reviewed, although the content, duration, and intensity of this training varied extensively. One wonders about the possibility of linking all enhancement activities statewide or nationwide to specific, commonly agreed-on indicators of quality. As they currently exist, some interventions seem too minimal and too diffuse to achieve the desired effects.

Another trend in the infrastructure services developed by these projects is that the services are increasingly comprehensive; they attempt to meet many of the providers' needs by offering financial and social supports as well as training and other opportunities for skill improvement. The most promising approaches have been increasingly sustained and long lasting. In contrast, so-called "inoculation methods," or short-term quick fixes, seem to have had only limited utility for affecting family child care practice. A comprehensive set of infrastructure services for family child care in a community must be able to provide initial and ongoing training and technical assistance to support quality services. This means sequenced programs of training and other services that address providers' needs and interests for as long as they are in the business of family child care.

Lessons from Other Fields

There are lessons from related and linked human service fields regarding the enhancement of service quality that may be transferable to the family child care arena. Lessons from home-visiting, family support, and nutrition programs are considered below.

Home-visiting programs that deliver parenting education and family support services have burgeoned in the last decade, with the proliferation of models such as Parents as Teachers, Home Instruction for Preschool Youngsters, and the Maternal Infant Health Outreach Worker program. The more developed home-visiting programs have shifted from their initial demonstration and evaluation phases to replication and institutionalization throughout entire communities and, in some cases, throughout entire states. These shifts have necessitated careful design of training and program management processes, affiliation structures, communication strategies, and methods for coordinating with other service providers. The lesson for the family child care field is that it too will have to make this shift to replication and institutionalization by using the most promising or proven strategies on a much larger scale.

Family support programs offer or coordinate—or do both—a range of services that include health care, parenting support and training, early care and education, employment and training, and assistance with securing benefits and housing. Family support programs have integrated their services into locations where eligible program participants reside or frequent. In addition, they deliver services with a great deal of flexibility, as they pay consistent attention to specific goals and objectives. Further, a number of states now have statewide family support initiatives, and broader state-level intermediary entities to provide and coordinate training and technical assistance to the community-based organizations. A number of lessons have been learned about family child care from the family support field—to reach high proportions of family child care providers, services may need to be delivered in providers' own and other providers' homes, as well as in houses of worship, schools, neighborhood agencies, and other locations that providers frequent; specific desired outcomes for providers should be spelled out from the start, although implementation may need to be flexible; and intermediary organizations and their responsibilities must be explicit, funded, and recognized by policy makers, service providers, and the public.

The Child and Adult Care Food Program, funded by the U.S. Department of Agriculture, also offers a number of important lessons for improving the quality of family child care. As Larner (1994) and others have noted, this program may be the most important vehicle currently available for supporting low-income family child care providers. The Child and Adult Care Food Program is structured nationwide with resources, education programs, and an accountability system. Providers receive reimbursement for nutritious meals served to children, participate in educational sessions—most often focused on nutrition, and agree to periodic monitoring visits in their homes by their sponsoring agencies. The most significant barrier to providers' participating in the program is that they must be regulated by the state. Creative combinations of outreach, financial incentives, training, and technical assistance have resulted in additional providers joining the program. A key lesson from the Child and Adult Care Food Program for the larger family child care field is the importance of coupling financial assistance with training and peer support. There must be monetary incentives, as well as opportunities for skill development and camaraderie, for many providers to participate and improve their services. A second lesson is the importance of the ongoing nature of assistance. This constancy provides consistent moderate pressure to keep services at a certain level of quality. Finally, the Child and Adult Care Food Program illustrates the importance of a home-based monitoring and technical-assistance structure for working with those who are more difficult to reach.[1]

The strength of the Child and Adult Care Food Program leads one to wonder about the potential for building more comprehensive family child care quality-enhancement strategies around it. These strategies could reach more providers of all income levels with training on numerous topics, including nutrition and a range of other supports. The program also offers an intriguing opportunity to develop community-based networks that link a range of infrastructure service providers to family child care providers, including child care resource and referral agencies, family child care associations, and other intermediaries and community-based agencies suggested by the Carnegie Corporation's (1994) recent task force on very young children. Some states and the U.S. military are already experimenting with such networks as structures for quality-enhancement and management activities.

Conclusions for Enhancing Quality

There are a number of strategies for enhancing the quality of family child care.

Taking Quality Enhancement to Scale

The next challenge facing family child care is to take to scale the types of quality-enhancement approaches reviewed in this chapter. To accomplish this, the place of family child care in the array of larger services must be more clearly established. For a major investment to be made in improving family child care quality, these programs would have to be viewed on equal terms with preschools, child care centers, and Head Start programs—that is, they would have to be seen as good environments for promoting children's optimal physical, cognitive, and social development. It would follow that family child care providers should be paid at rates comparable to those received by providers in other programs, and they should be eligible for the same benefits and opportunities. One concern related to promoting such equity within the early care and education field is that some of the less formally educated or more isolated providers may not be included if a more formal system is established.

Another key issue in taking these quality-enhancement strategies to scale is that mechanisms for initiating and maintaining community-based efforts must be developed and supported. This would require the public sector's, and possibly the private sector's recognition and adequate financial support for state-level intermediaries. The necessary structures and true costs of maintaining quality must be acknowledged.

Implementing the quality-enhancement infrastructure services described in this chapter on a large scale would also precipitate more informed program and policy debates about what constitutes quality and about what level of quality care society is willing to finance. The different hierarchies of demands for quality from parents, providers, policy makers, early child development specialists, and others must be considered. The base of knowledge remains quite limited regarding the optimal intensity, duration, and content of the quality-enhancement infrastructure services and the ways in which these services effect change in family child care–provider practices. There is still much to be learned about what interventions work for which providers under what conditions.

Finally, efforts to take promising quality-improvement infrastructure services to scale would more than likely prompt concern about the efficacy of exact replications. Attention must be directed to the level of adaptation that would be necessary to be responsive to demographic, cultural, and other community differences, as well as to the level of program fidelity that must be maintained to assure positive effects. Both the literature and the actual experience on program replication remain quite limited. The early care and education field needs to reach consensus about the level of strict replication versus local adaptation that is desirable to ensure quality infrastructure services.

Program Quality

Future definitions of early care and education quality that encompass family child care should not be derived primarily from the research and practice on center-based programs. More basic research is needed on family child care quality, especially on the important attributes of provider responsiveness and sensitivity, on programs in different cultural contexts, and on programs for children of different ages. Other possibly important characteristics of family child care, such as the types and intensities of the relationships between parents and providers and the effects of interactions among mixed-age children, also warrant much more research and consideration. A more complex definition of family child care quality, one that reflects these unique attributes and their interactions, is sorely needed. Recent efforts to develop quality criteria for family child care need to be taken to the next level and to be validated in varied settings. The field needs to build a consensus around a new definition of quality in family child care. The National Association for Family Child Care and the Center for Career Development in Early Care and Education, Wheelock College, are currently creating an accreditation instrument for family child care providers and their homes, which will build on existing instruments and meet some of this need.

In addition to being derived almost exclusively from center-based programs and to being relatively simple in terms of design, most current definitions of early care and education quality are based only on the desired outcomes for the child, as indicated by measures of cognitive and social development, or by the strength of the child's attachment to the practitioner, or by both. To measure the quality of all types of early care and education, a more complex set of outcomes would be preferable, ones that take into account desired child, parent, family, provider, and community outcomes simultaneously.

Future definitions of quality in early care and education also need to be much more flexible than current ones, so they can accommodate the wide range of family child care arrangements. Different proxies for providers' characteristics in various settings may be very appropriate. Measures of provider or environmental characteristics at a single point in time may not be that meaningful or reliable. They may not offer much information about the typical behavioral style or motivational abilities of the providers. Also, little is known about how the individual attributes of a provider and the quality of the environment interact; nor is much known about the potential for strong attributes to compensate for weaker ones.

The possibility of having a universal definition of quality in the early education and care field, one that could accommodate all variations in arrangements—in both homes and centers—may be more desirable than having separate definitions for different types of settings, given the state of the field and the need for a more collaborative system. The articulation of such a definition would challenge service providers, researchers, and policy makers both to quantify and to qualify their visions for the field. Establishing such a universal definition of quality in early care and education would require integrating various approaches, ranging from good parenting at one end of the spectrum to good formal center-based programs at the other end. This will be no small feat.

Quality-Enhancing Infrastructure Supports

A comprehensive early care and education system in a community must be able to provide initial and ongoing training and technical assistance to support quality services. This means sequenced programs of training that address providers' needs and interests for as long as they are in the business of offering care. The content of the training and technical assistance must be carefully shaped by the knowledge available regarding the predictors of quality. Attention must be focused on the processes by which quality child care is delivered, not just on what quality care looks like. More training on the management of the family child care business and the behaviors of providers is also necessary.

Experience in improving family child care has shown that training programs are much easier to implement than are services aimed at helping providers become accredited or achieve other credentials. These latter services require more intensive and sustained activities and may be appropriate for only a portion of the provider population. It should be understood that a goal of training is to encourage providers to meet the requirements necessary for accreditation or credentialing. Training, accreditation, and credentialing should be viewed as part of an ongoing process that has both short- and long-term objectives. Regulation, basic training, accreditation or credentialing, and advanced training are landmarks in this process.

Promoting quality in all types of early education and care arrangements in a community must be intentional. The use of intermediary organizations—such as child care resource and referral agencies, family child care provider associations, and community colleges—has been shown to be essential to meeting this goal. At the national, state, and local levels, the necessity of these intermediary structures must be recognized so that financial support for their initial development and their ongoing operations is provided. Determining what types of intermediary entities make the most sense for a community will depend on a number of characteristics, including the community's demographics, history, and leadership.

Infrastructure supports must devote some attention to the issues of financing if they are to influence the quality of family child care. There are numerous examples from demonstration projects in which providing financial or in-kind resources for specific purposes—from purchasing equipment to making safety improvements in the home—triggered more dramatic quality improvement than did providing training and technical assistance alone. Financial barriers are often perceived by the providers as the hardest to overcome. Community organizations that sponsor infrastructure services for family child care should consider new, viable forms of financing, such as group purchasing, utilizing the Child and Adult Care Food Program (or whatever new form of nutrition assistance may take place in states), and taking advantage of the Community Reinvestment Act and other public funds to enhance the quality of family child care.

Other infrastructure services that are particularly necessary for improving and maintaining the quality of family child care include mechanisms to recruit and support providers, especially those who are unregulated or geographically isolated. Many providers may need concrete incentives such as money or material to become involved in the regulated system. Ideally, once the providers are engaged, incentives should flow naturally through the ongoing training and technical-assistance process. However, the front end of this process will have to be intentionally "primed" for some time to come because few providers are regulated.

Effecting Change

Changes in early education and care systems that are relevant to family child care would be hastened by the intentional organizing of family child care around the previously described intermediary organizations. This would begin to ensure that all family care providers are part of larger systems and that there are effective and efficient mechanisms for delivering essential services to them. Much can be learned from home-visiting programs and from the family support field about ways to reach and to engage home-based family child care providers and to maintain basic levels of quality. There must be substantial support for intermediary organizations, however, both from within and without the early care and education community. A dramatic increase in the need for quality early care and education services precipitated by welfare reform could provide this impetus to support intermediary organizations, if the opportunity is clearly perceived and carefully managed.

Changes in the quality of family child care could also be hastened by more inclusive leadership in the early care and education field. Leaders need to accept family child care as an integral part of the array of early care and education programs and conscientiously include those with expertise in family child care in program and policy development activities at the national, state, and local levels. Significant attention needs to be directed to the representation of family child care issues in public advocacy and education. Although a number of national organizations include family child care in their purviews, it is a major focus of only a few, including the National Association for Family Child Care and the National Association of Child Care Resource and Referral Agencies.

There is clearly much to be learned about building a supportive infrastructure for family child care from demonstration projects to improve the quality of family child care and from the best practices in related fields. The challenge remains to implement these strategies on a large scale, in order to affect significant percentages of providers and ultimately to affect significant percentages of young children and families.

Organizations to Contact for Further Information

The Family-to-Family Project, The Dayton Hudson Foundation, 777 Nicollet Mall, Minneapolis, Minnesota 55402

The American Business Collaboration, Work/Family Directions Development Corporation, 930 Commonwealth Ave., West, Boston, Massachusetts 02215–1212

The National Family Day Care Project, The National Council of Jewish Women Center for the Child, National Council of Jewish Women, 53 West 23rd Street, New York, New York 10010

The California Child Care Initiative, The California Child Care Resource and Referral Network, 111 New Montgomery St., San Francisco, California 94105

The Child Care Development Project, Coastal Enterprises, Inc., P.O. Box 268, Wiscasset, Maine 04578

The Child Care Initiative, Two Liberty Square, Boston, Massachusetts 02109

The Neighborhood Child Care Network, Save the Children's Child Care Support Center, 1447 Peachtree St., N.E., Atlanta, Georgia 30309

Note

1. Current congressional discussion of major revisions in funding and administrative approaches to human services may result in significant changes in the Child and Adult Care Food Program. Whatever the future of this program, the lessons learned from it can be used more widely in the family child care field.

References

Carnegie Task Force on Meeting the Needs of Young Children. (1994). *Starting points: Meeting the needs of our youngest children.* The report of the Carnegie Task Force on Meeting the Needs of Young Children. New York: Carnegie Corporation of New York.

Cohen, N. E., & Modigliani, K. (1992). *The Family-to-Family Project: Results, best practices, and lessons learned.* New York: Families and Work Institute.

Collins, M. I. (1990). *Portraits of child care: An examination of availability, quality, and cost.* Portland, Maine: University of Southern Maine, Child and Family Institute.

Dombro, A. (1994). *Select initiatives to improve the quality of family child care.* New York: Families and Work Institute.

Dombro, A., & Modigliani, K. (1993). *The Family-to-Family Project: Accomplishments, emerging issues, and next steps*. New York: Families and Work Institute.

Galinsky, E., Howes, C., & Kontos, S. (1995). *The family child care training study: Highlights of findings*. New York: Families and Work Institute.

Galinsky, E., Howes, C., Kontos, S., & Shinn, M. (1994). *The study of children in family child care and relative care: Highlights of findings*. New York: Families and Work Institute.

Larner, M. (1994). *In the neighborhood: Programs that strengthen family day care for low-income families*. New York: National Center for Children in Poverty.

National Council of Jewish Women Center for the Child. (1992). *The final report of the NCJW's National Family Day Care Project (1988–1992)*. New York: National Council of Jewish Women.

Willer, B., & others. (1991). *The demand and supply of child care in 1990: Joint findings from the national child care survey 1990 and a profile of child care settings*. Washington, D.C.: National Association for the Education of Young Children.

Part Three

Implementing Change

Chapter Twelve

Media and Mass Communications Strategies

Kathy Bonk
Meredith Wiley

Introduction

The formation of public opinion and the development of the public policy agenda are complex processes, in which media play a central role. Considering that public attitudes and beliefs increasingly influence governmental actions, media and mass communications are important resources in advancing any social agenda, including improving the quality of early care and education programs that serve young children. This chapter explores media's role in effecting policy and social change in a range of fields, considers ways for advocates to use media effectively, reviews the current public view of early care and education, and then builds on the lessons learned to make recommendations for strategic communications in support of major social change in early care and education.

The terms *media* and *mass communications* are used throughout the chapter. The term *media* is used to describe the press; it includes all forms of news and commentary, such as documentaries, features, and panel discussions among journalists. The term *mass communications* is much broader in scope; it encompasses all forms of large-scale dissemination of information, including entertainment, magazines, advertising, and the new technologies of the information highway.

Media's Role in Shaping Attitudes and Policy

The information provided by media is an important factor in the formation of individual attitudes on policy issues. Will Rogers once said, "All I know is just what I read in the papers." This comment, updated to include television, summarizes much of what U.S. citizens know about the public policy agenda: most of us deal with a secondhand reality. For the most part, our primary concerns are the routine matters of daily living and our own personal experiences, such as job and financial security, neighborhood safety, and the well-being of family and friends. At the same time, however, we form an opinion as to whether we should enter a free-trade agreement with Mexico and Canada or send troops into Bosnia, or whether the size of the national debt presents a threat to the U.S. economy.

Policy Agenda

Walter Lippmann characterized the connection between public events and private life as "the world outside and the pictures in our head." He argued that the citizen's political world is by necessity a pseudoenvironment, which is largely shaped by media because, "the real environment is altogether too big, too complex and too fleeting for direct acquaintance" (Neuman, Marion, & Crigler, 1992, p. 1). Because we do not take part in the reality of most news stories, we depend on information and analysis provided by media. As a result, media have enormous power to shape public thinking. As one observer wrote, "The press is significantly more than a purveyor of information and opinion. It may not be successful much of the time in telling people what to think, but it is stunningly successful in telling its readers what to think *about*" (Cohen, 1963, p. 13).

The media influence the priorities that Americans—voters and policy makers alike—attach to national problems. This in turn influences policy and can prompt and support social change. Many issues compete for attention; only a few are successful in getting it. The first step in policy making is the decisions, conscious or unconscious, that determine the issues that *will* receive government attention out of those that *could* receive attention. At any given time, the policy agenda consists of no more than five to seven issues (McCombs, 1993). Though the link between public opinion and governmental policy is not always immediate, ultimately government does respond to bring majority purpose and public action into harmony (Iyengar & Kinder, 1987).

The media signal the salience of an issue via a variety of cues, such as story placement, headlines, and the amount of space or airtime given. The most powerful cue, however, is repetition. Numerous studies have shown that voters' agendas reflect the overall coverage of the preceding week's news; nearly two hundred studies conducted around the world at the local and national levels, combined with survey research and focus groups, document the connection between news coverage and voters' concerns (McCombs, 1993).

Although media are a powerful force in shaping public attitudes, they are not the only force. The process by which people learn about public issues is complex. A recent study found that what individuals may learn from a few news stories about an issue is only about 5 percent of what they already know (Neuman, Marion, & Crigler, 1992). The process of learning about an issue is interactive and cumulative. Most people pick up information and ideas from a wide mix of media—television, radio, and print, as well as from personal conversations and experiences in their daily lives.

Context and Timing

The success of policy reform and social change depends on the structural readiness for change; it encompasses political and socioeconomic forces as well as organizational preparedness: structural readiness makes the consideration of a particular problem possible. Major policy shifts occur when there is a confluence of these factors. This concept of opportunity is summarized by political strategists as "timing." Media coverage and mass communications can be important tools for ripening a concern into an issue—by generating public interest, discussion, and understanding, and by helping build consensus on solutions.

In looking at the social and institutional forces in the present political environment, during the late 1990s, several factors point to the possibility of an unprecedented readiness for a change in public attitudes toward the importance of early care and education, particularly at the state and local levels. First, the movement of the violence issue to the center of public concern highlights the need for children, especially young children, to be with a trusted adult twenty-four hours a day. Growing public concern about violence also presents an opportunity for educating the public that prevention of violent behavior is most effective if begun in earliest childhood. Second, the public is increasingly willing to support intervention in families when a case can be made for a compelling societal interest, such as child or spouse abuse. And third, states are increasingly moving in this direction. Some states, such as Hawaii, Oregon, Ohio, Missouri, and Kentucky, are working to design, pass, and implement comprehensive child and family legislation that encompasses early childhood strategies, such as home visitation, intensive family preservation services, violence prevention programs, comprehensive child care programs, and expanded Head Start.

Maximizing Media Effectiveness

A sophisticated, well-planned communications effort is an essential element in moving the national policy agenda on early childhood issues. Such an effort should be built by formulating a broad communications strategy, rather than by simply contacting journalists working in traditional media outlets. To gain maximum impact, early care and education advocates should marshal allies, pool resources, and mobilize advocates, who together can use mass communications as a tool for change. The following are several key obstacles to harnessing the power of media and several approaches to addressing them.

Obstacles to Media Effectiveness

There are substantial communications barriers to the placement of any particular issue, including early care and education, on the policy agenda.

Audience Fragmentation
The explosive expansion in media and all mass communications is splintering information sources into a bewildering array of

choices. In 1970, television in the United States consisted of only three commercial broadcast networks and public television. Just twenty-five years later, we are in the midst of an unprecedented information proliferation, with the possibility of five hundred television channels. These new technologies present both an upside and a downside to communications efforts. The upside is that there are more outlets and more opportunities. The downside, however, is potentially steep—a self-selected narrowing of information sources by both broadcasters and viewers. The days of the "electronic hearth," when most citizens could be reached relatively simply through the three major networks and public television, are disappearing. Selective access to news and information makes it easier for people to isolate themselves from what they find disturbing or deem unimportant. Providers of programming are "narrowcasting," or targeting audiences by demographics and individual interests. These tendencies make it increasingly difficult to reach a wide audience. At the same time, however, people are increasingly feeling bombarded and confused by the bewildering volume of information available—in the news media, on cable, on the Internet, and in their mailboxes. Not only is the volume of material overwhelming, but recipients somehow have to find meaningful patterns in disjointed stories and out-of-context information.

Prevailing Public Attitudes

There are serious attitudinal barriers to effecting major policy shifts and social change on early care and education issues. According to opinion polls, there are several basic public attitudes to consider when developing communications strategies for child and family issues (Columbia University Graduate School of Journalism, 1992). First, for the most part, when advocates talk about improving the status of children, voters tend to think about one specific issue area, education. Second, Americans view children as being primarily the responsibility of their families; they worry about our ability to make social policy without violating family sanctity. Third, there is a significant gap in public sympathy between children who are categorized as poor and children in general. People are not as receptive to supporting programs and services for children they perceive as poor, and they tend to view many of the problems of children and families as isolated to inner-city neighborhoods. There is a tendency for a large segment of the public to equate programs for poor children with welfare and to see "children's issues" as code words for tax increases. Fourth, people are not certain about solutions, and there is no consensus on what should be done. And finally, people worry that money targeted for children will become bogged down in bureaucracy, waste, and inefficiency.

Framing the Issues

The differences that appear in responses to public opinion polls when children are perceived as poor clearly illustrate that how an issue is framed affects how it will fare in the long run.

Powerful Phrases

Careful framing of an issue is crucial to minimizing the barriers presented by existing public attitudes. The words, phrases, and themes used to discuss issues are extremely important in how issues are perceived and whether they will have staying power, a fact that advertisers have spent many millions of dollars demonstrating with market research. A well-framed issue captures the attention of media, the public, and policy makers alike. It conveys complex concepts in simple code words that are widely understood. Powerful phrases developed in recent years include "secondhand smoke" and "designated driver." Graphic code words create a common frame of reference and an image with staying power. They enable a formerly unrecognized problem to be culturally identified through a unifying concept that reveals the pattern underlying seemingly unrelated facts or stories. For example, the issue of child abuse leaped onto the national policy agenda in 1962 when C. Henry Kempe labeled child abuse the "battered child syndrome." The code words "battered child" effectively communicated a complex set of factors, including a pattern of ongoing familial violence and physical and psychological harm to children, which prior to this labeling did not coherently exist in the public's conscience as a social problem.

Positioning Issues

The public's understanding of an issue is also affected by how it is positioned. Positioning is determined by such factors as who the primary advocates or spokespeople are—such as teachers, doctors, and parents; how the problem is cast—such as welfare-to-work transition, poverty prevention, and school readiness; and whether the issue is cast positively or negatively. During the debate on family and medical leave, for example, opponents from the business community framed the proposal negatively: they were against federal mandates imposed on business. Proponents and leading spokespeople, including teachers, parents, and pediatricians, framed the proposal positively: they characterized it as offering "minimum job protection" and being "pro-family." Like the minimum wage and child labor laws, family leave would provide minimum benefits for children and families at critical times for newborns and seriously ill children.

Assigning Responsibility

The framing of an issue also shapes how the press, public, and policy makers assign responsibility for both the genesis of a problem and its solution. For example, the complex factors of domestic violence against women have been given a cohesive framework by the code phrase "battered woman." Advocates are now beginning to realize, however, that the battered-woman frame tends to place responsibility in the public's mind on the victim. Many ask, Why doesn't she leave him? Some advocates now argue that a semantic change in how the issue is framed—to "battering man"—would shift the responsibility from victim to perpetrator.

Framing the issues that affect children and families in ways that overcome the cultural tendency to blame the poor for their plight is one of the greatest challenges to advocates for many social programs. Assignment of responsibility for both the causes and the treatment of problems is particularly important in understanding the shaping of public policy (Iyengar, 1991). There is a strong cultural belief in the United States that poor people are responsible for their plight and can change their status simply by working hard. This attitude is deeply rooted in tradition and such folklore as the rugged individualist, rags-to-riches immigrants, and the Puritan work ethic. Unfortunately, this simplistic and often inaccurate view of poverty is widespread and is strongly reflected in policy debates.

Tying to Science

Who the public identifies as the main spokesperson for an issue has a powerful impact on how a particular issue is framed. For example, Americans have great faith in scientific research. As a result, scientific experts have considerable access to media and frequently shape how an issue is positioned. Medical experts, in particular, have played an important role in shaping the news agenda since World War II. Many behaviors formerly viewed as social or ethical problems have been successfully reframed as medical deviances, for example, child abuse, smoking, and drug addiction. Alcohol addiction has been particularly medicalized, moving from being viewed as sinful, criminal, reflecting a lack of character, or as a labor issue to being seen today primarily as a disease. The framing of a problem as medical shapes public attitudes and policy decisions by shifting responsibility for the problem away from individuals and onto the external social system. Policy makers appear to be more willing to place problems on the policy agenda when they are framed as diseases.

The Information Highway

In the coming years, it will be imperative that social policy advocates understand and consider both the communications opportunities and the special challenges of the rapidly evolving information highway. The information highway is a shorthand term for systems of communications and information accessed via computers, modems, and telephones with voice, data, and video transmission. For example, companies such as America Online, CompuServe, Lexis/Nexis, and Prodigy provide hundreds of services, ranging from banking, shopping, and entertainment to direct connection with journalists, reference libraries, and media outlets, as well as internal communications among organizations and coalitions. The potential for advocacy and policy organization afforded by this technology is enormous.

The information highway is literally being created day to day with staggering and as yet unclear implications for society. Vice President Albert Gore has been a powerful advocate for a proposed National Information Infrastructure—an integrated high-speed network for voice, data, and video services that would connect "everyone." A wide cross-section of people and interest groups, including members of Congress, computer company executives, telecommunications lawyers, federal communications commissioners, and science fiction authors are now debating the implications of the superhighway and how it will be built. In examining the staggering implications of new highway technology information systems, Sheldon Mains questions where the information super highway will take us, noting that the results of the debate will help determine the shape of our society (Mains, 1994).

There are fundamental social questions and socioeconomic issues embedded in this debate. Who will the information highway systems serve? Who will have access and at what cost? How will it shape society? Who will control content? As one computer industry commentator, Patricia Schnaidt noted, "Some barriers to the superhighway are technological, but most are economic and social. The biggest challenges will be the people themselves—getting groups to cooperate, finding funding for public service and educational applications, ensuring access to people who can't afford to pay, delivering quality content where the super highway delivers public services, and providing access devices that people can use easily" (Schnaidt, 1994, p. 6).

The information systems likely to be developed in the late 1990s will have a major impact on the development of communications strategies for interest groups. For example, as advocacy groups work toward policy change, technology systems can make communication among organizations and individuals—from one to one thousand—a simple task. Numerous transmission options will be available—beyond simply sending written reports through the mail—for the dissemination of data, research, and policy reports to elected officials, journalists, and policy makers. It could also become a serious barrier to achieving major policy changes should these systems be available only to those who can afford access or if issue leaders are unprepared to take full advantage of emerging technology.

Public Opinion of Early Care and Education Issues

Any communications effort must be grounded in the current reality of both public opinion and the media's perception of the issue. The Child Care Action Campaign's studies of media coverage and public opinion of early care and education between 1988 and 1993 (Child Care Action Campaign & Communications Consortium Media Center, 1994a, 1994b) show that there has been steady public support since 1988 for the general proposition that government should provide more support for early care and education services to working parents. However, it is important to distinguish between government *services* and government *assistance* when talking about child care. Support for government assistance may not be support for government actually providing services. Early care and education advocates should be aware that the specific language of the questions posed in public opinion polls may have a significant impact on the responses given. In addition, since passage of the 1990 Child Care Development Block Grant, child care has become a second-tier political issue, and its saliency has varied depending on media coverage.

Taken together, the information gathered on early care and education from this public opinion research points to the need for advocates to develop long-range political strategies. There is potential public support for major social change in early care and education, which can be furthered with well-planned media coverage. Republican and Democratic pollsters alike believe that the key to increasing the political power of family issues may lie in the development of a family of issues, a *cluster*, which could be used by advocates on multiple fronts to raise the political visibility of family and children's issues and to develop public support. Essential elements of such a cluster could start with support and reform of education, which in 1994 was identified as the top children's issue in the minds of most Americans (Child Care Action Campaign & Communications Consortium Media Center, 1994b). Information about related issues, such as early care and education, might be more readily received by the public if framed as part of a larger education reform debate.

While such a coordinated effort may have a substantial impact in the legislative arena, advocates should also become involved in the elections process at all levels of government. The bottom line is that until races are won or lost on a politician's position on family policies, issues such as child care and parental leave will remain in the second tier of the public policy agenda. Unlike the issue of health care reform, which is perceived as having both elected and defeated members of Congress, family policies are still considered "soft" and of limited consequence.

Recommendations for Advancing Early Care and Education

Sustained media coverage rarely just happens. To mount a successful effort to promote policy and change, early care and education leaders must make mass communications a high priority. The following factors are important in the development of effective mass communications strategies for early care and education.

Identify a Positive and Clear Course of Action

It is easier to gain consensus and public support when voters believe that there is a compelling need and that there is a comprehensible course of action that taps into a vein of common sense. Rather than tackling all the issues that affect early care and education at one time, begin the communications effort by focusing on one or two proactive steps that policy makers might adopt to build consensus or a broad enough base of support to succeed. For example, providing good early care and education could be positioned as a step in reducing dropout rates, and consensus could be built around a simple phrase such as "good early care and education helps prevent later school failure."

Identify Allies and Resources

Combining forces in a coordinated effort can leverage effectiveness and resources. Activists should assess the individual and collective communications capabilities of advocacy groups, academic and other research centers, professional associations, and others who might be part of an early care and education network. This *communications audit* should identify existing media skills, functions, and activities, including publications, newsletters, information kits, media outreach efforts, staffing patterns, technology expertise, and contacts with journalists. The plan should identify and assess what efforts and resources already exist in the early care and education field that could be coordinated, as well as new resources that will be needed to implement a comprehensive media plan. Activists should also identify and initiate partnerships with compatible organizations to create a cluster of family issues and to design and implement collaborative outreach campaigns, advocacy strategies, and efforts.

Generate Sustained Media Interest and Coverage

People learn a little at a time from a wide variety of media sources. Ongoing media coverage is essential to this learning. One potentially powerful strategy for gaining sustained media coverage would be to develop and implement a long-range plan to capitalize on all scientific research that could be linked to early childhood issues. For example, a key to the sustained coverage of child abuse was the ongoing role of research from different voices and perspectives, such as law, health, and crime (Nelson, 1984). Each is a different media beat, and all are research sources that media like to cover. Reporters' interest in stories on scientific research coming from multiple disciplines has implications for early care and education that are often overlooked. Advocates could look for this link and consistently feed scientific perspectives into breaking stories. A continuous stream of research from multiple disciplines can be used to expand discussions about early childhood issues from various perspectives, such as child care, child psychology, child development, and education. In addition, generating coverage of research provides an opportunity to link early care and education to a larger set of concerns, such as child abuse prevention, school success, and quality of the workforce.

Look for opportunities to play into breaking stories and national policy debates. Activists should be alert to early care and education–related breaking issues or national policy discussions. Riding an existing wave of media and public interest is much easier than trying to generate one.

Include Media Decision Makers in Target Press Audience

Activists should target editors and midlevel managers who make the daily news decisions. The demographics are changing in the newsrooms as a younger, more diverse, and potentially more receptive group of reporters move up the ranks, and older, more conservative editors retire. In addition, economic forces and demographic trends are pushing coverage toward stories about family concerns. Female consumers are key to newspaper and television and radio station long-term profitability. News outlets are beginning to search for ways to be more relevant to women's lives. Be prepared to demonstrate that it is good business practice to cover early childhood issues in news stories and programs.

Base Communications Strategies on Public Opinion Research

Good public opinion research provides a realistic picture of the existing political climate and should be used to shape the basic strategy. Media outreach is effective only if guided by a knowledge of public attitudes, based on periodic information gathered from focus groups, polls, and other public opinion sources. If the research shows that there is already a broad understanding and majority support among the American public for early care and education's goals and approaches, the need is to mobilize support. If research shows that there is little understanding and little favorable consensus on early care and education goals, a different strategy is called for—educating the public, building a consensus, and changing opinions.

Develop Messages That Resonate

Messages should be based on public opinion research and then tested for their effectiveness at achieving clear communications goals. The messages should speak to the public's and the policy makers' deepest concerns. When people move beyond their personal experiences and direct observations, new information plays into what they already know and believe. It is easier for people to receive and process information when it relates to their common experience and daily lives. Though not all information can be simple, taking account of how people learn must be a fundamental goal of any communications effort.

Create Memorable Images

Code words simplify complex concepts and allow people to see patterns. Powerful labeling helps build the public recognition and the support necessary to transform a social condition into an issue worthy of attention and resources. Messages should be phrased in language that engages the public. Language and phrases should envelop the concept of family rather than focusing just on the child (Breglio, 1992). Research also shows a strong response to messages based on the concept of prevention (Family Violence Prevention Fund, 1993).

Frame the Debate Carefully

Determine whether the issue will be positioned positively or negatively; for example, *for* a public policy (of quality early care and education) or *against* a current system (that does not value children or families). In addition, avoid trigger words that raise red flags. For instance, many people believe that "child care" is a family responsibility. Finding language that can successfully transcend this philosophical quagmire and then reframing the discussion are basic challenges for early care and education advocates. Also, find ways to help journalists, particularly television journalists, look beyond the predominant story frames of children as either villains or victims.

Take Advantage of New Communications Technologies

Although the new technologies present many challenges, they also offer expanded opportunities. Technology is becoming much less expensive, and there is wider access to information and more opportunities to link people—for example, linking communities together on the Internet for an interactive dialogue on what works in early care and education, or linking advocates together to share ideas, information, and legislative alerts.

Understand the Limited Role of Media in Setting the Policy Agenda

The main role of media in our society is to sound the alarm and to educate. But a steady stream of information by itself is not enough. It is also important to find ways to deal with value conflicts and to create forums for public discussion and debate. Most important, early care and education advocates must give people compelling reasons to act and specific action-steps they can take.

Conclusion

Clearly, media and mass communications are powerful forces in setting the public policy agenda and influencing the ultimate outcome of how an issue is dealt with in the political process. Effective use of the increasing opportunities available to disseminate widely strategically planned and well-presented information must be a basic component of attaining fundamental changes in public policy on important social issues.

National policies can and do change when a majority of the public reaches agreement that a social condition has become a problem and supports or demands particular identifiable approaches to alleviating it. Building such a base of popular support for a quality early care and education system should be the ultimate goal of a communications effort.

References

Breglio, V. (1992). *Family groups speak out.* Report for the Department of Social Services, State of Missouri, by the Kauffman Foundation. Kansas City.

Child Care Action Campaign & Communications Consortium Media Center. (1994a). *Media analysis of 20 leading newspapers covering child care issues, 1988–1993.* Washington, D.C.

Child Care Action Campaign & Communications Consortium Media Center. (1994b). *Polling analysis of child care issues, 1988–1993.* Washington, D.C.

Cohen, B. (1963). *The press and foreign policy.* Princeton, N.J.: Princeton University Press.

Columbia University Graduate School of Journalism. (1992). *Focus on children: The beat of the future.* Report of Columbia University School of Journalism media conference. New York.

Family Violence Prevention Fund. (1993). *Men beating women: Ending domestic violence.* San Francisco: Family Violence Prevention Fund.

Iyengar, S. (1991). *Is anyone responsible? How television frames political issues.* Chicago: University of Chicago Press.

Iyengar, S., & Kinder, D. (1987). *News that matters: Television and American opinion.* Chicago: University of Chicago Press.

Mains, S. (1994). Where will the super highway take us? *MAIN.* Newsletter of the National Alliance for Media Arts and Culture. New York.

McCombs, M. (1993). *What is the media's role in the agenda setting process?* Presentation at the Annenberg Washington Program, Seminar on Mass Communication and Social Agenda-Setting, Washington, D.C.

Nelson, B. J. (1984). *Making an issue of child abuse: Political agenda setting for social problems.* Chicago: University of Chicago Press.

Neuman, W. R., Marion, R. J., & Crigler, A. N. (1992). *Common knowledge: News and the construction of political meaning.* Chicago: University of Chicago Press.

Schnaidt, P. (1994). Cruising along. *Interoperability.* Supplement to Lan Magazine.

Chapter Thirteen

Citizen Participation
Transforming Access into Influence
Christopher Howard

One of the distinctive features of U.S. politics is the ease with which ordinary citizens gain access to policy making officials and institutions. Any country with eighty thousand governments is bound to create opportunities, and citizens have responded in many ways. The number of opportunities to run for elective office is unparalleled. In few other countries are interest groups as prevalent or contacts between individual constituents and elected officials as common as in the United States. Nor do many established democracies have a comparable history of mass demonstrations and riots. If obtaining access is easy, however, wielding political influence is quite difficult. In this chapter, I identify several of the primary obstacles that separate access from influence and then describe general strategies for overcoming those obstacles.

Citizens influence public policy, I argue, by discovering the right combination of ideas, interests, institutions, and instruments. That is to say, citizens advance *ideas* about what government should do and about the nature of social problems; they mobilize particular groups—or *interests*—for or against public action; they make demands on certain *institutions* like courts and legislatures; and they choose from a variety of policy *instruments,* ranging from regulations to vouchers and consumer information. Putting together the right combination of ideas, interests, institutions, and instruments involves as much art as science. There is no one right way. More than one combination may work for a given policy, and more than one combination is certainly needed across different policy domains. In some cases, there may be no right combination.

This chapter begins by sketching some fundamental features of U.S. politics that impede citizens who wish to effect change. The heart of this chapter is the subsequent discussion of the role of ideas, interests, institutions, and instruments in overcoming these obstacles. In the conclusion, I apply these insights to a hypothetical case involving the early care and education of children.

Barriers to Influence

Probably the most serious barrier to citizen influence in the United States is the fragmentation of formal authority. James Madison's "compound republic" distributes power between the national and state governments and then again among branches of the national government, giving each branch some power to check the others. Although this design creates numerous access points, it also creates numerous veto points, meaning numerous opportunities to block change. Legislation can be overturned by the courts or vetoed by the executive; states can balk at implementing national policies, as some have with the Goals 2000 education initiative. This design was intended to create a bias in favor of the status quo, a bias that persists today. It favors deliberation over decisiveness, compromise over clarity.

Interest representation is likewise fragmented. The traditional mechanisms for aggregating interests in democratic societies— political parties and labor unions—have historically been frail in the United States. Party ties have weakened further over the last few decades, as more citizens call themselves independents and more elections are decided by issues and candidates' traits. Fewer than one in six workers is a union member. The void left by strong parties and unions has been filled by interest groups. Traditional peak associations like the National Association of Manufacturers have been joined by literally thousands of specialized groups, such as the Center for Law and Social Policy, the Children's Defense Fund, and the National Association for the Education of Young Children. No single interest group can currently claim to represent a majority of citizens, and most claim a small but committed number of supporters. As a result, it is easy for specific interests to be expressed but difficult for them to be influential on any major policy debates.

Another important barrier to influence is that all forms of political participation are skewed in favor of citizens with more education, higher incomes, and higher-status occupations. Disadvantaged citizens are less likely to vote, less likely to be campaign workers, and far less likely to be campaign donors, interest group members, or advisory board members than the rest of the population. Remarkably, the poor are also less likely to engage in protest than are better-educated and more affluent citizens. For every march of welfare mothers, there are several on behalf of AIDS research or the environment. The main reason for these disparities is that *all* of the relevant political resources—especially time, money, and civic skills—are distributed unequally. Some interests are consistently better represented than others, a violation of the principle of political equality (Verba, Schlozman, & Brady, 1995).

Overcoming Barriers

Citizens have historically overcome these obstacles by pursuing, more or less simultaneously, four strategies—ideas, interests, institutions, and instruments.

Ideas

Political scientists have recently rediscovered the impact of ideas on policy making—principally, ideas about the proper scope of government and the definition of public problems. In order to place their issues on the public agenda, citizen advocates need at a minimum to establish that government has the necessary technical capacity to address the issues. Calling for an earthquake prevention policy, for example, will probably fall on deaf ears. The more vexing problem is establishing the propriety and advantages of government involvement in a country founded on the principle of limited government. Government action is commonly justified to provide public goods that cannot be parceled out readily to individual consumers and sold through a market (such as national defense), or to correct for the negative effects of market transactions on third parties (such as pollution). Government action also may be justified on some noneconomic grounds, such as equity or human dignity (programs that move individuals above the poverty line, for example). At bottom, advocates have to explain why government is better able to address their problem than the market, voluntary associations, or the family (Weimer & Vining, 1992).

It is one thing to persuade people that government should do something about a problem, quite another to generate agreement concerning the precise scope and causes of that problem. Defining public problems is a highly political act, one that influences both the range of interests involved and the solutions chosen. In the words of Deborah Stone, "Problem definition is never simply a matter of defining goals and measuring our distance from them. It is rather the *strategic representation* of situations. . . . Problem definition is strategic because groups, individuals, and government agencies deliberately and consciously design portrayals so as to promote their favored course of action" (1988, p. 106). Opponents and proponents of gun control know well the importance of problem definition. The National Rifle Association wants to portray gun ownership primarily as a constitutional issue and secondarily as a law-and-order issue. After initially accepting these definitions and losing the battle, advocates of gun control have tried to redefine gun ownership as a public health issue. By citing the numbers of people, and especially children, who have been killed by guns accidentally or in the heat of passion, they have managed to generate greater support for gun control (Sugarman, 1987).

The definition of problems helps determine whose interests are activated. As a constitutional issue, gun control remained a narrow debate among lawyers. As a public health issue, it involved medical and law enforcement officials and appeared more accessible to the general public. Reframing the problem, as gun control advocates did, is one of the first steps that the losing side in any policy debate will take to entice powerful actors to join their side (Schattschneider, 1960).

Interests

Mobilizing individuals for political action used to be considered a simple matter. According to pluralist scholars writing in the immediate postwar era, citizens with common interests would join together spontaneously. They did not have to be enticed. Later scholars discovered that certain kinds of groups are inherently easier to form than others. For instance, many grassroots organizations of citizens in the postwar era were created to *prevent* rather than *promote* government action. Notable examples include opposition to the so-called renewal of urban neighborhoods in the 1950s and 1960s, to busing in the 1970s, and to the siting of jails, hazardous waste dumps, and nuclear power plants in the 1970s and 1980s (Howard, Lipsky, & Marshall, 1994).

Nevertheless, all groups are hampered to some extent by "free rider" problems. The economist Mancur Olson (1965) argued that individuals join groups when the benefits outweigh the costs. If people think they can enjoy the benefits of a group's efforts without joining, they will not join. This problem arises repeatedly because groups typically work for policies that benefit a general class of citizens or companies and not just group members. To reduce the number of free riders, group members can restrict their policy demands to those that would benefit group members only, a technically difficult task. More likely, they can offer potential members additional reasons to join and remain part of the group. The most common benefits available only to group members are material goods such as publications and discounts. The American Association of Retired Persons is a classic example of a large interest group that employs a host of material incentives to sustain membership. Scholars also discovered that whereas some groups rely on selective material benefits, others depend on individuals' dedication to a cause or desire to associate with like-minded individuals. These nonmaterial benefits are particularly important to groups whose members lack occupational or industry ties.

Forming and sustaining the group, however, is different from wielding political influence. The two objectives may in fact collide if groups become dominated by professional staff and large donors. Policy makers may begin to question the depth of interest group support. To bolster their credibility, interest groups often need to mobilize their members and other interested citizens to contact public officials directly about specific issues. But public officials have learned to distinguish, in the words of one former senator, "between grass roots and AstroTurf" (Stone, 1993, p. 755). As a result, cultivating the grassroots has become more sophisticated in recent years as interest groups have learned to vary the timing and content of their appeals. Again, strategy and political savvy matter. Much as defining problems involves the strategic representation of ideas, wielding political influence involves the strategic representation of interests.

For major debates such as welfare reform and health care reform, individual interest groups often need to coalesce to be influential. As mentioned previously, the decline of political parties and unions and the proliferation of interest groups have led many citizens to pursue their policy objectives through narrow interest group channels. When issues arise that cut across established interest groups, ad hoc issue coalitions may be created (Costain & Costain, 1983). Coalition members openly state that although they do not agree with their colleagues on all issues, they have temporarily banded together to advance one issue of common concern. Ideally, such coalitions unite groups with complementary sets of political resources, which can then pressure a larger number of public officials from a greater variety of angles.

Institutions

Once individuals have managed to form an interest group or ad hoc coalition, they need to decide which institutional arenas—primarily legislatures, executives, bureaucracies, or courts—appear most favorable to their demands. Each arena exists at the national, state, and local levels. Each arena overlaps to varying degrees with the others. Each arena is biased toward certain interests at different points in time.

To understand the direction of this bias, advocates need first to assess the motives of public officials within each arena (that is, legislators, presidents, governors, mayors, cabinet officials, civil servants, and judges). The most basic motives are promoting one's own career in office and making good policy. What constitutes good policy changes over time as individual officials change, and the direction and magnitude of that change is fairly obvious. The less obvious but more durable source of bias originates in the structure of institutions. Since 1990, for example, Congress and the president have imposed fixed caps on annual appropriations and required any new entitlements to be fully paid for with spending cuts or increased taxes. This budgetary rule creates more of a zero-sum contest among spending priorities and makes policy instruments like consumer information more attractive than income transfers.

The Executive Arena

Since at least the time of Franklin Roosevelt, the executive branch has been the most important arena for setting the public agenda, the first stage in the policy process (Kingdon, 1984; Van Horn, Baumer, & Gormley, 1992). The president is widely viewed as the center of government. He is the one official elected by the entire country, a fact that appears to give his actions greater legitimacy than those of unelected judges and bureaucrats or elected members of Congress. Governors and mayors occupy similar positions at the center of state and local governments, though their dominance is often less pronounced than the president's. Issues raised by executives at all levels of government almost always rise to the top of the public agenda.

The executive arena is also important in generating policy alternatives, the second stage of the policy process. These alternatives tend to originate with staff rather than with the individual executive. The importance of this arena declines in later stages of the policy process, as responsibility for implementation shifts to the bureaucratic arena. The main exceptions are such crises as war or depression; executives are often directly involved in implementing policy in these areas because other arenas lack the capacity to act as swiftly and decisively.

The executive arena is commonly believed to be relatively receptive to redistributive policies. With a broader constituency, fewer reelection pressures, and a stronger desire to establish their places in the history books, executives are less beholden to specific interest groups than are legislators. This freedom enables executives to consider the needs of individuals who are not well represented by interest groups. Just as President Johnson initiated a series of antipoverty programs in the 1960s, President Clinton led efforts to extend medical coverage to the uninsured in the 1990s.

The Legislative Arena

For the last two decades, the legislative arena has typically been portrayed as a microcosm of the polity—highly fragmented, easily accessed, but not easily influenced (Arnold, 1990; Baumgartner &

Jones, 1993; Kingdon, 1984). Dozens of committees and subcommittees, some with fuzzy boundaries, make it relatively easy for policy advocates to find a forum in which to voice their demands; assembling a majority coalition of legislators, however, is difficult. The same committee system that facilitates access creates a long series of procedural hurdles that help prevent nine out of every ten bills introduced in Congress from being enacted (Stanley & Niemi, 1994). Generating majority coalitions is particularly difficult when party discipline is weak or when an issue is highly visible and contentious.[1] In these circumstances, it may be necessary for legislation to be so vague that different actors can support it for different and sometimes contradictory reasons. In these cases, the real burden of determining policy shifts to the bureaucratic and judicial arenas. Alternatively, legislators may spread the costs and benefits so broadly as to maximize support and minimize opposition from specific interests. If the executive arena is conducive to redistributive policies, the legislative arena favors distributive policies.

The legislative arena tends to be more important in the early stages of the policy process, in which agendas are set and decisions made. (Legislative influence over implementation and evaluation, via bureaucratic oversight, is more indirect.) Lacking strong parties, legislators constantly seek out issues to champion in order to distinguish themselves in the eyes of their constituents. The more savvy advocates search for legislators who would benefit from advocating their positions and who have sufficient power in the right committees.

Legislators tend to be most receptive to those claims that increase their chances of reelection. This goal is not their only one, but it is a prerequisite for accomplishing other objectives, such as making good public policy. Legislators' sensitivity to reelection pressures depends in part on the frequency of elections and in part on the perceived threat of losing their seats. Legislators in safe districts, especially longtime incumbents, generally enjoy greater latitude in deciding issues on their merits than do legislators in more competitive districts, who must focus on the immediate electoral consequences of their actions.

Because running for office is expensive, legislators are receptive to those groups capable of contributing significant funds to their campaigns. Perhaps even more important than money are votes. If advocates can successfully demonstrate that their issue affects a significant number of constituents willing to vote based on that issue, then legislators are inclined to be supportive. Here is one place where problem definition, interest mobilization, and institutional bias intersect.

The Bureaucratic Arena

Although some analysts contend that the bureaucratic arena is heavily insulated against outside pressures, thus enabling bureaucrats to twist public programs to fit their individual needs, the more widely accepted view is that the bureaucratic arena is open to political pressures from a variety of directions (Wilson, 1989). Far from being aloof, bureaucrats are constantly trying to cultivate support among legislators who oversee their activities—high ranking members of the executive branch, service providers in the private and nonprofit sectors, and interest groups. Bureaucrats' desire to build a loyal constituency has, if anything, increased in recent years as budget deficits have prompted cuts or leveling of funding in many programs.

The bureaucratic arena is influential at the alternative-generating, policy-implementing, and policy-evaluating stages of the policy process. Although bureaucrats seldom set the public agenda, they are solicited for solutions to problems identified in the executive and legislative arenas. Bureaucrats tend to define these problems narrowly and to propose incremental changes. Thus, citizens seeking significant changes to the status quo are better off directing their efforts to executive and legislative staff members. Bureaucrats also tend to respond better to technical arguments about program efficiency or effectiveness than to passionate arguments about rights or justice.

Like the legislative arena, the bureaucratic arena has become more open to citizen participation in recent decades. Beginning with the Community Action Program of the 1960s, governments increasingly mandated citizen participation in the implementation of public programs. Participation typically took the form of citizen advisory boards, open-meeting laws, and procedures designed to elicit public input concerning proposed actions. Though on the surface these developments were quite positive, some citizens have benefited more than others. Several studies have demonstrated that effective participation in this arena requires certain resources, principally time and civic skills (technical expertise, ability to navigate through bureaucratic channels), that lower-income citizens generally lack. Practically the only way in which disadvantaged citizens have been able to participate fully in the bureaucratic arena has been when public authorities provided them with financial or technical assistance (Berry, Portney, & Thomson, 1993; Howard, Lipsky, & Marshall, 1994).

The Judicial Arena

The judicial arena is more important in the United States than in any other advanced capitalist democracy (Baum, 1989). Courts have been instrumental in a wide variety of policy domains, ranging from interstate commerce to civil rights. Their decisions can be influential, directly or indirectly, at every stage of the policy process. Particularly at the national level, judges and their clerks have considerable discretion over which cases to hear. The Supreme Court renders full opinions on fewer than one in twenty cases submitted to it. Nor are judges above politics. Federal judges are appointed by the president, almost always from the same party, and many state judges are elected. Party identification is still a good predictor of judicial opinions. Judicial philosophy matters, too, particularly judges' willingness to engage in judicial activism or restraint. It is quite possible for judges holding conservative policy positions to uphold previous decisions issued by more liberal judges because they believe that courts should not stray too far from established precedents.

One advantage of participating in the judicial arena is that the costs are generally lower than mounting a comparable legislative lobbying campaign. This is one reason that disadvantaged groups have often sought recourse in the courts, aided by organizations like the National Association for the Advancement of Colored People Legal Defense Fund and the American Civil Liberties Union. One disadvantage is that courts seldom have the power to implement their decisions, thereby shifting the debate at the end of the policy process to another arena.

Alternative Arenas

If we do not limit definitions of institutions as organizations that are accompanied by formal buildings, then citizens have a couple of other institutional arenas in which to advance their claims (Van Horn, Baumer, & Gormley, 1992). Elections are important in setting the public agenda because certain issues can rise to prominence during the campaign. Ross Perot's presidential campaign in 1992 is widely credited with forcing Democratic and Republican officials to pay more attention to deficit reduction. Special elections, initiatives, and referenda generally convey more precise messages than general elections, as individuals can voice their approval or disapproval for individual policies. States' and localities' uses of such elections vary. In California, the formal barriers to placing issues on the ballot are low, and policy is often made through referenda. In other states, however, there are sizable hurdles.

Finally, advocates can make their claims in the arena of public opinion, which includes opinion polls, conferences and seminars, and protest. All of these techniques reach the public at large through the mass media. Activating the audience is the common aim. These techniques tend to be most influential in the early stages of the policy process; they help shape the definition of public problems and compel policy makers to "do something" about an issue. Each of these techniques requires different resources. Opinion polls are expensive, particularly as they become more precise in linking specific group interests to specific issues. Conferences and seminars likewise require money, as well as the knowledge of how best to disseminate the results. Protests appeal to groups short on money and long on civic skills. These groups rely on their powers of organization, inspiration, and disruption to elevate issues on the public agenda. They do so by creating a sense of outrage or empathy in more powerful actors, who in turn pressure policy makers for change (Lipsky, 1968).

Levels Within Arenas

Citizens must choose both an arena and the appropriate level within it. Though it is easy to overstate the case, the national level is generally more conducive to redistributive policies than are the state and local levels. State and local officials fear that if they engage too heavily in redistribution, employers and wealthy individuals will move to another jurisdiction, thereby depleting the local tax base. Equity, they believe, can only be achieved at the expense of growth. States and cities will generally concentrate on developmental policies—such as streets, sewers, and education—

that improve the entire community's prospects for economic growth, and they will aggressively compete with each other for corporate investment. Redistribution pursued at the national level, in contrast, does not place any single state or community at a competitive disadvantage (Peterson, 1995).

The national level is attractive to interests seeking widespread change, yet lacking political resources or a widespread federated structure. These interests find it easier to fight one battle in Washington than fifty in the states or five thousand in local communities. Interests who desire uniformity in policy also find the national level better suited to their causes.

Shifting debate to the state and local levels makes sense if advocates wish to experiment with programs that are novel or contentious. The Robert Wood Johnson Foundation, for example, has been underwriting a series of health care reforms in the states, the results of which they hope will be incorporated into national legislation. Their efforts are part of a larger trend in which states serve as policy laboratories. Other recent examples of this approach include child-support enforcement in Wisconsin and workfare programs in Massachusetts and California.

Instruments

Policy instruments (or tools) are the mechanisms by which government delivers goods and services. Income transfers, criminal laws, and regulations are the best-known instruments, but not the only ones (Salamon, 1989). Governments contract with third parties to provide job training and health care. They create loans and loan guarantees for housing and education, and quasi-public organizations like Amtrak and the National Science Foundation. Tax incentives subsidize everything from oil exploration to child care and retirement income. In some cases, the government provides consumers with more information (for example, food labeling laws) or tries to persuade citizens not to engage in certain kinds of behavior (for example, drinking and driving).

Each of these tools lends itself to certain kinds of ideas, interests, and institutions. For instance, when market values are ascendant, policy makers will be biased in favor of marketlike tools such as tax incentives. Such tools rely on inducements rather than commands, and they appear to promise less government intervention and less red tape than, say, regulation. One of the major sticking points delaying passage of the Act for Better Child Care in 1990 was the mix of government regulation, direct government spending, and tax incentives. Traditional children's advocates were openly skeptical of the potential for tax incentives to produce quality early care and education, particularly for poor families. They encountered a conservative president, Bush, committed to addressing social problems via the tax code, and a Democratic party intent on proving that it was capable of harnessing the private sector for public ends. The final bill contained a far higher proportion of tax incentives than these advocates would have preferred (Howard, 1994).

Effective use of each instrument requires certain types of expertise. Monitoring the performance of loans and loan guarantees, for instance, requires an understanding of how banks make lending decisions. If advocates lack this understanding and cannot develop it quickly, they might choose a different tool. The choice of instruments also affects which interests become part of the program's constituency. A loan guarantee program will activate bankers; a tax incentive program will activate accountants and tax lawyers; contracting out will activate third-party providers; and direct provision will activate government bureaucrats. When choosing their policy instruments, citizens need to anticipate the political interests they will activate. Can they work with the people who will implement the program? Will these new actors have complementary or competing objectives?

Conclusion

Suppose that one wanted to influence policy concerning the early care and education of children. This case presents immediate difficulties because the barriers separating access from influence are greater than average. Responsibility for the early care and education of children is highly fragmented, in Washington and among national, state, and local governments. Multiple agencies administer dozens of programs, many of them relatively small and specific. Whereas the elderly have the Social Security Administration and program, there is no public institution comparable in size or political clout that focuses exclusively on children. In addition, young children lack the resources needed to participate effectively: they cannot vote, rarely show up on lists of major campaign contributors, and lack the capacity to organize and protest that even older children have. About the only resource available to them is their capacity to generate compassion and empathy in other, more powerful actors.

To establish the appropriateness of government action, advocates could claim that although the household historically provided the early care and education of children, it is less able to do so today. Changes in the economy and in family structure have made the two-parent family with one wage earner and one caregiver a decided minority. A growing number of single- and two-parent families need help in caring for their young children. One might also argue that all children can benefit from improved early care and education and that the country needs smarter, healthier children to compete in the global economy. Therefore, government action would not be a threat to the household or the market; it would provide crucial support to these other realms (Stanfield, 1993).

One of the most important decisions advocates will make concerns problem definition. If they portray early care and education as a children's issue, they will limit the number and range of actors who become involved. Although this strategy may make sense if only small changes are desired, it may antagonize people without children at home (the majority of the population), who might perceive that the costs of such programs exceed the benefits. If, however, advocates portray the issue more broadly, they may generate more support and make it harder for opponents to hammer away at the details. Policy makers would be forced to focus more on general policy objectives and leave the specifics to experts in and out of government. By portraying early care and education as a family issue, for instance, advocates may be able to form coalitions with groups advocating expanded health insurance coverage, better parental leave, and flexible job arrangements. Alternatively, framing the issue in terms of human capital, in which better-educated children today become better workers tomorrow, might lend itself to alliances with advocates of job training and retraining. It might persuade employers as well as citizens worried about the future solvency of Social Security to offer their support. These definitions are not mutually exclusive, and some calculated ambiguity may well be useful.

It would seem unwise to target poor or minority children, even if they are receiving worse or less early care and education than other children. A targeted program is more likely to be considered welfare reform rather than a children's or family issue (Skocpol, 1991). The goal would be to enable poor mothers to work rather than to serve the needs of children (Stanfield, 1993). In addition, there is a considerable distrust among policy makers of anything that remotely resembles a Great Society program. However effective such programs may be in directing aid where it is most needed, these programs are politically vulnerable. Advocates may wish to target specific populations within some more inclusive program, but they should do so when hammering out the details of legislation or regulation and not when setting the public agenda (Skocpol, 1991). Otherwise, they will need to devote some of their political resources to demonstrating conclusively that programs created in the 1960s were indeed successful.

The leading advocates for change would likely be service providers, foundations, and academic policy experts. These individuals possess technical expertise, established relationships with policy makers, and national networks of communication. They would speak on behalf of children and their parents, neither of whom has effective interest group representation. Nevertheless, to wield influence these advocates will need to mobilize a wider community of parents and employers—to cultivate, from above, grassroots support. The alternative is to risk being dismissed as a special-interest group motivated solely by the prospects of economic gain or greater professional power.

Choosing the right institutional arena(s) is the most difficult task facing advocates, given the rapid recent changes in Washington. During the 1980s, children's advocates worked primarily through Congress to elevate concern for the problems of young children and to achieve favorable policy decisions. That strategy proved inadequate, if only because Presidents Reagan and Bush stood ready to veto most proposals. The election of President Clinton and a Democratic Congress in 1992 opened new doors: Hillary Rodham Clinton had an active interest in children's issues, and President Clinton named Donna Shalala to head Health and

Human Services. Both had close ties to the Children's Defense Fund. It appeared quite logical for advocates to work through the executive in setting the public agenda, then combining strengths in the executive and legislative arenas to propose alternatives and pass legislation.

The ascension of congressional Republicans in 1994, however, has made innovation at the national level far less likely. Leaders of the new Congress are committed to a smaller national government, stronger state governments, and a traditional vision of the nuclear family. Many Republicans also appear to be skeptical of economic and scientific expertise, preferring instead to base their decisions on ideology and personal experience. Though President Clinton has opposed many of their proposals, he and the more conservative wing of the Democratic party have been receptive to enhancing the role of the states. At least in the near term, state legislatures and executives would seem to be the logical arenas to start many policy initiatives. This approach works best if advocates possess the kind of geographically widespread strength that the Chamber of Commerce enjoys. This approach also makes sense if there is uncertainty concerning the best policy solution and if advocates wish to conduct different experiments in different states.

The choice of instruments follows in part from the definition of the problem. An emphasis on improving quality would lead to more direct forms of government involvement, such as the regulation of early care and education facilities. These instruments are probably well known to children's advocates and their implementation easier to influence. Such instruments might appeal to moderate and conservative policy makers if they require few new monies, but not if they seem to augment the power of (liberal) professionals at the expense of families. The importance of local control and local variation would probably have to be stressed. An emphasis on quantity implies greater spending, which can be addressed through direct or indirect tools. To the extent that indirect tools are used—such as tax credits to parents—advocates would need to develop the capacity to monitor their implementation. Such capacity might be developed internally or acquired through a coalition with groups having expertise in public finance and the tax code.

Though far from complete, the above scenario indicates how one could use the framework of ideas, interests, institutions, and instruments to approach a policy problem. As dedicated advocates become more adept at these strategies for transforming access into influence, they will improve their initially slim chances of success.

Note

1. The Congress that was elected in 1994 stands in stark contrast to the typical portrait of an undisciplined, fragmented body. The Republican members have acted more like a cohesive majority party than any in recent memory, have dramatically reduced the scope of deliberation, and have pushed forward a number of significant policy proposals. Although these changes may be temporary, they do build on preexisting efforts to centralize power in Congress.

References

Arnold, R. D. (1990). *The logic of congressional action.* New Haven, Conn.: Yale University Press.

Baum, L. (1989). *The supreme court* 3rd ed. Washington, D.C.: Congressional Quarterly.

Baumgartner, F. R., & Jones, B. D. (1993). *Agendas and instability in American politics.* Chicago: University of Chicago Press.

Berry, J. M., Portney, K. E., & Thomson, K. (1993). *The rebirth of urban democracy.* Washington, D.C.: Brookings Institution.

Costain, A. M., & Costain, W. D. (1983). The women's lobby: Impact of a movement on congress. In A. J. Cigler & B. A. Loomis (Eds.), *Interest group politics* 2nd ed. (pp. 191–216). Washington, D.C.: Congressional Quarterly.

Howard, C. (1994, Spring). Happy returns: How the working poor got tax relief. *The American Prospect, 17,* 46–53.

Howard, C., Lipsky, M., & Marshall, D. R. (1994). Rise and routinization: Citizen participation in urban politics. In G. E. Peterson (Ed.), *Big-city politics, governance, and fiscal constraints* (pp. 153–199). Washington, D.C.: Urban Institute Press.

Kingdon, J. W. (1984). *Agendas, alternatives, and public policies.* New York: Little, Brown.

Lipsky, M. (1968). Protest as a political resource. *American Political Science Review, 62,* 1144–1158.

Olson, M. (1965). *The logic of collective action.* Cambridge, Mass.: Harvard University Press.

Peterson, P. E. (1995). *The price of federalism.* Washington, D.C.: Brookings Institution.

Salamon, L. M. (Ed.). (1989). *Beyond privatization: The tools of government action.* Washington, D.C.: Urban Institute Press.

Schattschneider, E. E. (1960). *The semisovereign people.* Austin, Tex.: Holt, Rinehart and Winston.

Skocpol, T. (1991). Targeting within universalism: Politically viable policies to combat poverty in the United States. In C. Jencks & P. E. Peterson (Eds.), *The Urban Underclass* (pp. 411–436). Washington, D.C.: Brookings Institution.

Stanfield, R. L. (1993). Child care quagmire. *National Journal, 25,* 512–516.

Stanley, H. W., & Niemi, R. G. (1994). *Vital statistics on American politics* 4th ed. Washington, D.C.: Congressional Quarterly.

Stone, D. A. (1988). *Policy paradox and political reason.* Glenview, Ill.: Scott, Foresman.

Stone, P. H. (1993). Green, green grass. *National Journal, 25,* 754–757.

Sugarman, J. (1987, June). The NRA is right: But we still need to ban handguns. *Washington Monthly,* 11–15.

Van Horn, C. E., Baumer, D. C., & Gormley, W. T. (1992). *Politics & public policy* 2nd ed. Washington, D.C.: Congressional Quarterly.

Verba, S., Schlozman, K. L., & Brady, H. (1995). *Voice and equality.* Cambridge, Mass.: Harvard University Press.

Weimer, D. L., & Vining, A. R. (1992). *Policy analysis: Concepts and practice.* Englewood Cliffs, N.J.: Prentice Hall.

Wilson, J. Q. (1989). *Bureaucracy.* New York: Basic Books.

Chapter Fourteen

Organizing Communities and Constituents for Change

Ernesto Cortés, Jr.

The Industrial Areas Foundation (IAF) is the center of a national network of broad-based, multiethnic, interfaith organizations in primarily poor and low-income communities. Created over fifty years ago by Saul Alinsky, it now provides leadership training for over forty community-based organizations, representing nearly one thousand institutions and over one million families nationwide. The role of the IAF organizations is to build the competence and confidence of ordinary citizens and taxpayers so that they can reorganize the relationships of power and politics in their communities.

With the mentoring of professional IAF organizers, thousands of community leaders have mobilized local resources to improve schools, coordinate youth programs, build homes, create job-training programs, and make their neighborhoods cleaner and safer. As leaders have coordinated efforts with other local organizations, they have worked to influence public policy and effect change at the state and national levels.

The IAF sees community organizing as part of a larger effort to revitalize local institutions and rebuild a civic culture. Within a

Note: Parts of this chapter are similar to those in "Reweaving the Fabric, The Iron Rule and the IAF Strategy for Power and Politics," a chapter in *Interwoven Destinies,* edited by Henry Cisneros and forthcoming from W. W. Norton. They are used with permission of the publisher.

civic culture, ordinary citizens take part in public life; they begin to take ownership of their neighborhoods and shape the public decisions that impact their families. Not only does their quality of life improve, but more important, their involvement begins to change the very nature of power and politics in their communities. No longer are the bureaucrats, policy experts, and elected officials the sole decision makers. As ordinary citizens join officials at the decision-making table, they become effective leaders and can begin to bring about lasting change in their communities.

This chapter focuses on community organizing as it relates to public education and youth issues. It elaborates on core principles that have proven to be highly effective in organizing citizens around issues of public concern. It then details more specific strategies for organizing citizens around their concerns for public education that may be applied to the field of early care and education. It concludes by highlighting successful IAF education organizing efforts in Texas.

Children, Families, and Community Institutions

Any effort to improve the quality of early care and education must be connected to the revitalization of the social and political institutions in our communities. The core institution of our society is the family. Ideally, families provide nurturing and educational environments for young children. Yet today, approximately ten million American children—more than 40 percent—live in families with low incomes (National Center for Children in Poverty, 1994). For minorities, the number is two in five. The parents of these children are working longer and harder to make ends meet, as their living standards continue to decline.

As these families are forced to work more, they need more help providing for their children, especially when the children are young and require extra attention and care. Traditionally, these families looked to local institutions for help in difficult times. Parents could find supportive networks of friends and neighbors in churches, in schools, at work, in civic clubs, and in local organizations like the Parent Teachers Associations (PTAs) and the Boy Scouts. Not only did the support from these institutions ease the burdens of daily life, but being connected to such networks helped families stay in touch with one another and with the issues in the community. In this way, they learned to become leaders in their communities.

Today, however, these community institutions have all but disappeared in low-income areas. Economic decline, coupled with a disinvestment in the inner city over the past three decades, has put pressure on these institutions. As William Julius Wilson explains, many residents of the inner city with the resources to move have followed economic opportunities to the suburbs, separating themselves from the plight of the truly disadvantaged in the inner cities. As these middle-class residents left, they took with them not just their financial and political resources but also their participation in community affairs and their leadership responsibilities, thereby weakening the schools, churches, and other local institutions (Wilson, 1987). Christopher Lasch argues that these suburbanites have also withdrawn internally: they have resigned from the business of public life altogether. They live in private communities and send their children to private schools, comfortably secluded in a "culture of contentment" (Lasch, 1995, pp. 25–49). Thus, working families in low-income urban areas have become increasingly disconnected from the power and money they need to rebuild and maintain their communities. Without strong institutions, families living in inner cities are simply unable to provide or arrange for the basics needed by their families, including early care and education for their young children. More damaging than that, the decline in mediating institutions has removed an avenue for these citizens to participate in public life. Without a connection to neighborhood churches, schools, and civic associations, these families are isolated and rendered powerless to effect change.

Basic Principles of Community Organizing

Community organizing revitalizes these community institutions that support and defend families. Within strong institutions, families can create the space, time, and resources to nurture their children. To strengthen these mediating institutions, community leaders need to act collaboratively instead of acting in isolation. Parents, service providers, and community leaders must come together, engage one another in debate and discussion over important issues, make decisions about how to improve their community, and act on them.

The approach to bringing communities together that the IAF has found to be most effective is hiring and training professional organizers. The organizers initiate conversations with community members to identify the most pressing issues in their neighborhoods and the potential for leadership. The organizers work closely with local churches, teaching citizens how to work with one another and with local governments to address the issues that matter to them. The leaders then work to bring other organizations into communities' institutional networks. This strategy strengthens the relationships among citizens, and in the process, strengthens their community institutions.

Through its fifty years of experience in community organizing, the IAF has relied on a few core principles—following and teaching the *Iron Rule,* having a proper understanding of politics and power, building social capital, and working through broad-based community organizations to implement these principles.

The Iron Rule: The First Rule of Organizing

Central to effective community organizing is the Iron Rule: "Never do for others what they can do for themselves." The IAF has won its victories not by speaking for ordinary people but by teaching them how to speak, to act, and to engage in politics for themselves. The IAF has found that the potential of ordinary people emerges when they engage one another in the serious business of the *polis*—the fundamental issues of family, property, and education. Following the Iron Rule, community organizers have developed thousands of ordinary people into powerful community leaders. Housewives, pastors, bus drivers, secretaries, nurses, and teachers have learned how to participate as partners with businessmen, politicians, and bureaucrats, who are normally thought of as our society's sole decision makers.

The Iron Rule is the practical consequence of Alfred North Whitehead's warning about the danger of teaching inert ideas, "ideas that are merely received without being utilized, tested, or thrown into fresh combinations" (Whitehead, 1929, pp. 1–2). Inert ideas make people the passive receptacles of disconnected information. The Iron Rule recognizes that the most important aspect of intellectual development is self-development. According to John Stuart Mill, if a person has common sense and experience, his own way of living his life is the best alternative, not because it is *the* best way, but because it is *his* way (Thompson, 1976).

The Iron Rule is about developing people's confidence in their own competence. It is central to any good teaching of adults or children. It is a process that stimulates curiosity, inquiry, judgment, and mastery of new areas of understanding. It recognizes that people can only learn confidence through competent participation: we learn by doing.

The Nature of Politics and Power

Aristotle said that we are political beings: there is a part of us that emerges only to the extent that we participate in public life. Sheldon Wolin described our birthright as our political identity, which involves our capacity to initiate collaborative action with other human beings (Wolin, 1989). This kind of action enables citizens to open schools, change the nature of schools, create job-training programs, and initiate flood control programs, and by so doing recreate and reorganize the way in which people, networks of relationships, and institutions operate.

Politics, properly understood, is about collective action, which is initiated by people who have engaged in public discourse. Politics is about relationships that enable people to disagree, argue, interrupt one another, clarify, confront, negotiate. Through this process of debate and conversation, they forge a compromise and a consensus that enables them to act. Armed with a proper understanding of politics, people join together to confront public officials in efforts to improve their schools and their neighborhoods. Ordinary citizens learn how to participate in politics to achieve not just short-term results but also long-lasting change in the political culture of their communities.

Instead of focusing on the relational and deliberative process involved in politics, our current political culture teaches us to focus on the least-important elements of political action—voting, elections, and turnout. Yet voter participation is the wrong measure of the health of a democracy. In fact, voter turnout is not a problem in many totalitarian countries. A more classical conception of politics is one that maintains that elections are held not just to register preferences but also to ratify decisions and actions that citizens have reached through extended argument and deliberations. In focusing exclusively on elections, we have reduced people to mere voters or clients rather than allowing them fuller identities as citizens and neighbors. As a result of this narrow focus, we have ignored the ways in which citizens have been impoverished and rendered incompetent. We have trivialized their political participation by disconnecting them from real debate and real power, from forums in which they can be real actors, not just passive viewers of an electronic display. If there is to be real politics in this country, there must not only be different understandings of its nature; there must also be opportunities for ordinary people to initiate action about matters that are important to their interests.

In order to understand the true sense of politics, there must be an understanding of the nature of power. Oftentimes, people shy away from the discussion of power. The IAF believes, as did Lord Acton, that power tends to corrupt. Yet powerlessness also corrupts, perhaps more pervasively than power itself.

There are two kinds of power. *Unilateral power* is that in which one party of authority treats the other party as an object to be instructed and directed. One-sided power tends to be coercive and domineering. *Relational power* is more complicated. It is developed subject to subject and is transformative, changing the nature of the situation and of the self. Power that is imbedded in relationships involves not only the capacity to act but also the reciprocal capacity to allow oneself to be acted upon. In this context, relational power involves the use of calculated vulnerability, an understanding that there is a meaningful exchange that involves getting into the other person's subject and allowing him or her to get into yours.

This notion of calculated vulnerability relies on a vision of autonomous yet interdependent persons who respect one another and appreciate the values of reciprocal accountability. Healthy relationships in public life are developed through this back and forth of conversation, in contrast to the one-sided communication that our modern world directs at people in much of daily life. In the same way that our conversations demand listening as well as speaking, our public relationships demand reciprocity. They are processes that demand an openness, a willingness to suspend judgment, a willingness to argue and to adjust one's own views. Public relationships involve a willingness not only to act but also to be acted on, and to be transformed in the process. One enters into a public relationship not with self-righteousness, but with a commitment to the dignity and respect of the other. As in a conversation, a relationship does not have a foreclosed beginning and ending. Rather, it represents a moment in a longer-term relationship. The goal of a relationship is not a short-term transaction, but rather a longer-term collaboration.

There is no power without relationships: two or more people come together, express and argue their concerns, develop a plan and the intention to exercise that plan, and take some sort of action on it. Now the question is, how can people get enough power to do the things they think are important? This can happen through two routes—organized people or organized money. Obviously, the poor have more of the former than the latter. Two, or even ten, people by themselves may not be able to do much. But as they begin to build coalitions with other people and to learn the rules of politics, relational power, and reciprocity, they gain the capacity to make real changes.

In every community throughout the nation, there are literally thousands of people with the potential to participate successfully in public life. Reform strategies will not work unless they recognize and draw on the resources of these people and their ties to community institutions. The value and strength of these public relationships are what economists and social scientists now label "social capital."

The Importance of Social Capital

Broadly defined, social capital is the value of a community's relationships. In contrast to human capital, which is a product of the skills of individuals, social capital is a measure of how much collaborative time and energy people have for one another—how much time parents have for their children, how much attention neighbors give to one another's families, what kind of public relationships people have with one another in churches, PTAs, civic organizations, scout troops, and the quality of the many other potential networks of relationships in communities. Harvard political scientist Robert Putnam documented that where civic associations and networks of public relationships are strong, local government is the most effective. In other words, social capital makes communities "work" better (Putnam, 1993).

To think of relationships as capital suggests a different way of thinking about people. To create capital, we must invest labor, energy, and effort today to create something for later use. We expend energy now in creating a tool, learning a skill, or saving money in order to put it to use in the future. Similarly, investment requires the ability and the discipline to defer gratification and to invest energy not only in the needs or pleasures of the present but also in the potential demands of the future.

Building capital also requires maintenance and renewal. Workers find that their tools wear out with use and rust with disuse. Knowledge and skills must be updated and refined. The partners in a venture must renew the means of trusting one another. Neighbors in a community or members of a family must maintain their relationships to renew the social capital they represent.

Sociologist James Coleman described one dimension of social capital in the lives of children as attention from responsible adults, which students receive in the various institutions of their daily lives—their schools, families, churches, and neighborhoods. Coleman studied public, Catholic, and non-Catholic private schools in Chicago and found that Catholic schools were more successful at educating students than either public or non-Catholic private schools. Even when he took into account the advantages and disadvantages of varying family backgrounds and incomes (that is, different levels of human and financial capital), students at Catholic schools had slightly higher achievement rates on math and verbal skills and dramatically lower-dropout rates. Coleman argues that the strong, informal adult-student relationships of Catholic schools and communities were responsible for the significantly lower-dropout rates. Even when children had relatively diminished attention from adults at home, the Catholic schools were able to keep them coming to class. He suggests that adults in the Catholic community were attentive to the children's growth and willing to intervene early when they saw trouble. They provided role models and mentored children. They were available for help or guidance.

They taught children how to relate collaboratively with others (Coleman, 1989).

The concept of social capital places credence in the quality of relationships among people, not just in the number or availability of relationships. Social capital implies a richness and robustness of relationships; the members of a community are willing and eager to invest in one another. To build, expand, and agitate the social capital that is imbedded in the networks of human relationships, organizers work through broad-based organizations.

Broad-Based Organizations: Developing Citizens

A broad-based organization is a network of citizens, rooted in community institutions—local parishes, congregations, synagogues, and social groups. These isolated institutions come together to constitute the broad-based organization, grounding it in the traditions and patterns of the community. With the training of the IAF, these broad-based organizations cultivate curiosity, imagination, and a vision of what is possible for citizens and their families. They become public spaces in which ordinary people learn how to engage others in conversations and arguments, how to reflect on their actions, and how to make informed political judgments.

Broad-based organizations are different from traditional service organizations, which tend to focus on service delivery. Service organizations do not expand the capabilities, vision, and political acumen of community residents. Although these organizations can help provide important services to families, their services often only alleviate immediate problems rather than addressing the underlying causes. Broad-based organizations seek to address underlying causes by teaching citizens to alter the power relationships in their community. For example, whereas service delivery organizations, such as an early care and education center or a referral agency, can provide crucial services to parents and practitioners, broad-based organizations can connect parents to community institutions like churches, where they build long-term relationships with other parents and community leaders. Parents learn how to become engaged in public life, how to discuss their concerns with others, and how to act on them collectively. The work of broad-based organizations is long-term, so it is important that there be social service organizations to help families obtain needed services in the interim.

A broad-based organization is essentially a formal affiliation of congregations that includes anywhere from twenty to fifty local churches, synagogues, schools, or other neighborhood organizations. These member organizations pay dues to be a part of the broad-based organization so that the network can become a financially self-determining, independently incorporated organization. A broad-based organization has its own governing board, consisting of one or two leaders from each member congregation, which exercises collective leadership over the organization. It also has a smaller, core executive committee made up of a few outstanding leaders from member organizations, who are elected by the rest of the members. Leaders are defined as men and women who have a following and can consistently deliver that following; leaders deliver either people or dollars to the broad-based organization. Leaders also commit to participate in training and to expand the number of fellow leaders in the interest of collective power.

The local broad-based organization has a contractual relationship with the IAF: in exchange for dues to the IAF, the leaders of the broad-based organization are mentored by the IAF organizers and attend IAF training sessions. Although the broad-based organization defines its own goals and agenda, it chooses to work with the IAF because it shares the IAF philosophies and strategies for community organizing. The IAF organizers work with leaders of the broad-based organizations to develop their leadership abilities.

Essentially, broad-based organizations teach people how to be citizens. Too often, our citizens have become professional clients and plaintiffs, who are unwilling to engage their fellow citizens and neighbors in any serious conversations about public affairs. The role of the broad-based institution is to assist citizens in making the kind of informed judgments that are necessary for participating in the political process. Rather than selecting a number of predefined options, citizens must learn to define the public conversation. This entails more than just choosing a candidate and casting a vote. Making political judgments is an art that must be practiced.

Broad-based organizations teach people to act on their judgments and decisions. "Action" is not just displacement of energy, not just reaction to crisis, but rather what the Greeks called *praxis*—

action that is aimed, calculated, and reflected on. Broad-based organizations plan actions—public dramas in which large groups of people meet with local officials to address common issues. At the action, the community leaders ask their elected officials to make firm, public commitments to work with the community to address urgent issues.

In that they are teaching institutions, broad-based organizations act like "mini-universities." Not only do they teach people the art of citizenship and the skills of public life, they also create the type of public space in which people can initiate meaningful dialogue about common issues of concern and engage one another in constrained conflict. In forums provided by broad-based organizations, citizens learn to acknowledge and welcome public conflict. If societal tensions are repressed, the result may be violent outbursts. Teaching people how to engage in public discussion tempers conflict to a manageable level.

Like a good university, a broad-based organization does not just teach people skills; it provides them with a broader perspective on society, and thus imparts a civic education. As William Galston said, a civic education is essentially about the character formation of individuals. As individuals, we do not learn our values in isolation. We learn them only in relationships with others, in the context of our history and traditions (Galston, 1989). Because character development occurs within a context, individuals need institutions, be they familial, religious, or political, which can help shape their values and perspectives. Broad-based organizations provide individuals with an interpretive framework in which character development, leadership development, and civic education can take place. In this way, broad-based organizations develop individuals into citizens who fully understand their community and who can effectively participate in public life.

Organizing for Early Care and Education Reform

In the larger effort to revitalize civic culture and strengthen community institutions, the IAF has organized citizens around their concerns for the education of children in their communities. The IAF has demonstrated that those concerned about the quality of education can significantly improve school climate and student achievement by drawing on the principles of community organizing. Having recognized the importance of the Iron Rule, the role of social capital, the nature of politics, and the importance of working through broad-based organizations, IAF leaders and organizers have developed a specific strategy to connect communities to schools in a way that transforms schools into effective centers of learning. Aspects of this strategy may be relevant to early care and education.

This strategy hinges on leadership development: the IAF organizers provide ongoing, effective leadership training to the community leaders, parents, teachers, and administrators involved in public school reform efforts. IAF education organizers start from an institutional base: they work through churches and broad-based organizations to develop relationships between the school and community. These relationships create the social capital that sustains local school reform efforts. Although the IAF has organized communities primarily around elementary, middle, and high schools, these strategies can be applied to the field of early care and education as well. The following is a discussion of these specific strategies that follow from the broad philosophical organizing principles outlined in the first part of the chapter.

Institutional Bases

In building constituencies for education reform, the IAF works through local broad-based community organizations. IAF organizers have found that the churches that constitute these broad-based organizations are uniquely situated to play an important role in the school improvement efforts. To an extent unmatched by other modern institutions, churches work to foster the formation of constructive values and provide support to families who are trying to nurture those values. They are often the only institutions with which members of disadvantaged communities have maintained supportive ongoing ties. This is often especially true in predominantly minority communities.

Working with clergy, educators, and lay leaders, IAF organizers identify existing networks of relationships that might become the building blocks of school improvement efforts. Regular contact with institutions such as the church allows parents to meet other parents, establish themselves as part of a community network, and build long-term public relationships. For parents who might feel uncomfortable attending a meeting in a school that seems intimidating, the church provides a more neutral environment in which to develop leadership skills and begin involvement in public life.

Leadership Development: Building Social Capital

In keeping with the Iron Rule, organizers do not implement a predetermined reform plan in schools; they teach parents, teachers, and principals how to create and implement an improvement plan themselves. This is the key to the success of community-organizing efforts to reform education. Organizers nurture the capacity of parents to become leaders and experts in reform efforts. As they connect these parents and community leaders to leaders in the school, they build the social capital that sustains reform efforts.

When parents and community leaders first become involved in public education reform efforts, they are often unfamiliar with basic aspects of school structure, including those of the individual school, the district, and the state. This is especially true of families who are recent immigrants or who have had negative experiences with schools. Without adequate knowledge of how schools operate, and without the skills necessary for effectively working within the public sphere, parents cannot be strong and competent participants in decision making concerning their children's education. Effective organizers do not simply impart knowledge and develop leaders' skills; their close mentoring instills and builds self-esteem and self-confidence, creating opportunities for new leaders to become effective and powerful persons in the public arena.

In communities in which a strong tradition of public action has not been developed, efforts to develop community leadership and to encourage school-community collaboration take time. Parents and community leaders must learn the skills of public life—how to identify and research issues, how to put together action teams, and how to engage in public debate and negotiation. They must learn how to work in constructive ways with school personnel. Sometimes, school personnel themselves do not know how to collaborate with parents and community leaders, especially with parents from a different cultural or economic background. They, too, can benefit from training. As parents and community leaders begin to interact differently with schools, their attitudes change from distrustful to supportive.

To build this collaborative atmosphere and capacity for change, IAF organizers hold regular meetings and training sessions in churches, schools, and homes. Meetings are held often enough to sustain conversations within the community about important issues, but not so often that they impinge on family time and become burdensome. These meetings are designed to let individuals develop not only their leadership skills but also an awareness of their interdependency, which is basic to the development of social capital.

Individual Meetings

Leadership development begins with a serious, one-to-one conversation in which the leader and organizer exchange views, judgments, and commitments. In individual meetings, organizers meet one-to-one with administrators, teachers, pastors, community leaders, and parents. These are not surveys but conversations that involve true dialogue between parties. The organizer identifies leaders' concerns, their willingness to participate in reform efforts, and their ability to teach others. The organizers see themselves as teachers, mentors, and agitators who cultivate leadership that sustains broad-based organizations. These individual meetings create the foundation of personal relationships on which collective work around school issues can be built.

Community Meetings

As individual meetings continue, organizers and leaders also begin a process of holding group meetings, or house meetings, with neighbors and parents who have expressed interest in school reform. Networks of relationships become established, and concerns around which groups might take action are identified. As key leaders emerge, they convene a team of parents, teachers, principals, administrators, and other leaders to address their concerns in an organized way. Based on a situational audit of the strengths and weaknesses of the school, and on much deliberation, the team begins to hold strategic-planning sessions. In these sessions, they develop a plan of action, guided by a collaborative vision for the future of their school. As they translate their vision for school improvement into a step-by-step plan of action, the community leaders constantly reevaluate their plan. As IAF recognizes, all successful organizing is constant reorganizing. The core leadership team then presents its plan to the larger community in a neighborhood meeting with community organizations, churches, businesses, elected officials, school officials, parents, and school personnel. When the community ratifies the plan, or a version of it, all of these stakeholders make a public commitment to implement it.

Training Sessions

Organizers continue leadership development through community-training sessions. Organizers hold regular training sessions for parents and community leaders to explain the basic workings of the education system and to provide the opportunity for leaders to have ongoing conversations about their concerns. In these sessions, parents and community leaders discuss their ideas about how to improve the school and discuss new ways parents can become involved. They learn to act collaboratively, negotiating compromises when differences arise. As they strengthen their leadership skills, they plan neighborhood meetings around issues that affect the well-being of the entire community, organize door-to-door outreach campaigns to speak individually with each parent, and implement their plans for school and community improvement.

Leaders develop their own abilities and build the power base of their organization when they first begin to tackle small, winnable issues, such as repairing streetlights and putting up stop signs. With the experience of success, they gather the confidence to take on larger concerns, such as curriculum reform and making the school a safe and civil place for children to learn. Soon, new leaders have developed the capacity to set agendas for capital improvement budgets, strategize with corporate leaders and members of city councils on economic growth policies, and develop new initiatives in job training, health care, and public education.

Successful IAF School Improvement Efforts in Texas

Trained in the skills of public life and versed in the intricacies of education reform, parents and community leaders have become capable partners who do more than just participate in reform efforts: they shape them. Over the last eight years, parents have worked with IAF organizers, educators, administrators, and public officials to improve schools all over the Southwest. In Texas, seventy schools in twelve cities formalized their partnerships with the local IAF organizations as part of the Alliance Schools Initiative. These Alliance Schools have each made a public commitment to collaborate fully with parents and community leaders to restructure their schools in ways that improve student achievement. Many of these schools are eligible to receive grants and waivers from the state education agency to implement their own ideas for education reform. These are schools that have built a strong constituency in the community, strong enough to leverage the political support for these waivers and grants.

At the most successful Alliance Schools, standardized test scores have increased, dropout rates have declined, attendance rates have improved, and parents now attend meetings at the schools in record numbers. These schools have been successful because they have changed the very culture of their schools from bureaucratic to collaborative. Through hundreds of conversations, meetings, and negotiations, a different understanding of the "system" has begun to emerge. The rule-driven, hierarchical, command-and-control mentality formerly governing these schools has given way to a more relational, collaborative atmosphere. Principals no longer see themselves as compliance officers of the district, but as leaders of a team. Teachers learn how to negotiate rules and regulations and can contribute their creative ideas to the classroom. Parents learn how to be equal decision makers at the table with teachers, principals, and officials. It is this collaborative atmosphere that sustains reform efforts.

Roosevelt High School is an Alliance School in Dallas that has partnered with one of the local IAF organizations, Dallas Area Interfaith (DAI). Working with families in sixty congregations from diverse faiths and ethnic backgrounds, DAI has proven to be a powerful new force in the city's public arena. Over five thousand community leaders from DAI congregations have successfully negotiated with city, state, and corporate institutions to direct public and private resources toward a multitude of pressing issues. In 1994 alone, DAI leaders designed a unique job-training program and leveraged over $2 million in public and private funds to support the initiative. DAI leaders also secured public commitments from city officials to provide infrastructure improvements and community policing in low-income neighborhoods whose residents were concerned with health and safety issues.

In 1992, DAI began to work with the principal of Roosevelt High School. For years, Roosevelt had been recognized as one of the worst schools in the Dallas Independent School District. Located in the "bottom," an economically depressed inner-city neighborhood in the shadow of downtown Dallas, Roosevelt has a student body that was 99 percent minority; well over half of the students come from economically disadvantaged homes. Gang violence and discipline problems had been epidemic at the school. In 1993, a student was killed there. When the district threatened to close the school, the principal knew Roosevelt needed to act quickly to improve dramatically. So he turned to Dallas Area Interfaith for help.

DAI sent an organizer to begin working with the principal, parents, and teachers at Roosevelt to help them reimagine their school. As soon as the organizer arrived, she began to have hundreds of individual conversations with teachers, parents, staff, coaches, janitors, students—everyone in the school. She then encouraged teachers and parents to begin having conversations with one another about what was wrong with their school and what they could do to change it. Before the principal invited DAI into his school, discussions about the school usually took place privately, if they took place at all. Some teachers who had been in the school almost twenty years had never talked to one another. As the organizer described it, there were different camps of parents and teachers: the band parents, the football parents, the cheerleader parents. No one shared ideas.

The discussions on how to change the school were difficult at first: parents and teachers wanted to blame one another for failures, and each person had a different opinion about what was wrong. But gradually, after many lengthy conversations, people began to discover that they had a common concern: they wanted a better school. In the next few months, parents and teachers began to have regular meetings and put together a core leadership team of parents, teachers, and staff. They began to research ways in which Roosevelt might improve.

The organizer connected them with other schools in the IAF's statewide reform initiative. At an Alliance Schools conference, Roosevelt learned of the success of the block-scheduling program at Davis High School in Houston. Roosevelt sent a team of leaders to Davis to research how the program was implemented there, and the team discussed how to begin such a program at Roosevelt. After considerable deliberation, Roosevelt voted to introduce block scheduling at their school. Roosevelt's campus leadership team obtained the necessary waivers from the district and switched to a block-scheduling program in the fall of the 1993–94 school year. By December 1994, attendance had improved dramatically, and the school district awarded Roosevelt $52,000 for having the largest increase in attendance in the district.

With the taste of success, Roosevelt decided it was time to share its accomplishments and vision for change with the district and the surrounding community. In January 1995, a Roosevelt teacher led a delegation of 350 parents who filled the room at a school board meeting to present their vision of campus improvement. This was the first major action as a school, and it proved to be the turning point. Throughout the spring, parents and teachers attended workshops together, organized tutoring programs, reached out to neighboring churches for support. They strengthened their partnership with Dallas Area Interfaith: Roosevelt parents and teachers attended DAI organizational meetings to help win support for DAI's job-training program and neighborhood revitalization plans, and DAI congregational leaders lent their support to Roosevelt's improvement efforts. In April, DAI even chose Roosevelt as the site for their organization-wide meeting with candidates for city elections, and over fifteen hundred DAI delegates attended. Parents worked side by side with DAI leaders to get out the vote for the elections.

In September 1995, Roosevelt hosted DAI's education conference. This meeting was pivotal for Roosevelt because it established itself as a leader in DAI's school and community improvement efforts. Nearly four hundred congregational leaders, parents, teachers, and principals from eight area schools spent a Saturday morning attending workshops, listening to speakers, and planning the future of the education initiative strategy. Roosevelt representatives told their story of transformation to representatives of other schools who attended. Roosevelt announced that it had been taken off the Texas Education Agency's (TEA) list of low-performing schools due to the fact that the number of students passing all sections of the state standardized academic achievement test jumped from *13 percent* in 1993–94 to *40 percent* in 1994–95. TEA evaluators who visited the school in April publicly congratulated the parents, teachers, and the principal for the most dramatic improvement they had seen in a school in one year. Roosevelt now sees itself not only as a successful institution of learning but also as a leader in the community.

Conclusion

The success of IAF organizations in building a constituency for education reform shows that parents, working together with public officials, teachers, principals, and community members, can improve education for their children. Broad-based organizations are essential in the constituency-building process, because they can simultaneously develop community leaders, spearhead innovative public policy connected to ordinary families, and rebuild neighborhoods. Learning from these strategies discussed here, those involved in early care and education reform can educate and involve parents in their efforts, build constituencies capable of altering public policy, and ideally effect long-term change in the quality of early care and education.

References

Coleman, J. S. (1989, November). Schools and communities. *Chicago Studies.*

Galston, W. (1989). Civic education in the liberal state. In N. Rosenblum (Ed.), *Liberalism and the moral life.* Boston: Harvard University Press.

Lasch, C. (1995). *The revolt of the elites and the betrayal of democracy.* New York: Norton.

National Center for Children in Poverty. (1994). *Young children in poverty: A statistical update.* New York: National Center for Children in Poverty.

Putnam, R. D. (1993). *Making democracy work: Civic traditions in modern Italy.* Princeton, N.J.: Princeton University Press.

Thompson, D. F. (1976). *John Stuart Mill and representative government.* Princeton, N.J.: Princeton University Press.

Whitehead, A. N. (1929, 1957). *The aims of education.* New York: Free Press.

Wilson, W. J. (1987). *The truly disadvantaged.* Chicago: University of Chicago Press.

Wolin, S. (1989). *Presence of the past.* Baltimore: Johns Hopkins University Press.

Chapter Fifteen

Understanding the Complexities of Educational Change

Ann Lieberman
Diane Wood
Beverly Falk

Introduction

This chapter presents historical and contemporary views of schools and attempts to change them. The focus is on teachers and teaching, schools and school cultures, and how processes of change affect them. It also focuses on the approaches to change that facilitate real, lasting, and meaningful reform (Cohn & Kottkamp, 1993; Fullan, 1991; Goodlad, 1984; Lieberman & Miller, 1992; Sarason, 1990; Wise, 1988). Throughout, we consider how the lessons that have been learned in schools can be applied in the early care and education field. Although we are in the midst of a major era of reform in education, it is unfortunately true that American schools are still struggling with contemporary versions of some of the same old education problems—how to teach individuals and groups; how to set high standards without standardizing all students and all classrooms; how to attend to students' special needs and interests without forfeiting excellence; how to teach subject matter engagingly for today's students; how to deal with the tension between facts and discovery; and how to make schools sites for individual and societal improvement, not repositories for social ills.

The current rhetoric about the need for addressing these problems is strong, but so too is allegiance to the status quo. Although there are examples of successfully reformed schools, described later in the chapter, most schools still are governed by centralized authority and elaborate bureaucracies. They structure learning around teacher-centered pedagogy; depend on "batch processing" of students; emphasize only individual learning; tend to isolate teachers in classrooms; and adhere to rote learning of facts instead of learning content through problem solving, thinking, and experiencing (Goodlad, 1984; Lortie, 1975; McLaughlin & Talbert, 1993; Resnick, 1987; Sarason, 1990; Tyack, 1974).

Unfortunately, many of the struggles for solutions to these problems have culminated in one-right-way answers, leading to conceptions of one best system for educating all students in all places (Tyack, 1974). We argue that such thinking is ultimately futile for both schools and early care and education. In its place, we offer a conception of democratic practice, one that makes schools and early care and education programs communities of learning that are grounded in their own specific contexts and the realities of contemporary society. These effective schools and programs inquire into and try out approaches to teaching and learning that are aimed at promoting optimal learning for *all* students. To support this, we try to synthesize what has been learned from over a century of school reform efforts. First, we provide a historical perspective by looking at earlier models of educational change. Second, we discuss new social, political, cultural, and economic conditions that have led to new knowledge and interpretive frames that are themselves pressing schools toward change. Third, we describe an organic view of school reform that leads to learner-centered schools, with examples of how such schools are taking shape. Last, we examine key understandings about educational change that have been drawn from our review of school reform.

A Historical View of School Change: Opposing Visions

Perhaps a central insight for students of educational change is recognizing that individual schools have histories (Altenbaugh, 1992; Bolin & Panaritis, 1992; Tyack, 1974). To assume that reforms have never been tried or to introduce old ideas as if they were new not only builds resistance and cynicism (Sergiovanni, 1993) but also ignores shared experiences (good and bad) that have become the traditions on which school cultures are built (Sergiovanni, 1993; Sykes, 1992).

How and What Children Should Learn

Learner-centered schools have an historic tradition, rooted in ideas of the late nineteenth century that gained momentum in the early twentieth century and into the 1930s (Cremin, 1964). These ideas, associated with progressive education, contrast with a more traditional view. Whereas early progressive educators, such as Colonel Parker and John Dewey, argued for centering curriculum around real experiences, interests, and needs of learners (as well as around contemporary social problems), other reformers, such as William T. Harris, argued that students should be taught the great books and traditional academic disciplines (forms of knowledge that they considered to be the nation's cultural heritage). Progressive educators urged an education of the whole child, which meant that all aspects of students' needs—intellectual, social, physical, and artistic—had to be considered in relation to schoolwork. In contrast, traditional educators focused on children's intellects and discipline, emphasizing the importance of education as a preparation for students' futures as adults. Progressive educators saw education as a process of growth, which must continually adapt to individual students, to learning communities, and to society—all of which were in states of continual change. Traditionalists argued for efficient methods to give time-tested knowledge to students (Goodlad, 1984; Tanner & Tanner, 1980). These opposing worldviews have spawned conflicting and frequently contradictory reform efforts over time, and this same debate continues today. The early care and education field has experienced similar struggles between developmentally appropriate practice and more traditional approaches of instruction.

Process of Reform

In addition to traditional and progressive assumptions about what children should be taught and how they learn, there have also been a variety of beliefs about how reform takes place and the role of the teacher in that reform. Derived from themes of scientific management, early efforts at reforming schools represented top-down, linear approaches to change (Darling-Hammond & Wise, 1981; Elmore, 1991). Change was seen as an undeviating journey, on a straight road toward a clearly defined goal. Teachers were viewed as technicians who simply had to be trained to adopt and accept the right ideas. Judgment of the success of an innovation was based on the teacher's fidelity to the idea.

Bennis, Benne, and Chin (1961) challenged this approach. They realized that no amount of analysis and planning can be effective without attending to social processes, including the interpersonal relationships among people and the learning that takes place as a part of any change effort. Furthermore, during the 1970s, Rutter and his colleagues (1979) studied secondary schools in England and found strong relationships between school processes and student attainment. Responding to the Coleman Report's (1966) finding that schools made little difference in students' lives, Rutter and colleagues countered with their finding of the importance of a school's *ethos* to student learning and engagement: the school's social organization mattered significantly for students. They found that in urban schools, students did better when they observed positive adult modeling, recognized school values in everyday practice, received regular feedback on their work, undertook social responsibilities, and experienced shared activities with both teachers and peers. This evidence turned the direction of reform toward social reform in local schools.

This focus on the social aspects of schools was soon eclipsed, however, when *A Nation at Risk* (National Commission on Excellence in Education, 1983) became widely publicized. The report led a widespread call for schools to get back on track, return to basics, and reinstate the perceived higher standards of a bygone era. School reform, it was claimed, needed to be based on "excellence," as determined by standardized solutions and standardized tests. Generic "best-way" methods were again being sought, despite increasing evidence that teachers needed more—not less—autonomy with students whose academic and social needs could not be met by standardized solutions (Cohn & Kottkamp, 1993; Darling-Hammond, 1993; Fullan & Hargreaves, 1991, 1992; Tyack, 1974).

Similar fluctuations—though not as dramatic—characterize the history of early care and education, with shifts in focus from behaviorist to constructivist orientations.

Teachers and School Cultures

For many years, studies of teachers had been based on the search for discrete teaching behaviors and specific curricula that appeared to produce requisite high test scores (Denham & Lieberman, 1980). Good teaching became defined as teaching that efficiently transmits skills and knowledge as measured by standardized test scores. Improving schools became a matter of training teachers in these "best" practices, carefully supervising their work to ensure faithful adoption, and assessing teacher performance and school accountability via test scores (Bolin & Panaritis, 1992; Darling-Hammond, 1992). Competency-based education, teacher-proof curricula, and management by objectives are only three examples of top-down reforms that characterize this period (Shor, 1987; Shulman, 1987).

The "effective schools movement" made another attempt to include school culture by incorporating Rutter and colleagues' (1979) conception of the school's social arrangements. They maintained that "best" teachers needed an environment that supported school improvement. Their generic characteristics of effective schools included the principal as a strong instructional leader, curriculum aligned with the school's goals, regular feedback to and from students and teachers, and ongoing opportunities for faculty evaluation and development (Griffin, 1990; Steller, 1989).

Teaching had often been described as an occupation for people not as bright as other professionals, for women just interested in a job subordinate to marriage, or for "unmarriageable women and unsalable men" (Waller, 1932, p. 379). But it was not until Lortie's classic study in 1975 that the *contexts* of teaching were clearly and poignantly explained. By finding out how teachers felt about the rewards of teaching (the excitement when students *get it*), about the connection between their own teaching and student learning (its *endemic uncertainties*), and about their lack of connection to other adults, Lortie began to unlock and give conceptual richness to the social realities of teaching and the problems of change. The most important things teachers were supposed to do for their students—create the conditions for their growth and learning—were being denied to them by their own schools (Lieberman, 1992).

In addition to Lortie's work, the Rand Change Agent Study of federally funded school improvement projects fundamentally changed how many educators viewed school improvement efforts (Berman & McLaughlin, 1978). This national study linked process issues—such as commitment of teachers, rewards for staff involvement, and opportunities and support for teacher learning—with outcomes—such as changed teacher practices, student growth, and project continuance. Using additional research a decade later, researchers defined a perspective on change demonstrating that although policies could enable outcomes, important factors (such as will, motivation, and commitment) were locally defined and largely beyond the reach of policy (McLaughlin, 1987).

Sarason's work (1982), published at about the same time as that of Lortie and Berman and McLaughlin, provided further explanation of the contradictions between the continual pressure for school reform and the powerful norms that tied a school's culture together, lessons that are beginning to be understood in early care and education. These norms, both "behavioral and programmatic" (p. 95) included, for example, regular patterns of teacher behavior during lunch hours and faculty meetings (behavioral) and the programming and organizing of schools into grade levels and discrete subject areas that dictated particular sequences at particular times (programmatic). Sarason was saying that schools have cultures and that cultural change is far more complex than simply delivering new curricula or pedagogical techniques to schools and including them in teachers' practices. The regularities of school culture were at the heart of what authentic change was all about, and these regularities involved not only subject matter, pedagogical techniques, and new technologies but also people, their values and aspirations, their understandings, and their commitments (Lieberman, 1992).

These insights into the contexts of teaching, coupled with the emerging conceptions of change as a social process, produced new approaches to changing schools and entirely different responses to *A Nation at Risk* (Bennis, Benne, & Chin, 1961; Havelock, 1971;

Miles, 1993; Rutter & others, 1979; Sarason, 1982). Claiming that schools never had veered from the track of teaching basic skills and traditional subject matter, these second-wave reformers argued that it was time to rethink, reframe, and reconceptualize school change (Cuban, 1990). This approach was reinforced by the Carnegie Forum on Education and the Economy's *A Nation Prepared* (1986), a report that called for restructuring schools with teachers at the center of the reform effort.

This thinking spawned an approach to change and a research agenda that inquired into the realities of schools as the participants saw them and then developed strategies for change based on this knowledge (Elmore, 1991; Fullan, 1993; McLaughlin, 1991; Sykes, 1992). These researchers argued that without teachers' commitment to and ownership of new methods and content, which involved providing time and opportunities to learn, little could be accomplished.

Unlearned Lessons from History

These ideas were not totally new. In *Democracy and Education,* Dewey emphasized the inextricable relationship between positive change and social processes (1916). For him, the sharing of common interests characterized the ideal social arrangement. Social groups must continually move toward developing further interests—both collective and individual. Schools, as social institutions, need to provide structures for exchanging ideas and defining collective visions, always open to renegotiating and redefining these visions according to the needs of the community.

Having seen the misapplication of some of his own ideas, Dewey pointed to the dangers of allowing a vision to become dogmatic. In their attempts to defend progressive ideas against more traditional views, some of his followers adopted a form of "either-or" thinking: "Mankind likes to think in terms of extreme opposites. It is given to formulating its beliefs in terms of 'either/ors' between which it recognizes no intermediate possibilities" (1938, p. 17). To progressives, education had become solely "development from within," whereas to traditionalists, it had become a process of "formation from without" (1938, p. 17). To Dewey, it was both. It was transmitting past knowledge and making sense of present experience, preparing for the future and living life meaningfully in the present, receiving and acting, thinking and doing, mastering past knowledge and constructing new knowledge, developing the individual and the learning community, viewing forms of knowledge as timeless and changing, honoring student freedom and adult authority. Educators would have to face the continuing challenge of negotiating the balance between these tensions.

Indeed, if such tensions are to be resolved, educators must stop looking for the one best way to operate schools. School communities must have the freedom to devise their own structures, to articulate their own educational goals, and to tailor curricula and instructional approaches to their own contexts and students within the framework of a democratic society (Elmore & McLaughlin, 1988).

The interrelationship of all facets of schooling—the nested relationship among nation, state, district, school, and classroom, combined with the social realities of teaching—implies the need for support from all levels of the policy structure (Fullan & Hargreaves, 1991; Lieberman & Miller, 1992; McLaughlin & Talbert, 1993; Sarason, 1990). Indeed, any significant change in a school must be authentically owned by individual communities, must be supported by district and state policies, and, to last, must grow organically with the participants who live in the culture (Fullan, 1992; Lieberman, Darling-Hammond, & Zuckerman, 1991; McLaughlin, 1990). The same is clearly true for significant change to occur in early care and education programs.

The Changing Social Context: New and Varied Frames of Understanding

Despite Dewey's 1938 call for "both-and" thinking to replace either-or conceptions of education, the either-or swings in educational reform have continued unabated (Passow, 1986). Social conditions, however, having changed dramatically in the last three decades, have created the need for a new synthesis, for new frames of understanding, and for new methodological and conceptual tools to help interpret and redefine the relationships between society, schools, and the processes of change.

New Conditions for Schools

Schools, as in earlier eras, absorb increasingly heterogeneous student populations with widely divergent attitudes, belief systems, experiences, and worldviews (Estrada & McLaren, 1993). Today, society is not in the process of expansion and asserting its assumptions. Instead, it is a society in the process of making major adaptations to a changed global economy (Hargreaves, 1994). Concurrently, schools—and early care and education programs—are trying to cope with the breakdown of family life, increased drug and alcohol use, violence outside and inside the school, and the competing demands on students' time and attention from pervasive media attractions. Widely held conceptions of morality and common sense have, for many, lost their legitimacy.

Context, Knowledge, and Learning

Like their colleagues in early care and education, educators are asking critical questions: What is knowledge? Whose knowledge counts as legitimate? What do we really mean by collaboration and colleagueship? Who should drive the agenda for change? How can we talk about universal truths when there are such enormous differences in educational settings? What do we do with educational settings that, for complex reasons of history, culture, and context, do not or cannot change? How do we listen to the competing voices of teachers, principals, parents, and the community? Whose reality do we act on? (McLaughlin & Talbert, 1993; Mishler, 1979). Knowledge cannot simply be a matter of describing a world out there waiting to be discovered. Knowledge emerges from acting and doing in the world, a very Deweyan notion. As early childhood educators understand and as Minnich also notes, to know is also to experience in context, to interpret from a particular frame of reference, and to create meaning from one's own experience (Minnich, 1990).

Implications for education reform become clearer. If knowledge is both constructed and dependent on context and perspective, then multiple perspectives and multiple contexts are necessary for wide participation in the construction of knowledge about schools and school reform. Research and changed practice must come not only from academic scholars but also from school-based educators who live the daily realities of school life (Cochran-Smith & Lytle, 1990; Cohen & Barnes, 1993). When school personnel decide to change, they need to build their vision for change together, and they must include all perspectives—district, administrators, teachers, students, parents, and community (Newmann, 1993). As these participants work to change their schools and classrooms, the efforts themselves become a form of learning, which not only enhance a change effort but also result in the shaping of a community of knowledge that can have lasting significance (Grimmett & Crehan, 1992).

Knowledge, when seen this way, has implications not only for how students learn but also for how teachers teach. Knowledge building for teachers becomes as much a matter of building community around shared ideas and reflecting on actual practice as it is of seeking knowledge from others (Lieberman & Miller, 1990; Little, 1993; McLaughlin & Talbert, 1993; Schon, 1983).

Similarly, student learning occurs when students can make sense of curricular content, when they can connect it to their own experiences and knowledge, and when they can see its relevance to their present and future lives (Belenky, Clinchy, Goldberger, & Tarule, 1986; Resnick, 1987). There are new and different problems facing our society today, problems that call for students to become "independent thinkers and enterprising problem solvers" (Cohen & Barnes, 1993, p. 207). Information must be joined with problem solving and other creative ways of thinking, framing problems, and generating solutions (Cohen, McLaughlin, & Talbert, 1993; Hargreaves, 1994; Shulman, 1987). This kind of teaching, which encourages students' understanding and conceptual thinking, is part of the new synthesis of curriculum and pedagogy. This approach also necessitates rethinking and reorganizing teacher learning. In contrast to older styles of professional development, which depended solely on workshops or course work, professional development for teachers is now being organized to involve teachers in their own learning through teacher research, participation in school-university partnerships, and subject matter networks (Lieberman & McLaughlin, 1992; Little, 1993).

In the past, urban schools have demonstrated a disconnection between cognition and social realities. Unfortunately, American schools often have failed to educate substantial numbers of poor and minority students adequately (Goodlad, 1984, 1990; Tyack, 1974). Currently, as the diversity within school populations has grown, the challenge to create inclusive forms of schooling has become the cause of much conflict and confusion. Dewey's concept of both-and thinking may help provide some direction for negotiating an appropriate balance. Schools can find ways to help students recognize their common culture as Americans, as they still honor diversity (Banks, 1975). As Dewey also pointed out, democracies depend on education, but only an education that itself incorporates democratic processes can truly serve a democracy (1916).

A major voice missing from the educational reform dialogue over the years has been that of teachers. It is only in the recent past that the experience and knowledge of those who work directly with students have been seen to have value. There are a number of reasons for this omission. The history of teaching as "woman's work," under social conditions that maintained a restricted role for women, is certainly a major one. Women, historically socialized and rewarded for being obedient, conservative, and nurturing, filled the teaching ranks, as men dominated the administrative positions (Altenbaugh, 1992; Grumet, 1988; Lortie, 1975).

In recent years, researchers, as well as policy makers, have come to realize that the connection between teaching and learning is a critical one and that no meaningful change will take place unless teachers are intimately involved in both technical and experiential learning in the context of their own classrooms and also supported by school norms of inquiry and change. To change schools involves people—individually and organizationally, structurally and culturally, personally and collectively (Cooper, 1988; Fullan, 1991; Little & McLaughlin, 1993; McLaughlin & Marsh, 1990; Richardson, 1990).

Changing Teacher Organizations

Teacher organizations, having long fought for basic economic issues, are becoming increasingly involved in school reform.

Involving unions in shifting from win-lose stances to working collaboratively with management and the policy community involves radical changes that will affect every part of teachers' professional lives. These changes are *structural*—committees and teams of all kinds involving teachers in making decisions that heretofore have been made solely by management; *process oriented*—teachers learning to take authority and responsibility for areas as disparate as budgets, peer review, and conflict management, as well as for new approaches to teaching and instruction; and *personal* and *interpersonal*—traditional, clearly defined positions of management and labor blurring and evolving. This potentially powerful change in direction for unionized teachers, if it gains momentum and spreads beyond a few sites, will make possible a significant addition to the voices that support major school reform.

Contemporary Approaches to School Reform

Some scholars, having initiated school reform projects based on broad and comprehensive conceptions of change, are encouraging new voices and finding new ways to organize work and understand practice. Sometimes moving from theory to action, sometimes from practice to theory, sometimes creating strategies or documenting the conceptualization of strategies, they are illuminating both the possibilities and the limitations of the school reform movements.

Pilot Programs: From Research to Action

Some researchers, such as Comer, Fine, Gardner, and Sizer, are working in schools, testing their ideas about how children learn most successfully (Comer, 1990; Fine, forthcoming; Gardner, 1983, 1993; Sizer, 1984). For example, Comer, coming from a strong background in child development, has based his School Development Program on a rethinking of how teachers and parents can work together to improve children's learning. His longitudinal research in New Haven, Connecticut, has produced important understandings about how parents can and must be involved with their children's education both in and out of school. Working toward structures that encourage better connections between teachers and parents at home and at school, Comer suggests that attention paid solely to students' cognitive development is insufficient to engage them in the learning process. He finds four *pathways* that are critical to young children's intellectual and cognitive development. They are stimulation and growth through social interaction, psychological and emotional experiences, speech and language opportunities, and moral guidance. These pathways help form a framework within which to build the school as a community—a community in which students learn to interact and communicate with others.

Gardner's research on *multiple intelligences* led him to another way of framing a changing role for schools (Gardner, 1983, 1993). Educators have historically thought of education in terms of quantitative logic, linguistic ability, and spatial ability. Gardner has added kinesthetic, musical, and inter- and intrapersonal abilities. This different approach to studying intelligence suggests ways of thinking about schoolwork and ways for students to participate in learning that are far more encompassing than had previously been recognized. The Key School in Indianapolis is in the process of incorporating teaching to these intelligences into its practices. This approach is changing the way teachers think about the curriculum and how they structure the school day to implement these new perceptions of student learning.

Sizer's work (1984), based on a national study of high schools, found that teachers in schools across the country were busily involved in covering the curriculum, even as they were losing students' interest, engagement, and commitment to learning. Observing teachers' work lives, he found that their adaptations were in large part due to heavy teaching loads, which left little time for creative teaching and interacting with students, which in turn led to frustration and lack of engagement. To change these conditions, Sizer began the Coalition of Essential Schools, made up of member schools from all over the country whose leaders were interested in fundamentally reshaping their high schools. The coalition is based on a set of principles aimed at changing how school-based educators think about their purposes, about the roles of teachers, and about the way students and teachers work together. It has grown to include over two hundred schools nationwide. Sizer defined a broad set of values and ideas, and he encouraged the schools to interpret and refine them. For example, one of the principles, *less is more,* involves teachers in struggling for solutions to a perennial tension in classrooms—the tension between breadth and depth of coverage of subject matter in the curriculum. Rather than trying to solve this problem by themselves, teachers in coalition schools work together in departments and teams to organize the curriculum and plan how both to deepen and broaden student experience. When educators work on ideas and solutions of this magnitude, it makes public the tensions in teachers' lives, which have long been private.

Fine has written about and helped lead another effort, which seeks to transform radically large comprehensive urban high schools. In Philadelphia, small schools known as charters are being created; they function independently within large comprehensive high schools. In collaboration with the Pew Foundation, the board of education, and the Philadelphia Teachers Union, the Philadelphia Schools Collaborative has sought to involve educators and parents in restructuring governance, frameworks, instruction, assessment practices, parent and community relationships, and students' transitions from high school to work or to postsecondary education. Charters are made up of small communities of no more than three hundred to four hundred students and approximately ten to twelve teachers. They focus on a particular theme—health and physical education, academic approach to language, literature and theater, and so forth. To date, there are ninety-two charters, with more on the way.

Each of these examples represents a different approach to framing the problem of fundamentally changing schools. Each underscores the breadth and depth of the concern about schooling. It is important that these models for school change are seen as part of a larger reform movement, so they can complement each other rather than work in isolation.

Teacher Learning and Professional Development

In this period of intense reform, earlier notions of teachers as technicians or as passive recipients of experts' ideas are slowly giving way to a more robust and rounded view of how teachers learn (Lieberman & Miller, 1990; Little, 1990). As teachers begin to transform their curriculum and assessment practices, their teaching role undergoes transformation as well. As they observe and document student growth, they seek to learn more about human development and learning theories. As they plan classroom activities with students around themes or questions, they learn how to structure problem-solving activities and how to diagnose students' needs for basic skills in ways that are more consistent with how students learn. As they have opportunities to document what students do and how they go about doing it, they become researchers of their own practice. These changes, then, become the means for creating a learning community among peers, a place where student learning is legitimately seen as an opportunity for teacher learning and discussion and where teacher inquiry is a significant part of being a teacher (Little, 1992; Lytle & Cochran-Smith, 1992). Some of the ways these expanded roles have been carried out in various settings include joint preparation periods across grades or disciplines, financial reimbursement for professional development meetings during lunch or after school, exposure to current research and professional conferences, visits to other classes, and expanded opportunities for teachers to learn about new practices both within and without their own schools. Teacher learning and professional development become central to the teaching-learning process and integral to building learner-centered schools—*and* early care and education programs.

School Structures, Organization, and Leadership

It follows that changes in teaching and learning, practices, and the professional culture of schools necessitate changes in school and program structure, organization, and governance. One such structural change is the creation of small schools that are formed from or exist within larger ones or that are altogether new. Fifty new, small high schools are now being created in New York City. This is in addition to the several hundred that have been created as part of the Philadelphia Schools Collaborative and the Coalition of Essential Schools.

In small schools, it is far more likely that the focus will be on people and ideas rather than on trying to deal with the complexities of the hierarchy (Meier, 1989). Some schools, having reorganized their programs and staffing to lessen the fragmentation of students' and teachers' work, find that this helps them provide a more interdisciplinary, in-depth type of knowledge and learning. One of the forms this has taken, in both elementary and secondary schools, has been the provision of longer blocks of time for teachers to work with students. Some schools have altered the way students are grouped, adopting multi-age groups. This offers students a wider range of peers, increases opportunities for peer tutoring, and provides for naturally occurring differences in students' developmental ages. Such reforms, adapted to younger children, could be tried in early care and education programs as well.

As part of the changes in school organization, many schools have increased opportunities for teachers to participate in the process of school governance and decision making. Site-based management, shared decision making, expanded leadership roles for teachers, and participatory structures that allow school staff to have greater involvement in community life have resulted in a richer learning environment for all—despite the difficulties such changes present (Lieberman, Darling-Hammond, & Zuckerman, 1991; Lieberman, Falk, & Alexander, 1994). This approach could play a role in reforming early care and education programs.

Many schools have created close partnerships with parents, in which their commitments, goals, and strategies for children can be shared (Comer, 1990). Such partnerships help connect parents to schools in ways that serve multiple purposes. As parents are involved in understanding new modes of assessing student work, for example, important connections are created between school and home. Not only do parents become more involved in and supportive of their children's schoolwork, but they are also more likely to become supporters of and participants in the changes that are entailed by learner-centered schools. The early care and education field has a long history of valuing close staff-parent relations, and these school-based findings suggest renewed emphasis in this area.

Conclusion: Building Learner-Centered School Communities

Looking back on the history of reform in American education, one is struck by the power of either-or thinking that has kept us from developing a more comprehensive approach to school reform. Heaping contradictory reforms, one on top of another, has drawn our attention away from analyzing the complexities of school culture and seeking the knowledge—as well as building the structures—needed to change it. The perceived needs of our nation, however, as well as the perceived failures of previous piecemeal reforms, offer important incentives to build a new commitment to reform that is at once comprehensive and practical.

As staff struggle to create learning environments that are responsive and responsible to the needs of all children, they develop new understandings about the teaching and learning process. In so doing, they create new forms and structures. As learning-centered principles are applied, not only to children but to all participants in the school or early care and education community, a collaborative process of learning and growth takes place, which builds collective knowledge and a sense of community.

The process of building learner-centered communities is, however, a complex one, fraught with its own problems and conflicts. Those engaged in such efforts are called on to maintain a delicate balance between the needs of individuals and the interests of the group, trying to reflect the differing perspectives of people from diverse backgrounds and experiences. When new voices, which heretofore have not been heard, are given the opportunity to participate in the shaping of schools or early care and education programs, we can expect tensions to arise, as the community struggles to provide ways to think critically and creatively and simultaneously maintain respect for systematically accumulated knowledge. Although these tensions will not be resolved by formula or prescription—as each community must respond to internal conflict in its own way—the dissemination of knowledge gleaned from individual and collective experiences will help communities understand and deal with their own problems as they arise.

In using new frameworks to think about and organize learner-centered communities, differences and conflicts will surface over ways of thinking about the purposes of schools. Some of these challenges will inevitably form around the capacities of teachers to enact learner-centered practices, to build structures that support learner-centered teaching, to seek public understanding and support for changes in educational practice, to resolve the school's and community's differing conceptions of leadership, and to live the process.

Schools, early care and education programs, and communities cannot promote these kinds of changes on any large scale by themselves. They need the support of policies enacted at the district, state, and federal levels (McLaughlin & Talbert, 1993). Though it is true that "policy cannot mandate what matters most," that is, commitment, motivation, and will to change (McLaughlin, 1987, p. 172), schools and communities can be supported and encouraged rather than neglected and discouraged. Policies that create standards without standardization and encourage individual communities to adapt to their local conditions can help (Darling-Hammond, 1993). Instead of putting its resources into monitoring and inspecting, the state can broker, facilitate, and organize resources to support the commitments of local communities. In this way, policies can support democratic practices in schools and communities that are grounded in their own specific contexts and the realities of contemporary society.

In a changing world, one that requires workers who have developed problem-solving skills and higher-order thinking processes and citizens who share democratic values and practices, the move toward democratic practice in schools and early care and education programs can help define the territory and the commitment to larger goals for American education.

References

Altenbaugh, R. J. (Ed). (1992). *The teacher's voice: A social history of teaching in twentieth century America.* Bristol, Pa.: Falmer Press.

Banks, J. A. (1975). *Teaching strategies for ethnic studies.* Needham Heights, Mass.: Allyn & Bacon.

Belenky, M. F., Clinchy, B. V., Goldberger, N. R., & Tarule, J. M. (1986). *Women's ways of knowing: The development of self, voice, and mind.* New York: Basic Books.

Bennis, W. G., Benne, K. D., & Chin, R. (Eds.) (1961). *The planning of change: Readings in the applied behavioral sciences.* Austin, Tex.: Holt, Rinehart and Winston.

Berman, P., & McLaughlin, M. W. (1978). *Federal programs for supporting educational change: Implementing and sustaining innovations, Vol. 8.* Santa Monica, Calif.: Rand Corporation.

Bolin, F. S., & Panaritis, P. (1992). Searching for a common purpose: A perspective in the history of supervision. In C. D. Glickman (Ed.), *Supervision in transition: 1992 yearbook of the Association for Supervision and Curriculum Development* (pp. 30–43). Alexandria, Va.: Association for Supervision and Curriculum Development.

Carnegie Forum on Education and the Economy. (1986). *A nation prepared: Teachers for the twenty-first century.* New York: Carnegie Forum on Education and the Economy.

Cochran-Smith, M., & Lytle, S. (1990). Research on teaching and teacher research: The issues that divide. *Educational Researcher, 19,* 2–11.

Cohen, D. K., & Barnes, C. A. (1993). Pedagogy and policy. In D. K. Cohen, M. W. McLaughlin, & J. E. Talbert (Eds.), *Teaching for understanding: Challenges for policy and practice* (pp. 207–239). San Francisco: Jossey-Bass.

Cohen, D. K., McLaughlin, M. W., & Talbert, J. E. (Eds.) (1993). *Teaching for understanding: Challenges for policy and practice.* San Francisco: Jossey-Bass.

Cohn, M. M., & Kottkamp, R. B. (1993). *Teachers, the missing voice in education.* Albany, N.Y.: State University of New York Press.

Coleman, J. S. (1966). *The equality of educational opportunity.* Washington, D.C.: U.S. Office of Education, U.S. Government Printing Office.

Comer, J. P. (1990). Home, school, and academic learning. In J. I. Goodlad & P. Keating (Eds.), *Access to knowledge: An agenda for our nation's schools* (pp. 23–42). New York: College Board.

Cooper, M. (1988). Whose culture is it, anyway? In A. Lieberman (Ed.), *Building a professional culture in schools* (pp. 45–54). New York: Teachers College Press.

Cremin, L. (1964). *The transformation of the school.* New York: Vintage Books.

Cuban, L. (1990). A fundamental puzzle of school reform. In A. Lieberman (Ed.), *Schools as collaborative cultures: Creating the future now* (pp. 71–77). Bristol, Pa.: Falmer Press.

Darling-Hammond, L. (1992). Policy and supervision. In C. D. Glickman (Ed.), *Supervision in transition: 1992 yearbook of the Association for Supervision and Curriculum Development* (pp. 7–29). Alexandria, Va.: Association for Supervision and Curriculum Development.

Darling-Hammond, L. (1993). Reframing the school reform agenda: Developing capacity for school transformation. *Phi Delta Kappan, 74,* 752–761.

Darling-Hammond, L., & Wise, A. E. (1981). *A conceptual framework for examining teachers' views of teaching and educational policies.* Santa Monica, Calif.: Rand Corporation.

Denham, C., & Lieberman, A. (Eds.). (1980). *A time to learn.* Washington, D.C.: National Institute of Education.

Dewey, J. (1916). *Democracy and education.* In J. Boydston (Ed.), *The middle works of John Dewey, 1899–1924. Vol. 9.* Carbondale: Southern Illinois University Press.

Dewey, J. (1938). *Experience and education.* New York: Collier Books.

Elmore, R. F. (1991). *Teaching, learning, and organization: School restructuring and the recurring dilemma of reform.* Paper presented at the Annual Meeting of the American Educational Research Association, Chicago.

Elmore, R. F., & McLaughlin, M. W. (1988). *Steady work: Policy, practice and the reform of American education.* Santa Monica, Calif.: Rand Corporation.

Estrada, K., & McLaren, P. (1993). Research news and comment: A dialogue on multiculturalism and democratic culture. *Educational Researcher, 22,* 27–33.

Fine, M. (forthcoming). Chartering urban school reform. In *Chartering public high schools in the midst of change.* New York: Teachers College Press.

Fullan, M. G. (1991). *The new meaning of educational change.* New York: Teachers College Press.

Fullan, M. G. (1992). *Successful school improvement.* Philadelphia: Open University Press.

Fullan, M. G. (1993). Innovation, reform, and restructuring strategies. In G. Cawelti (Ed.), *Challenges and achievements of American education: 1993 yearbook of the Association for Supervision and Curriculum Development* (pp. 116–133). Alexandria, Va.: Association for Supervision and Curriculum Development.

Fullan, M. G., & Hargreaves, A. (1991). *What's worth fighting for: Working together for your school.* Paper commissioned by the Ontario Public School Teachers' Federation, Toronto.

Fullan, M. G., & Hargreaves, A. (1992). *Teacher development and educational change.* Bristol, Pa.: Falmer Press.

Gardner, H. (1983). *Frames of mind: The theory of multiple intelligences.* New York: Basic Books.

Gardner, H. (1993). *Multiple intelligences: The theory in practice.* New York: Basic Books.

Goodlad, J. I. (1984). *A place called school.* New York: McGraw-Hill.

Goodlad, J. I. (1990). Common school for the common weal. In J. I. Goodlad & P. Keating (Eds.), *Access to knowledge: An agenda for our nation's schools.* New York: College Board.

Griffin, G. A. (1990). Leadership for curriculum improvement: The school administrator's role. In A. Lieberman (Ed.), *Schools as collaborative cultures: Creating the future now* (pp. 195–211). Bristol, Pa.: Falmer Press.

Grimmett, P. P., & Crehan, E. P. (1992). The nature of collegiality in teacher development: The case of curriculum supervision. In M. G. Fullan & A. Hargreaves (Eds.), *Teacher development and educational change* (pp. 56–85). Bristol, Pa.: Falmer Press.

Grumet, M. R. (1988). *Bitter milk: Women and teaching.* Amherst, Mass.: University of Massachusetts Press.

Hargreaves, A. (1994). *Changing teachers: Changing times: Teachers' work and culture in the postmodern age.* New York: Teachers College Press.

Havelock, R. G. (1971). *Planning for innovation through dissemination and utilization of knowledge.* Ann Arbor, Mich.: Center for Research on Utilization of Scientific Knowledge.

Lieberman, A. (1992). The meaning of scholarly activity and the building of community. *Educational Researcher, 21,* 5–12.

Lieberman, A., Darling-Hammond, L., & Zuckerman, D. (1991). *Early lessons in restructuring schools.* New York: National Center for Restructuring Education, Schools, and Teaching.

Lieberman, A., Falk, B., & Alexander, L. (1994). Leadership in learner-centered schools. In J. Oakes & K. Quartz (Eds.), *Smart schools: Where all children can learn: The 94th yearbook of the National Society for the Study of Education.* Chicago: University of Chicago Press.

Lieberman, A., & McLaughlin, M. W. (1992). Networks for educational change: Powerful and problematic. *Phi Delta Kappan, 73,* 673–677.

Lieberman, A., & Miller, L. (1990). Teacher development in professional practice schools. *Teachers College Record, 92,* 105–122.

Lieberman, A., & Miller, L. (1992). *Teachers, their world, and their work: Implications for school improvement.* New York: Teachers College Press.

Little, J. W. (1990). Teachers as colleagues. In A. Lieberman (Ed.), *Schools as collaborative cultures: Creating the future now* (pp. 165–193). Bristol, Pa.: Falmer Press.

Little, J. W. (1992). The persistence of privacy: Autonomy and initiative in teachers' professional relations. *Teachers College Record, 91,* 509–536.

Little, J. W. (1993). Teachers' professional development in a climate of educational reform. *Educational Evaluation and Policy Analysis, 15,* 129–151.

Little, J. W., & McLaughlin, M. W. (Eds.). (1993). *Teachers' work: Individuals, colleagues, and contexts.* New York: Teachers College Press.

Lortie, D. (1975). *Schoolteacher: A sociological study.* Chicago: University of Chicago Press.

Lytle, S., & Cochran-Smith, M. (1992). Teacher research as a way of knowing. *Harvard Educational Review, 62,* 447–474.

McLaughlin, M. W. (1987). Learning from experience: Lessons from policy implementation. *Educational Evaluation and Policy Analysis, 9,* 171–178.

McLaughlin, M. W. (1990). The Rand change agent study revisited: Macro perspectives and micro realities. *Educational Researcher, 19,* 11–16.

McLaughlin, M. W. (1991). Enabling professional development: What have we learned? In A. Lieberman & L. Miller (Eds.), *Staff development for education in the 90's* (pp. 61–82). New York: Teachers College Press.

McLaughlin, M. W., & Marsh, D. D. (1990). Staff development and school change. In A. Lieberman (Ed.), *Schools as collaborative cultures: Creating the future now* (pp. 213–232). Bristol, Pa.: Falmer Press.

McLaughlin, M. W., & Talbert, J. E. (1993). *Contexts that matter for teaching and learning: Strategic opportunities for meeting the nation's educational goals.* Stanford, Calif.: Center for Research on the Context of Secondary School Teaching, Stanford University.

Meier, D. (1989, September 8). In education, small is sensible. *New York Times,* op. ed.

Miles, M. B. (1993). Forty years of change in schools: Some personal reflections. *Educational Administration Quarterly, 29,* 213–248.

Minnich, E. K. (1990). *Transforming knowledge.* Philadelphia: Temple University Press.

Mishler, E. (1979). Meaning in context: Is there any other kind? *Harvard Educational Review, 19,* 1–19.

National Commission on Excellence in Education. (1983). *A nation at risk.* Washington, D.C.: National Commission on Excellence in Education.

Newmann, F. M. (1993). Beyond common sense in educational restructuring: The issues of content and linkage. *Educational Researcher, 22,* 4–13, 22.

Passow, A. H. (1986). Beyond the commission reports: Toward meaningful school improvement. In A. Lieberman (Ed.), *Rethinking school improvement: Research, craft, and concept.* New York: Teachers College Press.

Resnick, L. B. (1987). Learning in school and out. *Educational Researcher, 16,* 13–20.

Richardson, V. (1990). Significant and worthwhile change in teaching practice. *Educational Researcher, 19,* 10–18.

Rutter, M., & others. (1979). *Fifteen thousand hours.* Cambridge, Mass.: Harvard University Press.

Sarason, S. B. (1982). *The culture of the school and the problem of change, second edition.* Needham Heights, Mass.: Allyn & Bacon.

Sarason, S. B. (1990). *The predictable failure of educational reform.* San Francisco: Jossey-Bass.

Schon, D. A. (1983). *The reflective practitioner: How professionals think in action.* New York: Basic Books.

Sergiovanni, T. J. (1993). *Moral leadership: Getting to the heart of school improvement.* San Francisco: Jossey-Bass.

Shor, I. (1987). Equality in excellence. In M. Okazawa-Rey, J. Anderson, & R. Traver (Eds.), *Harvard Educational Review Reprint Series, 19,* 183–203.

Shulman, L. (1987). Knowledge and teaching: Foundations of the new reform. *Harvard Educational Review, 57,* 1–22.

Sizer, T. R. (1984). *Horace's compromise: The dilemma of the American high school.* Boston: Houghton Mifflin.

Steller, A. (1989). One model for effective educational reform. In *Organizing for learning: Toward the 21st century.* Reston, Va.: National Association for Secondary School Principals.

Sykes, P. J. (1992). Imposed change and the experienced teacher. In M. G. Fullan & A. Hargreaves (Eds.), *Teacher development and educational change* (pp. 36–55). Bristol, Pa.: Falmer Press.

Tanner, D., & Tanner, L. N. (1980). *Curriculum development: Theory into practice.* Old Tappan, N.J.: Macmillan.

Tyack, D. (1974). *The one best system.* Cambridge, Mass.: Harvard University Press.

Waller, W. (1932). *The sociology of teaching.* New York: Wiley.

Wise, A. E. (1988). The two conflicting trends in school reform: Legislated learning revisited. *Phi Delta Kappan, 69,* 328–333.

Chapter Sixteen

The Synchrony of Stakeholders

Lessons from the Disabilities Rights Movement

H. Rutherford Turnbull
Ann P. Turnbull

Introduction

Expressing her faith in human capacity, Margaret Mead urges us to never doubt that a small group of committed people can change the world. She notes that it is the only thing that ever has. Nowhere is her admonition more apt than in the history of the Individuals with Disabilities Education Act (IDEA).[1] In every stage and in every branch of the federal government, as IDEA has been proposed, enacted (1975), and amended (as recently as 1990), there have been groups of people—parents, members of Congress, their staffs, and professional associations of special educators—strategically placed and passionately committed, who made it their mission to change the nation's laws and schools in order to improve the lives of children with disabilities. This chapter underscores that IDEA is the result of the synergy of multiple stakeholders and the three branches of federal government (La Vor, 1976a, 1976b).

Note: We are grateful to Sharon Lynn Kagan and her colleagues at *Quality 2000* for the opportunity to be part of their important work.

IDEA authorizes Congress to provide funds to state education agencies to carry out their obligation to educate children with disabilities, ages birth to three (Part H of IDEA) and ages three to twenty-one (Part B). The state agencies, in turn, pass the federal funds on to local educational agencies. Federal funding is conditioned on the agreement of state and local agencies to six basic principles—zero reject, nondiscriminatory evaluation, appropriate and individualized education, least-restrictive (most inclusive) placement, procedural due process, and parental participation in education decision making. This chapter reviews the roles played by presidents and the executive branch, Congress, and the courts, as well as parent and professional organizations, in the enactment and amendment of IDEA.

The history of IDEA teaches a powerful lesson to advocates for early care and education. In a nutshell, it is that the strategies that were effective in securing the passage of IDEA in 1975 are, with adaptations and accommodations, useful in today's advocacy for early care and education. These strategies include:

- A multipronged approach targeted on the Congress, the administration, and the courts
- The use of "insiders" in the Congress and the administration
- The mobilization of parents and families of students with disabilities
- A reliance on existing state capacities and needs for federally sponsored activities
- An articulation of compelling ideologies and their incorporation into the disability movement from other civil rights battlefields

Nowadays, as the federal role in early care and education is being reexamined, it seems that some of those strategies, augmented by others, may be particularly useful in preserving and even enhancing the federal role. This chapter describes the disability-related strategies, proposes new ones, and, ideally, sets out a modest proposal for early care and education.

The Presidents and Other Ultimate Insiders

The history of IDEA is replete with presidents and other influential policy makers who had personal ties to people with disabilities and were committed to a federal assistance role. President Kennedy's sister Rosemary has mental retardation, a circumstance that impelled him to form the President's Committee on Mental Retardation in 1961 to advocate for legal rights for people with mental retardation and other disabilities. The work of the committee was pivotal in Congress's enactment of federal laws creating programs for the benefit of people with disabilities. Vice President Hubert Humphrey was the grandfather of a child with Down syndrome and as a senator was a vigorous champion of laws that prohibited discrimination against people with disabilities. As important as these men have been, presidential appointees have also been very influential. One of the most powerful insiders in the Reagan administration was Madeleine Will, the mother of a son with Down syndrome and assistant secretary for special education and rehabilitative services. Thus, in disability policy, well-placed, committed family insiders have played pivotal roles. The election and appointment of such people is one effective strategy for change.

The Judicial Arena: The Courts and Their Decisions

Few, if any, decisions of the Supreme Court have had such an impact as the one rendered in *Brown* v. *Board of Education* (1954), which held that separate education for blacks and whites violates the Fourteenth Amendment's equal protection guarantee. *Brown*'s equal protection interpretation and the Court's later determination to expand it to benefit women and other traditionally disenfranchised groups led disability advocates straight into the courts.

During the mid-1960s and early 1970s, judges began to address the plight of people confined in unconscionable conditions in state institutions and psychiatric hospitals. The judges' decisions were based largely on *Brown*'s equal protection guarantee and on two other doctrines—*due process* and the *least-drastic means*. The former requires states to show compelling reasons to institutionalize a person with a disability, and the latter requires states to place and treat such persons in the least-intrusive effective ways.

Relying on these doctrines, parent advocates targeted not only state institutions but also states' public school systems. The parents' strategy—one of the first attempts to use the courts to open the schoolhouse doors to people with disabilities—consisted of five elements:

- Use the equal protection doctrine to pry the doors loose, relying on *Brown* as precedent.
- Shine a bright light on the number of children institutionalized and excluded from school.
- Assemble legions of parents to testify to their children's exclusion and the enormous costs of private education, making patently clear the inequality of educational discrimination and segregation.
- Assemble a cadre of professionals whose expert testimony would overwhelm the state's argument that some children cannot learn or that the schools already were providing an appropriate education in the least-restrictive settings.
- Solicit the help of the national organization of special educators—the Council for Exceptional Children (CEC)—and of other education associations to work toward federal legislation.

In Pennsylvania and Washington, D.C., the parents' lawsuits, *Pennsylvania Association for Retarded Citizens (PARC)* v. *Commonwealth of Pennsylvania* (1971, 1972) and *Mills* v. *D.C. Board of Education* (1972), succeeded in an extraordinary fashion, in reliance on the two doctrines and *Brown*. The courts ordered the state and District of Columbia to provide a free and appropriate public education, in the least-restrictive setting and subject to due process safeguards for all children in their jurisdictions.

Beyond doubt, *PARC* and *Mills* were the court-based wrecker's balls that battered down schools' discriminatory practices and persuaded Congress to construct a new house where one had only been planned but not yet designed. That new house was IDEA. Indeed, the courts' decisions justified a federal response: when courts find that the states are violating the federal Constitution's equal protection and due process guarantees, it is legitimate for Congress to enact laws that carry out these guarantees (Turnbull, 1994).

The Legislative Arena

The bulk of disability law reform has occurred in Congress. In Congress, the courts' decisions frontally raised the question of whether Congress should assist the states to implement federal constitutional guarantees. It was through Congress that presidential initiative—whether proposed law or veto—proved pivotal to IDEA's history. It was there—in the crucible of democratic government—that families, educators, and others successfully pleaded their special education causes.

Parent Advocates

Of the many people and organizations interested in a congressional response to *PARC* and *Mills*, few were more directly interested than the parents of students with disabilities and the organizations that represented them. These groups included The Arc (then the National Association for Retarded Children/Citizens), United Cerebral Palsy Association, Association for the Blind, Alexander Graham Bell Society, Association for Children with Learning Disabilities, and several others that had lesser impact. Unquestionably, The Arc was the most influential parent organization. Its governmental affairs office was staffed by an energetic, value-based former special educator (Paul Marchand). It benefited from the leadership of a dynamic and indefatigable parent (Elizabeth M. Boggs), who was particularly close to the chair of the Senate Committee on Labor and Public Welfare, which included the Subcommittee on the Handicapped.

The Arc was "at the table" all the time, shaping the legislation in every laborious step on its way to enactment. The Arc was also responsible for generating floods of letters from parents to congresspeople urging enactment of the new legislation. Because The Arc's state chapters (numbering about forty, with 150,000 to 200,000 members at any one time) had been active for many years in securing state special education laws, it had a collective capacity for effective lobbying and a close familiarity with state laws that had to be considered when Congress was thinking about its own laws. The Arc was a named plaintiff in the *PARC* suit and in other special education litigation. Students with mental retardation whose parents constituted The Arc often had been subject to educational discrimination and thus were the most visible beneficiaries of the courts' remedies. Finally, The Arc's goals were consistent with the *Brown*-based civil rights movement: dismantle the barriers that bar students with mental retardation from school or that admit them only to segregated programs.

Professional Advocates

No bill with as great an impact on schools as IDEA would have succeeded, however, solely on the basis of parent advocacy. Professionals were major stakeholders, and their relationship to parents and parent organizations was symbiotic: professionals needed parents in the halls of Congress just as much as parents needed professionals in the courtrooms and the legislative lobbies. When all was said and done, it was a professional organization that, in alliance with The Arc and other parent advocacy groups, led the way on IDEA. That organization was the Council for Exceptional Children (CEC), the professional association representing special educators (teachers, administrators, and university faculty concerned with educating students who have disabilities and those who are gifted and talented).

In no way was CEC a novice to special education law reform. In 1966, it had received two grants from the Bureau of the Education of the Handicapped, part of the Department of Health, Education, and Welfare, Office of Education. One grant enabled CEC to study state special education laws, propose model state legislation, provide training to the National Conference of State Legislators, and work closely with The Arc's state chapters in developing political power for state law reform. The other grant enabled CEC to establish a national clearinghouse and information center on students with disabilities. These two grants put CEC on the cutting edge of policy reform. Finally, CEC's governmental affairs staffers, Fred Weintraub and Al Abeson, were excellent students of the law, who had helped organize expert witnesses in *PARC* and other cases, had strategized with the counsel in the right-to-education cases, had written well-respected articles and chapters justifying and advocating a federal right-to-education law, and had worked closely with such professional associations as the

American Association on Mental Retardation and the State Directors of Mental Retardation, both CEC allies.

CEC could not have succeeded alone. Other professional associations were committed to securing a federal right-to-education law, including the Education Commission of the States, the National Education Association, the American Federation of Teachers, the Council of Chief State School Officers, the National School Boards Association, the Council of Great City Schools, and the National Association of Elementary and Secondary School Principals.

State and Local Governments as Advocates

The fiscal implications of the courts' orders were staggering. The remedies would cost more than the states were willing to pay. The groundswell against new local property taxes was under way, and some courts were requiring state legislatures to equalize their financial aid to school districts to avoid favoring wealthier areas. It was not surprising, therefore, that governors and state legislators testified in favor of federal laws and federal appropriation.

Congressional Advocates

No matter how strong the desires of parents, professionals, and state and local governments were for a federal law, nothing would have happened had it not been for a small but powerful and determined coterie of members of Congress and their staffs. These key members of Congress and their staffs had much in common:

- They were relatives of people with disabilities.
- Some also had disabilities themselves.
- Many had been longstanding advocates for people with disabilities.
- Some were close personal friends of advocates.
- Some were subjected to intense political pressures, especially when congressional hearings were held in their home districts.
- Some were influenced by Ford Foundation seminars on special education issues.

- Some strongly believed in a federal role in special education and for many years had sponsored federal education bills.
- Some were outraged by acts of local discrimination against people with disabilities.

In short, for many reasons and in many ways, there was a small but very powerful and active core of insider advocates in Congress for a much expanded, federal special education role.

State Precedents and Capacity

The state experience was also an important predecessor to the federal law. Some states already had enacted legislation to educate children with disabilities. Indeed, parent advocates had been successful at the state level and therefore had reason to believe that they might be successful at the federal level as well. Also, CEC had drafted a model state statute that could be easily adapted to become a federal law. In addition, the states had the capacity to sustain a massive federal intervention. State and local special education policies, practices, and personnel already existed; it was not necessary to build an infrastructure from scratch, although it clearly was necessary to adapt the existing infrastructure. Also, existing shared federal-state disability programs (for example, vocational rehabilitation) had established special education and other services for people with disabilities and were models for the new federal-state special education approach.

Ideological Precedents

Further, several congruent and compelling ideologies ascended to prominence (Turnbull, 1994). The New Frontier and Great Society agendas of the Kennedy and Johnson administrations rested on the political ideology of egalitarianism: disadvantaged status was inimical to the country's promise and potential. This perspective had its counterpart in the Supreme Court's assertion of the equal protection doctrine, authorizing the courts to undo the wrongs that unequal access to the political process had visited on individuals and groups disadvantaged by reason of their race, sex, economic condition, or other unchangeable traits, including disability. Also, the disability movement itself was converting to the normalization principle, which taught that, to the maximum extent possible, people with disabilities should have the same kinds of lives as nondisabled people (Wolfensberger, 1972).

Thus, stakeholders, precedents, ideologies, capacities, strategies, and ideologies converged around a single core idea—to provide a free appropriate public education to all students with disabilities, using massive federal aid and intervention to assist and direct the states. Multiple factors had serendipitously converged, and advocates had been alert and savvy enough to take advantage of them.

As time passed, it was inevitable that the courts would continually interpret IDEA and not always as child advocates would want. For each diluting interpretation, however, the advocates had a response: return to Congress to secure a clarifying or restoring amendment. This is exactly what they did, thus establishing a tripartite strategy—to advocate in the courts; or with the executive branch; or with the legislative branch. Their choice of forum was pragmatically dictated. This kind of political pragmatism is hardly new and undoubtedly also will be part of any strategy to reform early care and education, as Congress, the federal or state courts, the state legislatures, and the president and governors devise their own policies for children and families in an era of defederalized and block-granted social services.

Amending the Law for Infants and Toddlers

IDEA was strong and flexible enough to accommodate a new initiative, known as Part H—early intervention for infants and toddlers (zero to three). A small group of fewer than ten professionals were committed to legislation that would promote a family-centered orientation in early intervention. In a December 1984 midnight strategy session during the annual meeting of the Division of Early Childhood (a division of CEC), they began to formulate the key elements of Part H.

As fate would have it, this inner circle gathered a few months later at CEC's 1985 convention and received unwelcome catalytic news. A legislative aide for the House Select Education Subcommittee told them that there simply was "no way" for the early-intervention initiative to get off the ground when the Congress was hard-pressed for funds, and the Reagan administration was unwilling to expand domestic programs. The response of the professionals was equally direct: Surrender? Hell no! We've just begun to fight!

Again, key insiders made all the difference. In the case of the early-intervention legislation, it was Senator Lowell Weicker from Connecticut, whose son has Down syndrome and who had benefited greatly from early-intervention services. As Weicker engineered the legislation in the Senate, Representatives Pat Williams of Montana and Steve Bartlett of Texas did so in the House. Williams's niece is deaf—a fact that he noted when he accepted the Senate amendment to the House bill and began floor debate. During this time, parent organizations barraged senators and representatives with letters, telephone calls, and visits. They were the force that tipped the scales in Congress.

Again, context mattered. Congress was conscious of the disappointing outcomes of special education and of how expensive it was. Congress also realized how fiscally sound—and how advantageous for child development—it would be if programs could divert children from special education, reduce the time they spend in special education programs, prevent their institutionalization, and assist families in the development of their children (Hebbeler, Smith, & Black, 1991).

To avoid the risk that any amendments to IDEA's existing provisions for serving preschool children ages three to five would allow states to reduce or eliminate the law's requirements of them, advocates and legislators created a separate, wholly new program for children birth to age three and allowed it, and only it, to be debated. The new program sought to correct the mistakes in legal interpretation and service delivery that IDEA had inadvertently spawned. The new program was modeled on the early-intervention laws and programs enacted by some of the states themselves.

Infrastructure for Parent Advocacy: Implementing Laws

Just as the IDEA legislation grew incrementally, so too did a constituency of parents pushing for effective implementation. The parent movement now includes the traditional organizations that were early players in IDEA (for example, The Arc) and new federally funded and grassroots-sustained organizations that add a powerful presence to the advocacy movement—particularly to IDEA's implementation. This new segment of the parent movement includes Parent Training and Information Centers, Parent to Parent programs, Family-Directed Parent Resource Centers, and Partners in Policymaking.

Parent Training and Information Centers (PTIs), first authorized by Congress in 1983, train and provide information to parents of children with disabilities and to professionals who work with parents and children. There are sixty-seven such centers, with at least one in each state. Several of the centers work exclusively with minority parents and children. By law, the majority of the PTI governing boards must be parents. The centers receive technical assistance from a national center and from each other.

Currently, nearly twenty thousand families are being served by approximately 550 Parent to Parent programs in forty-seven states. There are sixteen statewide programs, and approximately ten states are developing statewide networks of local programs. Typically, the programs serve parents without regard to the type of disability their children have and are developed and run by volunteer parents on low budgets. The programs match a veteran parent who has successfully faced a certain challenge with a parent who is just beginning to deal with that challenge. The programs offer someone to listen and understand, information about the disabilities, information about community resources, assistance with referrals, and problem-solving support (Santelli, Turnbull, Marquis, & Lerner, 1993).

Partners in Policymaking is a program operating in forty states, in which state-planning councils on developmental disabilities teach families and individuals with disabilities to be community leaders. The councils provide participants with information, resources, and skills on such topics as the history of the parent movement and self-advocacy, rationales for inclusion of people with disabilities in generic services, state-of-the-art technologies and other services, strategies for analyzing county and state services, and strategies for identifying and acting on federal policy issues (Zirpoli, Hancox, Wieck, & Skarnulis, 1989; Zirpoli, 1992).

Parent-Directed Resource Centers merge the services of PTIs, Parent to Parent programs, Partners in Policymaking, and special projects. These new programs are comprehensive, community based, family centered, multifaceted, and family directed; they embody a one-stop-shopping strategy to meeting the needs of children with disabilities and their parents.

Efforts to create early care and education legislation can benefit enormously from the knowledge and political clout of the traditional and newer parent organizations.

Conclusion and Recommendations

One might be eager to leap to conclusions and recommendations for policy for early care and education in the 1990s, based on actions that led to federal special education policy. That would be a mistake: time, place, circumstance, and people are different.

The first significant difference is fiscal. At this writing in winter 1994, Congress has placed a cap on all discretionary spending and is attempting to cut spending on social services; at the very least, any new federal program must secure its funds from existing federal programs. From 1973 to 1975, however, when IDEA was first passed, there was no cap on discretionary funds, and there was a national willingness and capacity to raise and spend money.

Second, the ideology of the times is different. In the 1970s, the nation's mood was sympathetic to massive federal aid; liberalism, activist government, and a dominant central government role were acceptable. Today, a less activist federal government, privatization, and decentralization are barriers to federal initiatives.

Yet, there are lessons from IDEA's history that may be useful nowadays. Perhaps the greatest single factor in IDEA's success was the existence of a national movement. Parents, parent organizations, professionals, state and local officials, and members of Congress all coalesced around a single need and shared a single purpose—to respond to the discrimination that schools inflicted on students with disabilities. Moreover, they linked their alliance to the national priority of improved education and grounded their belief in the then unchallengeable ideologies of equal treatment, egalitarianism, and normalization. They relied on data about exclusion and misclassification. They took advantage of horror stories about institutional conditions and skillfully played them to the media. They used court victories to legitimize their legislative goals and built on existing state and local service-delivery capacities. Finally, they demonstrated the need for federal law and the capacities of state and local agencies to respond. Thus, adroit insider politics, fervid lobbying from key stakeholders, and strategically targeted local and regional congressional hearings were the keystones of a national movement.

The question is this: How can a national movement help the early care and education agenda? Federally funded and grassroots-initiated parent groups, such as Parent Training and Information Centers, Parent to Parent Programs, Partners in Policymaking, and Parent-Directed Family Resource Centers, could have benefits for families using early care and education services and could help create a special-interest constituency that could be quite formidable. Given the move to atomize decision making from a single federal source to fifty state capitals and simultaneously reduce federal funding of early care and education, it is clearly important for early care and education initiatives to create the capacities to influence decision making at the local, state, and national levels.

The development of IDEA makes the amend-and-expand strategy appealing for early care and education. There may be possibilities to extend the programs already authorized under IDEA to fund more early care and education. Also, early care and education programs may be funded in part from other existing appropriations for schools or health care. But, to succeed with any of these strategies, early care and education advocates must identify and support well-placed insiders in federal and local arenas. If block granting of federal funds is to be the new fiscal and regulatory approach, it is not inconceivable that the state governments themselves would adopt a similar laissez-faire approach, giving local governments and providers a great deal more leeway in early care and education decision making.

Assuming that defederalization and further decentralization are inevitable, it seems particularly important for early care and education advocates to create national networks—"interstate insider networks"—that facilitate sharing of information and policy initiatives. What works in Kansas or Nebraska may not be useful in New York or New Jersey, but one will not know that unless the early care advocates in these states can tap into one another's knowledge about policies, program delivery, and policy advocacy.

One of the greatest challenges in developing an empowered-parent movement for early care and education may be the perception of many parents that adequate services already exist for a finite period of time (birth to eight). By contrast, a primary motivation for the parent movement in the disability field was that no services or only deplorable services existed for an indeterminable period of time. Thus, the outrage created by unavailable and inadequate services and the chronicity of parental responsibility propelled parents to strong action. A long-term strategy in mobilizing a parent constituency for educational services for children from birth to age eight is to prepare people before they have children so that they can "hit the ground running" as consumer advocates when their children are young. This involves building motivation, knowledge, and skills in advance of parenthood.

Increasingly, diverse stakeholders in the disability field are practicing greater collaboration and sharing of diverse ideas and strategies to advance consumer goals. For example, a number of the professional organizations are encouraging the membership of families and policy makers. In addition, family organizations are reaching out more to include professionals in their training workshops and are developing models that foster partnerships. These approaches, too, could be useful in early care and education.

A major challenge is to develop energized and empowered leaders at all career levels, including senior leaders, midcareer professionals, young professionals, and the brightest and best high school graduates with whom exists the greatest opportunity for mentoring and leadership development. Patterning somewhat on the Partners in Policymaking model, a worthwhile effort would be to fund an annual "cohort," which would encompass people from each of the stakeholder groups, who would come together for advanced leadership and advocacy training. Training would emphasize early care education issues, state-of-the-art policy and service delivery options, process skills (including communication, negotiation, time management, balancing professional and personal responsibilities), and empowerment. Within each cohort, there could be responsibilities for a young child advocacy project. There could also be a collective project of national significance.

The program could be devised so that it would carry prestige and would offer unique learning opportunities, networking, and personal growth and professional development avenues.

A prime opportunity exists for early care and education to collaborate with parents of children with disabilities. Although in the past, disability advocacy has focused almost exclusively on children with disabilities, efforts are focusing increasingly on the responsiveness of typical programs to individual differences.

It could be helpful to replicate some of the activities that laid the foundation for IDEA and its amendments—private or public funding of interagency task forces, in-service education of congressional staff, policy analysis and model state laws, consultation by early care and education specialists with national and state public and private associations, demonstration programs, public and private study groups and political action committees (or their equivalents), development of legislative proposals (such as federal-state partnership laws like IDEA or tax incentive–based strategies for individuals or employers), and analysis and dissemination of information about state laws and programs that work. The key is to have a multipronged strategy for advocacy—one that addresses and builds on work in the federal and state government arenas and the private sector.

If anything is clear, it is that the history of IDEA—the synchrony of stakeholders in the law reform process—informs early care and education advocacy. Moreover, it is just as clear that, when the prospects seemed least promising or most challenging, advocates for IDEA redoubled their efforts. Today, as the very core national priorities are shifting, a redoubling of advocates' efforts for early care and education is necessary, but it may be inadequate without strategic planning based on history.

Note

1. Although some of the literature on the history of IDEA is cited in this chapter, a large part of the chapter relies on personal communications with key IDEA actors from the early to mid-1970s. They are A. Abeson, May 1993; T. Gilhool, May 1993; F. Weintraub, May 1993; J. Duncan, May 1993; P. Forsyth, May 1993; H. Leibergott, July 1993; J. Gallagher, May 1993; and B. Smith, May 1993. We are grateful to them not just for their assistance in the preparation of this

chapter but more especially for their intrepid advocacy on behalf of children with disabilities.

In the expanded version of this chapter, published by the Bush Center in Child Development and Social Policy, Yale University, we describe in much greater detail the history of IDEA and the implications that history has for early care and education policy advocacy.

References

Brown v. *Board of Education,* 347 U.S. 483 (1954).

Hebbeler, K. M., Smith, B. J., & Black, T. L. (1991, October/November). Federal early childhood special education policy: A model for the improvement of services for children with disabilities. *Exceptional Children,* pp. 104–112.

Individuals with Disabilities Education Act (IDEA), 20 U.S.C. Secs. 1400–1485 (Supp. 1995).

La Vor, M. L. (1976a). Federal legislation for exceptional persons: A history. In F. Weintraub, A. Abeson, J. Ballard, & M. L. La Vor (Eds.), *Public policy and the education of exceptional children* (pp. 96–111). Reston, Va.: Council for Exceptional Children.

La Vor, M. L. (1976b). Time and circumstances. In F. Weintraub, A. Abeson, J. Ballard, & M. L. La Vor (Eds.), *Public policy and the education of exceptional children* (pp. 293–303). Reston, Va.: Council for Exceptional Children.

Mills v. *D.C. Board of Education,* 348 F. Supp. 866 (D.D.C. 1972); contempt proceedings, EHLR 551:643 (D.D.C. 1980).

Pennsylvania Association for Retarded Citizens v. *Commonwealth of Pennsylvania (PARC),* 334 F. Supp. 1257, 343 F. Supp. 279 (E.D. Pa. 1971, 1972).

Santelli, B., Turnbull, A. P., Marquis, J., & Lerner, E. (1993, Spring). Parent to parent programs: Ongoing support for parents of young adults with special needs. *Journal of Vocational Rehabilitation, 3*(2), 25–37.

Turnbull, H. R. (1994). *Free appropriate education: Law and education of children with disabilities* (1994 rev.). Denver: Love.

Wolfensberger, W. (1972). *The principle of normalization in human services.* Downsview, Ontario: National Institute on Mental Retardation.

Zirpoli, T. J. (1992). *Partners in policymaking: Quantitative and qualitative outcomes the first five years.* Unpublished manuscript. University of St. Thomas.

Zirpoli, T. J., Hancox, D., Wieck, C., & Skarnulis, E. R. (1989). *Journal of the Association for Persons with Severe Handicaps, 14*(2), 163–167.

Part Four

Creating a Quality Early Care and Education System

Chapter Seventeen

A Vision for a Quality Early Care and Education System

Sharon L. Kagan
Nancy E. Cohen

The chapters in this volume have generated an abundance of provocative and promising ideas for improving the quality of early care and education programs and for building a quality infrastructure. The question remains, however: What would a quality early care and education system—including programs and an infrastructure—look like? In this chapter, we distill the thoughtful presentations in the preceding chapters, as well as four years of inquiry, analysis, and synthesis as part of the *Quality 2000* initiative described in the Preface, into a vision for a quality early care and education system that would meet the needs of children, families, and the nation. Stated briefly, the overarching goal of the vision is that by the year 2010, quality early care and education programs will be available and accessible to all children from birth to age five whose parents choose to enroll them, and the programs will be supported by a well-funded, coherent, and coordinated infrastructure.

The vision that follows is a systemic approach to solving the quality crisis in early care and education. It advances ideas to be refined and implemented over a fifteen-year period. It is not about reform that tinkers at the edges; it is an immodest proposal that challenges the nation to reform, redefine, and re-create enduring policies, structures, and networks. Some of the elements of the proposed vision will be quite controversial; others will be accepted more easily. Some are modest in scope and could be implemented relatively easily; others will demand Herculean reforms that will occur only with a dedicated national commitment. It is not about adding more disparate programs to what exists, although additional services and funds are essential to the vision. Rather, the vision should be regarded as a different approach to how we care for and educate young children in this country.

There is probably never a good time, politically, to discuss radically revamping early care and education nationwide—particularly when this change will require significant new funds. But 1996, the time of this writing, is arguably one of the worst times. A major shift in American federalism is being seriously debated, including the federal government's devolving responsibility for many social services to the states, reducing federal funding, and cutting taxes. The popularity of government and bureaucracies may be at an all-time low. This vision has been developed with the knowledge that a proposal requiring significant new funds, creating new institutions, and departing from business as usual is likely to meet with resistance. We are persuaded, however, that many Americans are disturbed by the inadequate programs in which young children spend long days; they are recognizing that learning and health begin in children's earliest months and years; and they are realizing that more coordination, higher standards, and increased intentionality are needed to achieve the quality programs that young children, their families, and the country need. A quality early care and education system must not be monolithic or inflexible; it should be agile and flexible, reflecting local needs and preferences.

At a time of volatile, politically motivated social service transformation, fundamental change in *any* direction is possible. At such a time, it is particularly important to have a concrete vision for a quality early care and education system that should and can be achieved. The vision begins with an expanded conceptualization of program quality and continues with a presentation of the components of a quality infrastructure—parent engagement, practitioner development and licensing, facility licensing and accreditation, funding and financing, and governance.

A Vision for Quality Programs

Quality early care and education programs are the centerpiece of a quality system. This vision specifies how conceptions of program quality need to be expanded to address a range of perspectives, as well as the broader contexts in which children-practitioner relationships—a key to quality—exist.

Use Child Results to Improve Pedagogy

By the year 2010, the effects that programs have on children's development must be integral parts of conceptions of quality in early care and education, expanding on traditional definitions of quality that have been based on program inputs, such as staff training and education, compensation, child-to-staff ratios, and group size. This shift from an emphasis on inputs to one based on results calls for practitioners and parents to observe youngsters and to collect information about them for the purposes of program and pedagogical planning and improvement. Parents, practitioners, and policy makers need to identify the results that they want children to achieve, results that cut across multiple domains of development, including physical well-being and motor development, language usage, social and emotional development, learning approaches, and cognition and general knowledge (Kagan, Moore, & Bredekamp, 1995). A thorough review of current assessment practices is also needed, discerning those that hold promise for elaboration or replication and identifying areas in which new assessments need to be developed.

Encourage Alternate Approaches to Organizing Staff and Children

By the year 2010, early care and education staff should have at their disposal an array of approaches for utilizing staff and grouping children, approaches that maintain warm, secure relationships between children and practitioners and that give programs more flexibility in using their resources to maximize quality in creative and cost-effective ways. Early care and education programs in a range of countries suggest that there are multiple ways to provide quality programs for young children. In addition, there is mounting evidence that individual structural indicators, including child-to-staff ratios, may not lead to quality in and of themselves (Hofferth & Chaplin, 1994; Howes & Marx, 1992; Phillips & others, forthcoming). Programs should be allowed and encouraged to work with children in mixed-age groups and to adjust child-to-staff ratios and group size for different activities and pedagogical purposes. In addition, we need to research carefully whether programs should be allowed to have higher child-to-staff ratios for three- to five-year-olds if staff are well trained and educated. However, under no circumstances should a call for research be construed as support for making linked changes in child-to-staff ratio and staff preparation requirements before the consequences of taking such an approach in the United States are understood.

Improve Organizational Climates

By the year 2010, the overall organizational climate of all early care and education programs should nurture staff, parents, and families and should support productive practitioner-parent relationships. To bolster the quality of early care and education programs for children, programs need to place greater emphasis on the nonpedagogical aspects of staff's work and on aspects of programs that are not confined to classrooms. Early care and education programs must also support practitioners (Jorde-Bloom, 1988), making them feel that they can turn to colleagues, administrators, and parents to ask questions and receive assistance; giving them opportunities for reflection and learning; and helping them meet their own family needs. The organizational climate of early care and education programs should create a mutually reinforcing positive environment for interactions among practitioners, children, and parents.

Consider Quality from Children's Perspective—Across Programs and Across Time

By the year 2010, early care and education programs and researchers need to expand conceptions of quality to take into account interactions among all the programs children attend, over the course of a day and over the course of years. Definitions of quality have traditionally been construed to reflect the quality of a program as it is assessed at a single point in time, not as it is experienced by a child in combination with other programs over time. Researchers should track children over the course of the day and over the course of their early years, noting the *cumulative* impact of early care and education experiences. Practitioners should assure that children make smooth transitions from one early care and education program to another on a given day, or from year to year, as well as from early care and education to school. Policy makers should craft legislation that minimizes transitions to those that benefit children and families.

Develop Multiculturalism

By the year 2010, early care and education programs need to respond effectively to the diversity of the children and families who use them. Multiculturalism is crucial to quality practice in early care and education programs. Whether very young children feel accepted or alienated sets the stage for subsequent attitudes about and performance in school (Phillips & Crowell, 1994). Quality programs need, at a minimum, to expose young children to people who are different from them, to promote cross-cultural understanding and respect among children, and to develop all children's primary language and cultural identity (Chang, Tobiassen, & Muckelroy, forthcoming; Derman-Sparks & the ABC Task Force, 1989). For programs to be truly multicultural, staff need to understand their own beliefs and biases and come to understand and appreciate the cultures of the families in their programs.

Link Family Child Care Providers with Supportive Organizations

By the year 2010, there needs to be an organization in every community with the responsibility for supporting all family child care providers. Although the quality of family child care is as problematic as that of center-based programs in this country (Cost, Quality & Child Outcomes Study Team, 1995; Galinsky, Howes, Kontos, & Shinn, 1994), family child care differs fundamentally in its decentralization, informality, and the isolation of providers. Based on successful efforts in a growing number of communities in the United States and abroad, community-based organizations (or collaboratives of organizations) are an efficient and effective way to provide supportive services to large numbers of family child care providers, to connect parents to family child care, and to serve as planning hubs for family child care—all with the ultimate goal of improving and maintaining the quality of family child care on a broad scale. Existing organizations with close ties to the community (such as child care resource and referral agencies, family child care–provider associations, community action agencies, and community colleges) should become family child care support organizations-collaboratives. Family child care support organizations-collaboratives, together with family and parent support programs in communities, could also offer supportive services to providers caring for related children.

Promote Integrated Services

By the year 2010, linkages should exist among early care and education programs and other child and family services in their communities to meet the comprehensive needs of children and families. Such linkages should include coordinating early care and education, health, social, and other services; facilitating child and family transitions among programs; and holding joint activities, from community events to staff training. Linkages can expedite and improve the quality of services for children and families, minimize duplication, and make the most efficient use of resources.

A Vision for Parent Engagement

Parents should be integrally engaged in a quality early care and education system and should be effective consumers, contributing to definitions of quality and being partners in programs. The vision for parent engagement builds on traditional conceptions of parent involvement in early care and education programs, which have, historically, been important to the field.

Help Parents Become Effective Consumers

By the year 2010, all parents of young children should have user-friendly information about the availability of early care and education programs, including how to distinguish good- from mediocre- and poor-quality programs and how to find the right program for their particular child. In our free market of early care and education, fueled by parent choice, the quality of programs children attend is dependent in part on parents being effective and discriminating consumers. The field needs to develop and expand strategies for helping parents choose programs, such as having well-trained child care counselors at workplaces and community organizations to help parents navigate the maze of early care and education programs; giving parents access to program ratings made by professionals and experienced parents; finding ways for parents to spend more time observing programs before they choose; giving parents more objective information about programs (such as levels of staff education and training, program accreditation, staff salary ranges, staff turnover, and facility-licensing reports); and conducting tours of high-quality programs. People who work with parents of young children, including pediatricians and their staffs, hospital staffs, and Lamaze teachers, need to understand the importance of early care and education and know where to refer parents for assistance. All consumer education activities need to evolve from being essentially one-way parent education (from professionals to parents) to two-way dialogues about quality.

Integrate Parents' Perspectives into Definitions of Quality

By the year 2010, in addition to expanding the definition of quality in the ways discussed previously, the definition must be expanded to integrate the needs and perspectives of families. Parents have opinions about how their children should be taught, about discipline, and about other more value-based practices, which may differ markedly from basic building blocks of professional practice (Powell, 1989, 1994). Researchers and professionals need to explore which aspects of professional practice are really crucial to positive child results in all cases and which aspects of professional practice could be more flexible in responding to parent perspectives. Parents need to be included in dialogues to develop quality definitions—such as those for child outcomes, accreditation, facility licensing, and teacher education curricula—so that their needs and perspectives will be better understood and addressed.

Promote Parents as Partners in Their Children's Programs

By the year 2010, all parents should be partners in their children's early care and education programs in ways that meet the needs of both parents and programs. This perspective transforms traditional parent involvement, in which parents are treated as helpers who learn from staff, into full-fledged parent engagement, in which the strengths of all parents are acknowledged and the flow of knowledge and assistance between parents and staff is two-way. To begin with, parents must feel welcome whenever they visit programs, and the best effort possible must be made to address their concerns and needs. Regular practitioner-parent communication about children—what happened during the day and what is going on in children's lives at home—is a basic building block of parent-practitioner partnerships. Additional effective roles for engaged parents include parents serving on decision-making bodies, observing and working with children, organizing and participating in activities for parents and families, participating in staff development and program accreditation, serving as program ombudsmen to resolve parent and practitioner concerns, and promoting service coordination and integration among neighborhood and community agencies (Epstein, 1995). Parents need to be given the resources to initiate activities that spark their interest and that meet their needs, as well as those of their children and of programs.

Make Workplaces Family Friendly

By the year 2010, all workplaces should be family friendly. This is a basic condition that business alone can assure for our nation's families. Family-friendly workplaces offer employees benefits that include having understanding and responsive supervisors; having flexibility in scheduling the workday; having time to find, monitor, and participate in children's early care and education programs and family events; having the option of part-time work with partial benefits; having paid sick days to care for sick children; and having job-protected and partially paid maternity and parental leave (Galinsky, Bond, & Friedman, 1993). Family-friendly workplaces recognize that workers who can balance work and family responsibilities are more effective at both.

A Vision for Individual Licensing and Professional Development

The practitioners who work with young children are the cornerstone of quality in early care and education (Whitebook, Howes,

& Phillips, 1989). The following vision calls for significantly increasing practitioner qualifications to provide a solid foundation for increasing the quality of programs (Galinsky, Howes, & Kontos, 1995; Morgan & others, 1993).

Require Staff Licensing and Establish a System

By the year 2010, all staff with responsibility for young children in both centers and family child care homes should be required to hold licenses, available on completion of high levels of training and education and demonstration of competency in working with children and families. Although there would still be open access to entry-level positions in the field, licenses—and the education, training, and competency that go with them—would be required for staff to have responsibility for young children and for staff to enter the profession. As Mitchell describes in Chapter Six, a variety of occupations in the United States demonstrate that the way to set standards for staff is by licensing them directly, not by including staff requirements in facility licensing. Licensing individuals would help ensure the basic quality of programs; would increase the efficiency of facility licensing; would demonstrate that early care and education is a profession; would help increase compensation for staff; and would facilitate training coherence and coordination, as well as career mobility (American Public Health Association & American Academy of Pediatrics, 1992). To create a system for licensing individuals, state laws would need to be passed that require individuals to be licensed. In addition, professional licensing boards (collaborative efforts of state governments and early care and education professionals) would need to be established to set the standards for each level of licensure, to approve the competency assessments, and to manage the overall licensing process.

Require Lifelong Learning

By the year 2010, continuing education—lifelong learning—should be required of all staff working with young children. Licensing systems need to require all personnel to continue to increase their knowledge and skills, whether staff remain in the same jobs or pursue new positions in the field. In addition to requirements, there should be incentives—such as increased compensation and jobs that have different or more responsibility—to encourage staff to pursue ongoing training and education.

Link All Training and Education to Academic Credit

By the year 2010, all training and education required for licensing should be of such quality that it carries academic credit. The goal is for all training and education that counts toward licensing to be integrated into the higher education system, in order to facilitate staff attaining initial and advanced degrees. In addition, institutions of higher learning should provide for assessment of prior learning, so that demonstrated skills and knowledge from valuable noncredit training and other experience can be granted appropriate credit. Training registries might be created to monitor the quality of informal training and workshops and to determine the level of credit that might be awarded. In addition, institutions of higher education need to create articulation agreements that enable students to transfer credits and apply degrees earned in one institution toward degrees in other schools.

Expand Training and Education Content

By the year 2010, the content of education and training should help staff develop the broad-based skills they need to serve children and families effectively. More transdisciplinary training, particularly at intermediate and advanced levels, needs to be developed. Curricula and sequences need to be revised and developed to address the broad-based knowledge and skills that staff need to be competent in today's early care and education programs. Specifically, training is needed in engaging and supporting parents and families; multiculturalism; observing and assessing children to improve staff practice; working with mixed-age groups, larger groups, and team teaching; working with infants and toddlers; and working with children with special needs (Morgan & others, 1993; Willer, 1994).

Make Training and Education Affordable

By the year 2010, all staff should be able to afford the education and training they need to secure individual licenses. Increasing practitioner wages in early care and education to levels comparable to roles in other fields that require similar levels of responsibility, education, and experience will be a huge step toward making training and education more affordable. (See Vision for Funding and Financing section for further discussion of compensation.) In addition, as early care and education training becomes better integrated into the higher education system, schools should step up efforts to connect early care and education students with traditional sources of funding, including government and private loans, grants, and loan-forgiveness programs. To facilitate the transition to a quality early care and education system, however, it will also be important to focus new, additional financial assistance on helping the current early care and education staff—low-income staff in particular—to increase their training and education to meet the new standards.

Promote Management and Leadership Expertise

By the year 2010, there should be adequate management and leadership capacity in the field to maintain the quality system described herein. Focused management and leadership development efforts, at the local, state, and national levels, should include professional associations, mentoring programs, advanced management degree programs and credentials, and "leadership for children and families" programs across the human services.

A Vision for Facility Licensing and Program Accreditation

The following vision describes an intentional, coherent, and coordinated approach to facility licensing and program accreditation to replace what has been deemed a haphazard approach (Adams, 1990, 1995; Center for Career Development in Early Care and Education at Wheelock College, 1995) and to ensure that the facilities and programs in which young children spend their days promote health, safety, and child development.

Develop Streamlined Facility-Licensing Standards with Options

By the year 2010, it should be a basic consumer right of parents that all early care and education programs are not harmful to children. Working hand in hand with licensing for individuals, facility licensing should prevent children from harm (Adams, 1995), including the spread of disease, the risk of fire, the risk of injury, and the risk of developmental impairment (Morgan, 1995). To this end, the areas that state regulations address should be streamlined to focus on basic health, safety, and development, regulating such aspects of programs as safety of physical facility and equipment; adequacy of health practices and supplies; quality of nutrition; thoroughness of child immunizations; and basic standards for unlicensed staff, such as criminal background checks. Facility licensing should maintain standards for staffing levels that allow programs alternatives to the traditional approach of low child-to-staff ratios, same-age groups, and static group size. Regulations might allow or make more explicit the ability of center-based programs to organize children in mixed-age groups; might regulate staffing levels in any program by group or program size to allow more flexibility in staff assignment throughout the day; and—if research demonstrates that well-qualified teachers can work with larger numbers of children and maintain or increase quality—might allow higher child-to-staff ratios for three-to-five-year-olds when staff are well qualified. States should not, however, give programs the option of raising child-to-adult ratios even if staff are well qualified until careful research demonstrates whether this approach can maintain quality. Though states should retain responsibility for setting and enforcing facility-licensing requirements, national regulatory coherence should be promoted via a set of national licensing guidelines, developed with broad-based participation.

Eliminate Exemptions

By the year 2010, all early care and education programs offering their services to the public should be required by law to be licensed. Although it is currently a widespread practice, legally exempting programs—including some family child care homes, church-based programs, part-day programs, and school-based programs—undermines the quality of the overall system, as well as public confidence and equity among sectors of the market. All programs that are available to the general public should be required to meet comparable standards. Although the vast majority of programs for young children should be licensed, there are care situations that states would not have an obligation to license, including people caring only for related children (care by "kin") and people caring only for the child or children of one friend (care by "kith"). These caregivers are offering services just to relatives or friends, not to the public at large. In addition, states would not be obligated to license people caring for the child or children of just one family (in the provider's home), because the parents are in effect hiring the provider to offer a service just to their family, similar to parents hiring a nanny or au pair to work in the family's home. The state should not be obligated to license such employer-employee situations.

Enforce Facility Licensing

By the year 2010, state monitoring and enforcement systems should employ positive, incentive-based strategies to support all programs in meeting basic licensing standards. Incentive-based strategies include calibrating the number of monitoring visits with programs' histories of violations; sharing licensing reports with all parents and publicizing to parents lists of programs in compliance with and violation of state standards; writing standards in simple language and giving programs options for implementation; coordinating the currently separate and fragmented protections of health, building safety, fire safety, and other requirements at the state and local level; exempting family child care homes from local zoning restrictions and conditional use permits; and encouraging staff to report program violations by using whistle-blowing laws to afford job protections (Center for Career Development in Early Care and Education at Wheelock College, 1995; Gormley, 1995). Programs in violation of standards need to be given the time and assistance to improve, but if they do not, licensing entities should invoke effective sanctions and penalties, such as posting licensing violations on the doors of noncomplying programs, imposing daily fines on programs that have violated basic requirements until the violations are fixed, and closing programs that present an immediate threat to children and do not address serious violations. To be effective, such a monitoring and enforcement approach needs to be implemented by a sufficient number of staff who understand the procedures and philosophies of early care and education programs, know how to provide supportive technical assistance to help programs meet standards, and have the legal training and resources to use more punitive measures if necessary.

Promote Accreditation

By the year 2010, half of all early care and education centers and a quarter of all family child care homes should be accredited, and additional add-on accreditation specialties should be available. Whereas facility and individual licensing should provide for basic quality, accreditation is needed to uplift mediocre programs to good and good programs to excellent (Bredekamp & Glowacki, 1995). Incentives need to be provided to encourage programs to become accredited. Add-on accreditation specialties—for example, family support, caring for infants and toddlers, caring for school age children, working with children with special needs, working with bilingual children—should be developed for existing accreditations to encourage programs to continue improving. The vision calls for half of all centers to be accredited by the year 2010, but just one quarter of the family child care homes, acknowledging that at present 80 percent to 90 percent of family child care homes are not even licensed (Willer & others, 1991).

A Vision for Funding and Financing

The proposal for funding and financing of a quality early care and education system is strategic. Quality early care and education is an economically powerful service. First, every dollar invested in quality early care and education promotes child development, leads to children becoming ready for school, and helps to assure their future success. Second, investment dollars create jobs for practitioners. And third, many of the dollars invested in quality early care and education support parents working. This vision is about increased costs but also about increased productivity, achievement, and successful lives.

Raise New Public Funds

By the year 2010, there should be mechanisms to raise the necessary public funds to support a single, comprehensive early care and education system, including a quality infrastructure, quality early care and education programs, and paid parental leave for the parents of very young children. In fiscal year 1992, about one-quarter of total annual spending for early care and education came from government expenditures or tax credits, and about three-quarters came from out-of-pocket expenditures by families (U.S. Department of Commerce, 1993). Community organizations and businesses made relatively small, though important, cash and in-kind contributions as well (Cost, Quality & Child Outcomes Study Team, 1995). This vision calls for the mixed funding of early care and education to continue but for the public at large—via the government—to pick up more of the tab. As is the case with school, parents cannot bear the cost of early care and education single-handedly.

The federal government should take the lead role in making early care and education programs affordable—in generating revenue—because the federal government is uniquely suited to raising funds across richer and poorer states and communities and to spreading the cost of programs across people's lifetimes. State governments are less promising candidates for being the prime funders of a quality early care and education system, because state governments are likely to have multiple, competing financial demands on them in the near future—including increasing school enrollments, more children in poverty, slower economic growth, and reduced federal investment in social programs. Though the federal government should raise the bulk of the funds for early care and education, state governments should continue and expand their support of early childhood programs, perhaps focusing on three- and four-year-olds. Federal spending should provide incentives for state spending by continuing requirements for matching federal funds and continuation of state funding efforts.

Multiple funding-generation mechanisms at the federal level will likely be needed to cover the costs of a quality early care and education system, and several approaches should be carefully considered, including individual and corporate income taxes; federal payroll taxes and trust funds; sales and excise taxes; savings-and-loan approaches; expenditure cutting in other areas; using Temporary Disability Insurance (a modified unemployment insurance system); and additional employer contributions to fund paid parental leave (Carnegie Task Force on Meeting the Needs of

Young Children, 1994; Hartmann, Yoon, Spalter-Roth, & Shaw, 1995). Another approach would be to raise funds for early care and education as part of a larger revenue generation package, which would raise funds for several social services with which families currently struggle, such as early care and education for young children and long-term care for the elderly.

In addition to the federal government raising funds from the public at large, business should contribute directly to a quality early care and education system via a payroll tax or corporate income tax. Business will benefit directly from a quality early care and education system and should contribute directly to the cost. Contributions and in-kind donations also should continue to be encouraged from community organizations, such as houses of worship, United Ways, and volunteer groups. These contributions promote quality programs and linkages and help weave the fabric of strong communities.

Shore up the Infrastructure

By the year 2010, a portion of all government funding for early care and education—we estimate about 10 percent—needs to be invested directly into building and maintaining the infrastructure. Funding for the infrastructure should help create and maintain mechanisms for parent information and engagement; for data collection, planning, governance, and evaluation; for practitioner professional development and licensing; for facility licensing and enforcement; and for program accreditation. Part of this 10 percent of funds should also support inventive financing approaches to improving and expanding the physical infrastructure—the actual facilities (centers and family child care homes) in which children spend their days.

Make Quality Programs Affordable

By the year 2010, a portion of the remaining 90 percent of government funding should be devoted to making quality programs available and affordable to all families with young children who choose to enroll in them. Government funding would make up the difference between what parents could afford to pay for programs, based on their incomes, and the full cost of quality programs. The full cost of quality programs would include increased salaries for early care and education staff, who must be compensated at levels comparable to what personnel with similar education and experience earn in other fields (Cost, Quality & Child Outcomes Study Team, 1995; Willer, 1990).

In this vision for increased public funding of early care and education programs, parents would continue to be able to choose among programs run by a variety of service providers, including nonprofits, for-profits, family child care, Head Start, schools, and houses of worship. As discussed in the licensing sections above, all programs would be required to have facility licenses and licensed staff.

In addition, some public funds for early care and education programs should be used to support directly programs in low-income communities, giving them the means to provide the comprehensive services needed by children and families living in poverty. These funds could be used to continue to support or to expand Head Start and other comprehensive, quality programs.

Make Paid Parental Leave Available

By the year 2010, a portion of the remaining 90 percent of public funds for early care and education should be devoted to making paid parental leave available to the parents of very young children. Although parents are the most appropriate caregivers for their infants, many do not have the financial resources to stop working when their children are very young. Paid parental leave is the major approach for providing care for very young children in most industrialized countries. Although parents should have the choice of enrolling their infants in early care and education programs while they work, working parents should also have the option of taking time off to care for their infants themselves.

A Vision for Governance

The following vision for governance is built on the premise that by the year 2010, federal, state, and local governments should have clearly differentiated roles in planning, coordinating, and supporting quality early care and education programs and a quality infrastructure, replacing the current division of labor that is rife with gaps and duplication (Gormley, 1995; Kagan, Goffin, Golub, & Pritchard, 1995; U.S. Advisory Committee on Intergovernmental Relations, 1994). This vision builds on Gormley's consideration (Chapter Nine) of which levels of government should be responsible for which aspects of a quality system, namely, that federal government should focus on *affordability*; state government on *quality*; and local government on *availability*.

Create Mechanisms for Results-Based Accountability

By the year 2010, the nation, states, and localities should have mechanisms in place to promote results-based accountability, including assessing and reporting outcomes for preschool children (ages three to five). In the vision for quality programs, we called for practitioners to assess child-based results of the children with whom they work, to help them improve their practice. In this vision for governance, we call for results-based accountability to provide the nation, states, and localities with information regarding the overall status of preschool children (ages three to five) and to hold programs, communities, states, and the nation accountable for the well-being of young children and their families. Currently, the nation, states, localities, and programs are held publicly accountable—at best—for the amount of services delivered, for the manner in which they are delivered, and perhaps for the cost. Under results-based accountability, they would be held accountable for concrete, measurable improvements in the lives of children and their families (Schorr, 1994). Results-based accountability systems must go beyond assessing child-based results and must also consider the contexts in which children develop. Child and family conditions, service availability and quality, and systemic outcomes must also be assessed and related back to child outcomes in order for professionals, parents, policy makers, and the public to understand the circumstances in which children are developing and how to improve child outcomes effectively.

The following steps are necessary to institute results-based accountability systems. First, appropriate child results must be identified (Kagan, Rosenkoetter, & Cohen, 1996). Second, data must be collected on these results, and the results must be measured appropriately (Shepard, 1994). Third, data must be reported to parents, policy makers, and the public at large in comprehensible terms. And fourth, programs that are not helping children achieve the desired outcomes need to receive assistance to improve their services, or funds need to be moved to other programs.

Promote Federal Government Roles Best Suited to Its Strengths

By the year 2010, the federal government should establish broad goals for child results; should coordinate the collection of uniform data on child results nationwide; should hold states accountable; should provide incentives for states and localities to develop governance bodies for early care and education; and should promote innovation, best practices, and information sharing among states and localities. These are roles for which the federal government has a comparative advantage.

First, the federal government should establish broad goals for child results, to guide states as they develop standards for child results and to guide communities as they develop benchmarks to meet state standards and national goals. Second, the federal government should coordinate the collection of uniform data on child results nationwide, to provide a national picture of progress useful for policy, planning, and accountability. Third, given that the federal government should raise the bulk of funds, it should also have the responsibility of holding states (and indirectly communities) accountable for moving toward and achieving the goals for child results. This will include developing a process to track state and community achievement, broadly publicizing the results, providing rewards for states (and indirectly for communities) that show continual improvement and targeting assistance to those that do not, and promoting public understanding of how America's children and families are faring and of the importance of development in the early years of life. Fourth, the federal government should provide incentives to states and localities to establish governance bodies for early care and education, such as the state early care and education boards and local early care and education boards described in the next section. Finally, the federal government is well suited to promoting innovation, best practices, and information sharing, by funding and evaluating demonstration projects, facilitating state and local networking to exchange information on best practices, and developing resources and providing other technical assistance to states and localities.

Create State Early Care and Education Boards

By the year 2010, every state should have a permanent state early care and education board to plan, coordinate, and administer early care and education statewide. State boards should institute an ongoing, consolidated state-planning process to improve the quality of early care and education services throughout the state and across the sectors. State boards should also establish state standards for results for preschool children (ages three to five) in early care and education settings, customizing the national goals to address the states' unique constellations of resources, strengths, needs, and priorities. In addition, state boards should make decisions concerning how to allocate the public early care and education funds for the infrastructure discussed earlier (approximately 10 percent of all public funds for early care and education), as well as how to allocate the remaining funds to help parents pay for programs and take paid parental leave (approximately 90 percent of all funds). State boards should also decide how funds reserved for building and maintaining the state infrastructure should be spent, including the development of integrated systems of facility licensing and individual licensing. Finally, given that they will be providing funds to the local early care and education boards for infrastructure development, state boards should hold the local boards accountable for achieving agreed-on local benchmarks and contributing toward the achievement of state standards and national goals.

Create Local Early Care and Education Boards

By the year 2010, every school district or county should have a permanent local early care and education board, autonomous from the school boards and responsible for coordinating the care and education of children birth to age five. Whereas school boards have responsibility for both governance and service provision of education for children ages five to eighteen, local boards would focus on the governance of early care and education for children birth to age five—influencing, shaping, and leveraging quality from the mixed-sector, free-market delivery system. Local boards would set in motion an ongoing planning process, involving consumers and other community members, to assess community needs, coordinate efforts, and address how remaining gaps in programs and the infrastructure should be addressed. Local boards should also establish local performance benchmarks for child results and services predicated on broad-based consensus among consumers and other community members, benchmarks that customize state standards and national goals for child results to local strengths, needs, priorities, and resources. In addition, local boards would make decisions about how local infrastructure funds are spent to promote the availability of programs, including coordinating existing programs, providing incentives for the development of new services to address unmet needs, and funding demonstration and ongoing projects to expand the supply of needed services.

Conclusion

The vision described herein for a quality early care and education system—quality programs and a quality infrastructure—would significantly help alleviate the quality crisis in early care and education. The vision builds on the responsive relationships between practitioners and children, calling for programs to meet expanded standards of quality as defined by both parents and professionals, which address the broad contexts in which children develop. Quality programs will help young children achieve positive outcomes. Parents will be fully engaged in the early care and education system, as effective consumers and partners in their children's programs. The vision calls for licensing requirements for both staff and facilities to reflect quality standards for early care and education. These standards should operate hand in hand to provide basic quality programs that protect children from harm and that provide parents with basic consumer protections. Program accreditation is recommended to build on individual and facility licenses, promoting higher levels of quality. Finally, the vision flows from the premise that all early care and education programs need to be funded and governed in ways that support quality—ensuring that resources are adequate and effectively utilized, shoring up the infrastructure, reducing fragmentation, promoting equity, strengthening shared decision making at the local and state levels, and holding programs accountable for results. In the next and last chapter, we describe the process of achieving this vision and how a range of players can help make the vision a reality.

References

Adams, G. (1990). *Who knows how safe? The status of state efforts to ensure quality child care.* Washington, D.C.: Children's Defense Fund.

Adams, G. (1995). *How safe? The status of state efforts to protect children in child care.* Washington, D.C.: Children's Defense Fund.

American Public Health Association & American Academy of Pediatrics. (1992). *Caring for our children: National health and safety performance standards—guidelines for out-of-home child care programs.* Washington, D.C. and Elk Grove Village, Ill.: American Public Health Association & American Academy of Pediatrics.

Bredekamp, S., & Glowacki, S. (1995). *The first decade of NAEYC accreditation: Growth and impact on the field.* Paper prepared for an Invitational Conference sponsored by the Robert McCormick Tribune Foundation and the National Association for the Education of Young Children. Wheaton, Ill.

Carnegie Task Force on Meeting the Needs of Young Children. (1994). *Starting points: Meeting the needs of our youngest children.* The report of the Carnegie Task Force on Meeting the Needs of Young Children. New York: Carnegie Corporation of New York.

Center for Career Development in Early Care and Education at Wheelock College. (1995). *Child care licensing regulation: Data compiled by the Center for Career Development in Early Care and Education.* Boston: Center for Career Development in Early Care and Education, Wheelock College.

Chang, H. N., Tobiassen, D. P., & Muckelroy, A. (forthcoming). *California Tomorrow early childhood project draft report.* San Francisco: California Tomorrow.

Cost, Quality & Child Outcomes Study Team. (1995). *Cost, quality and child outcomes in child care centers.* Denver: Department of Economics, University of Colorado.

Derman-Sparks, L., & the ABC Task Force. (1989). *Anti-bias curriculum: Tools for empowering young children.* Washington, D.C.: National Association for the Education of Young Children.

Epstein, J. L. (1995, May). School/family/community partnerships: Caring for the children we share. *Phi Delta Kappan,* 701–712.

Galinsky, E., Bond, J. T., & Friedman, D. E. (1993). *The changing workforce: Highlights of the national study.* New York: Families and Work Institute.

Galinsky, E., Howes, C., & Kontos, S. (1995). *The family child care training study: Interim report.* New York: Families and Work Institute.

Galinsky, E., Howes, C., Kontos, S., & Shinn, M. (1994). *The study of children in family child care and relative care: Highlights of findings.* New York: Families and Work Institute.

Gormley, W. T. (1995). *Everybody's children: Child care as a public problem.* Washington, D.C.: Brookings Institution.

Hartmann, H., Yoon, Y., Spalter-Roth, R., & Shaw, L. (1995). *Temporary disability insurance: A model to provide income security for women over the life cycle.* Paper presented at 1995 Annual Meetings of the American Economics Association and Allied Social Science Associations, Washington, D.C.

Hofferth, S. L., & Chaplin, D. (1994). *Child care quality versus availability: Do we have to trade one for the other?* Washington, D.C.: Urban Institute Press.

Howes, C., & Marx, E. (1992). Raising questions about improving the quality of child care: Child care in the United States and France. *Early Childhood Research Quarterly, 7,* 347–366.

Jorde-Bloom, P. (1988). *A great place to work: Improving conditions for staff in young children's programs.* Washington, D.C.: National Association for the Education of Young Children.

Kagan, S. L., Goffin, S. G., Golub, S. A., & Pritchard, E. (1995). *Toward systemic reform: Service integration for young children and their families.* Falls Church, Va.: National Center for Service Integration.

Kagan, S. L., Moore, E., & Bredekamp, S. (Eds.). (1995). *Reconsidering children's early development and learning: Toward shared beliefs and vocabulary.* Washington, D.C.: National Education Goals Panel.

Kagan, S. L., Rosenkoetter, S., and Cohen, N. E. (1996). *Considering child-based outcomes for young children: Definitions, desirability, and feasibility.* New Haven, Conn.: Bush Center in Child Development and Social Policy, Yale University.

Morgan, G. (1995). *Licensing and accreditation: How much quality is "quality?"* Paper prepared for an Invitational Conference sponsored by the Robert McCormick Tribune Foundation and the National Association for the Education of Young Children. Wheaton, Ill.

Morgan, G., & others. (1993). *Making a career of it: The state of the states report on career development in early care and education.* Boston: Center for Career Development in Early Care and Education, Wheelock College.

Phillips, D., & Crowell, N. A. (Eds.). (1994). *Cultural diversity in early education: Report of a workshop.* Washington, D.C.: National Academy Press.

Phillips, D., & others. (forthcoming). *Paths to quality in child care: Structural and contextual influences on children's classroom environments.* Washington, D.C.: National Research Council.

Powell, D. R. (1989). *Families and early childhood programs.* Washington, D.C.: National Association for the Education of Young Children.

Powell, D. R. (1994). Parents, pluralism, and the NAEYC statement on developmentally appropriate practice. In B. L. Mallory & R. S. New (Eds.), *Diversity and developmentally appropriate practices: Challenges for early childhood education* (pp. 166–182). New York: Teachers College Press.

Schorr, L. B. (1994). The case for shifting to results-based accountability. In N. Young and others, *Making a difference: Moving to outcome-based accountability for comprehensive service reforms.* Falls Church, Va.: National Center for Service Integration.

Shepard, L. A. (1994). The challenges of assessing young children appropriately. *Phi Delta Kappan, 76,* 206–213.

U.S. Advisory Committee on Intergovernmental Relations. (1994). *Child care: The need for federal-state-local coordination.* Washington, D.C.: U.S. Advisory Committee on Intergovernmental Relations.

U.S. Department of Commerce, Bureau of the Census. (1993). *Statistical abstract of the United States, 1992.* Washington, D.C.: U.S. Government Printing Office.

Whitebook, M., Howes, C., & Phillips, D. (1989). *Who cares? Child care teachers and the quality of care in America: Final report of the national child care staffing study.* Oakland, Calif.: Child Care Employee Project.

Willer, B. (1990). Estimating the full cost of quality. In B. Willer (Ed.), *Reaching the full cost of quality in early childhood programs* (pp. 55–86). Washington, D.C.: National Association for the Education of Young Children.

Willer, B. (1994). A conceptual framework for early childhood professional development. In J. Johnson & J. B. McCracken (Eds.), *The early childhood career lattice: Perspectives on professional development* (pp. 4–23). Washington, D.C.: National Association for the Education of Young Children.

Willer, B., & others. (1991). *The demand and supply of child care in 1990: Joint findings from the national child care survey 1990 and a profile of child care settings.* Washington, D.C.: National Association for the Education of Young Children.

Chapter Eighteen

Getting from Here to There
The Process and the Players

Nancy E. Cohen
Sharon L. Kagan

The last chapter focused on describing the *vision* of a quality early care and education system to be achieved. In this chapter, we consider *how* to go about implementing the vision and *who* should be responsible for doing what. To realize the vision will require strategy, organization, and mobilization. But above all, it will require a shift in public perception—the basis for any far-reaching social change. Recent decades have witnessed a number of dramatic shifts in commitment, policy, and practice throughout the country that seemed unthinkable right up to the moment they occurred, and today they seem obvious and inevitable. The early care and education field needs to build on these lessons. In this chapter, we present five ingredients of significant social change and apply them to early care and education. Then, we identify the players who can help achieve change and the roles they might play.

The Ingredients of Change

Drawing from the chapters in Part Three as well as from discussions throughout the four-year *Quality 2000* initiative described in the Preface, we have distilled five ingredients of successful social change in this country:

- Clearly defining the problem and the solution
- Identifying goals that are consistent with social beliefs but are placed in a new conceptual framework
- Working at multiple levels and in multiple systems to achieve synergy
- Assessing and capitalizing on the context
- Building on existing strengths

This list of ingredients is not meant to order the steps required for social change, nor is it meant to constitute an exhaustive list of change strategies. Rather, it suggests possible directions for bringing about reform in early care and education. We consider each ingredient in this chapter and explore how it might be applied to bringing about change in early care and education.

Clearly Defining the Problem and the Solution

The challenge of defining a problem and its optimal solution in terms that are clear and accessible forces reformers to foster some consensus on exactly what they want to change and the strategies to advance their goals. Defining a problem and its solution also forces reformers to delineate the scope of reform and the arena(s) in which it will occur, as well as the players who will shape the process. Moreover, the way the problem and the solution are defined shapes the constituency to be mobilized. In the following, we suggest an approach for the early care and education field to define the problem and the solution in its reform efforts.

Define the Problem as the Lack of Quality for All Children

The early care and education field needs to frame the problem as the lack of quality for the vast majority of families with young children. This represents a major shift from previous statements of the problem, which focused on the needs of low-income families. The old definition limited the constituencies that could be rallied for change and hampered reformers' efforts to command broad support. The popular assumption that low-quality early care and education is the problem solely of the poor is wrong; low-quality services pervade the field. To harness the attention and resources needed to sustain a long-term effort, we must expand the scope of the problem.

Define the Solution as a Quality System

We must also expand our definition of the solution. Historically, the field has confined improvement efforts to the classroom, promoting such program-level reforms as developmentally appropriate practice and antibias curricula. Over the last decade, there has been some movement toward framing solutions in terms of the infrastructure as well, but in most cases, narrow solutions have been put forward by single-issue organizations focusing on one element of the infrastructure—compensation, or professional development, or facility-licensing standards, or accreditation. In and of themselves, each of these approaches is too narrow; they are components of a more comprehensive solution.

The field needs an overarching solution, toward which all players can work single-mindedly until it is achieved. The field needs to frame the solution as developing and financing a quality *system*, with a focus on the *infrastructure*. Without a quality infrastructure, direct efforts to shore up program quality may result in short-term improvements but cannot bring about meaningful, sustainable reform. To this end, the innovative but fragmented reform efforts now under way need to be redirected toward the development of a coherent early care and education system. Creating consensus around an integrated agenda will not be easy, but it is critical to the change process.

Define the Solution Stressing Parent Advocacy

The field also needs to redefine the solution stressing the role of parents. If we frame the problem as the need to assure quality in early care and education programs for all young children, the solution will require the support of large numbers of parents. Major early care and education reform is unlikely to occur without the active support and advocacy of the broad-based constituencies that would benefit directly. Although parents have been involved to some degree in individual early care and education programs, they have not mobilized into a cohesive constituency for change in early care and education.

Identifying Goals Consistent with Social Beliefs, in a New Conceptual Framework

Revering the old, but ever infatuated with the new, Americans tend to support reforms that incorporate both traditional beliefs and new ways of thinking about a problem. Reforms that are consistent with social beliefs are more achievable than those that attempt to refocus or revise basic values. But how deep-rooted and powerful can a change agenda be if it stays safely within the confines of long-established norms? Successful change movements have shown that although America's adherence to values is strong, the nation's interest in innovation—a new construct or a new approach—can be equally potent. Building on these lessons, early care and education needs to ground its agenda in the common belief system. At the same time, it must create a new framework, new concepts, and new language to capitalize on America's penchant for innovation. Following are two specific suggestions for accomplishing this.

Invoke Beliefs in Education, a Competitive Economy, and a Strong Democracy

The early care and education field has already made significant advances in certain cases by tapping into deeply entrenched social beliefs. Emphasizing the democratic ideal of equal opportunity for all, early care and education has marshaled long-term support for Head Start. Numerous states have had similar success in gaining ideological and social support for state prekindergarten programs that serve at-risk children. Reform efforts need to build on the theme that early care and education is a cornerstone of a strong democratic society, helping ensure a well-educated future citizenry and a reliable workforce and helping reduce investments in costly remedial social services. In building on this theme, the early care and education field can gain much from our society's commitment to a free public education for all children—practically the only universal entitlement supported by most citizens. The challenge is to build on our society's commitment to universal public education without undermining that commitment or overstating its accomplishments.

Create a "New Think" for an Early Care and Education System and Infrastructure

As it builds on basic values, change efforts in early care and education must also reflect an innovative spirit. The solution discussed above—developing and financing a quality early care and education system with a focus on the infrastructure—must be framed in a way that offers a new conceptual framework for an old problem. A "new think" is necessary to persuade Americans that this solution is both feasible and desirable. Reformers need new phrases and terms to demystify what is meant by a system and an infrastructure, presenting these concepts as clearly and concretely as possible, linking them directly to how children, families, and the nation will benefit.

Working at Multiple Levels, in Multiple Systems, with Multiple Players to Achieve Synergy

An effective change effort requires clarity about where to concentrate efforts. Should effort focus at the federal, state, or local level? Should it focus outside the field with the hope of attracting new allies and resources? Or should it focus within one field? If it should focus within the field, what should be the role of various organizations—professional groups, advocacy organizations, special-interest organizations, and broad-based interest organizations? Following are suggestions for reform in early care and education, concerning the levels at which to work, the players to involve, and the systems in which to operate.

Given the present involvement of all levels of government in early care and education, it will not be possible to assure quality programs for all children by introducing reforms at only one level of government. Rather, reformers need to devise specific strategies for change at each level of government, based on the unique strengths of that level, generating a set of appropriate, explicit, nonduplicative, and coordinated goals. For example, as Gormley suggests in Chapter Nine, the federal government should focus its efforts on the affordability of early care and education—generating funds; state governments should take the lead on ensuring quality—including facility and individual licensing; and local governments should focus on availability—assessing needs and coordination.

Given that change must be fostered at all levels, a broad range of early care and education organizations and advocates for reform need to coalesce and work toward reform. National organizations are valuable because they can advocate for significant new federal funds and adjustments in federal roles. Moreover, they can take positions and secure visibility for critical issues. National organizations also have the responsibility to be beacons for new advances in the field and to help cross-fertilize effective efforts at the state and local levels. State and local organizations can respond to local challenges and needs and work effectively with state and local leaders in other human service fields. Closer to the pulse of change, state and local organizations also have the power to model effective systems and inform elected officials of real needs and priorities. They also monitor and influence state legislation, an increasingly critical role as more responsibility is devolved to the states.

Finally, should change efforts focus on the early care and education field or on a series of related human services? To be sure, the early care and education field faces a multitude of problems and needs significant internal reform. But at the same time, the field remains committed to meeting children's and families' comprehensive needs in a holistic fashion. The field needs to begin with direct significant attention toward internal reform. Such efforts should focus on the infrastructure and on continuing to enhance direct program quality. Working to support full-fledged parent engagement, create individual licensing approaches, revise facility licensing, expand accreditation, establish governance structures, and increase funding and financing are all efforts that need to begin immediately. At the same time, the field must devote some effort to linking its reform with change efforts in other fields, such as education, social services, and health care. Linking with the family support movement is a concrete strategy that promotes the field's goals as it extends the domain of early care and education endeavors. Linking with community organizers and community development initiatives—including housing and economic development—are other important strategies.

Assessing and Capitalizing on the Context

Successful change movements are nested in broader social, political, and economic contexts that set the stage for reform. Leaders of successful change efforts tacitly and explicitly assess contextual factors—both inside and outside of their fields—and capitalize on them in propelling change. Following are three suggestions for early care and education based on this lesson of capitalizing on the context.

Build on Auspicious Trends

Today, the social, political, and economic contexts for reform in early care and education are relatively promising. Over the last decade, five key factors have resulted in more sustained attention to this issue:

- Demographic trends, including the increasing number of mothers in the workforce and the increasing number of single-parent families
- Reform in related fields, particularly welfare reform
- Greater recognition of the need to ready children for school, promoted in particular by the National Education Goals (Goals 2000)
- Greater stress on the cost-effectiveness of prevention and early-intervention services (Schweinhart & others, 1993)
- Greater recognition of the relationship between quality early care and education and workforce productivity (Committee for Economic Development, 1993)

The challenge is to capture the opportunities associated with these trends to fashion a new public commitment to early care and education.

Work with the Media

Tapping the media is a key lever to propel reform, by building on and shaping the prevailing context. Generally speaking, the media have covered early care and education mainly when negative or sensational stories emerge. Working with the media to maintain and improve the context for change is a critical element of any reform agenda. The media can keep issues in the public consciousness and on the agendas of policy makers, as they emphasize the need for change by publicizing catastrophes. The field needs to make the most of media's tendency to cover crises, encouraging reporters to follow up with stories on the system and the infrastructure and how they can be improved. The media can illustrate both the urgency of the problem and the hope of a solution.

Use Court Strategies

Court action has often been the key to effecting durable systemic reform in the United States, for example, in education, special education, and civil rights. In contrast, early care and education has rarely looked to the judicial arena as a means of advancing change. In part, this may reflect that judicially propelled change can be slow, often requiring years of litigation, diligent monitoring after court decisions, and numerous follow-up lawsuits. In spite of these obstacles, the early care and education field needs to consider the strategic use of court action to augment other reform efforts. Our nation is a litigious society, and early care and education could benefit from this context in pursuing its agenda.

Discrimination is one possible basis for judicial action in early care and education, aimed at extending programs to more young children. For example, state and local governments throughout the country may be discriminating against younger children by investing so much more in the education of older children from age five to age eighteen. Another possible avenue is to pressure states to implement and enforce existing facility-licensing laws and regulations. In some states, facility licensing may effectively be discriminating by race, national origin, and geographic location by leading to the concentration of licensed programs in white, middle-class neighborhoods (*Doe* v. *Obledo*, 1985); court efforts could seek the more equitable distribution of services. Finally, language in legislation that makes early care and education services an entitlement has proven to be a strong statutory basis for litigation. A series of lawsuits concerning the early care and education entitlement in the Family Support Act of 1988 compelled noncomplying states, including California, Illinois, Massachusetts, and Wisconsin, to provide the guaranteed services (O'Brien & Stevenson, 1994).

Building on Existing Strengths

Reform efforts often pay too little attention to saving or bolstering existing efforts that are functional, or even exemplary. After achieving reform, fields are often faced with trying to reinstate aspects of traditional practice and programs.

The early care and education field has multiple strengths that should be safeguarded and nurtured as the reform process moves forward. First, early care and education allows most parents who pay for services to choose the programs they want for their children from a variety of nonprofit and for-profit providers. The recent expansion of voucher systems has extended parent choice to increasing numbers of low-income parents. Most concur that parental choice is an element worth retaining; some argue that elementary and secondary education should emulate the choice afforded to parents in early care and education. Second, early care and education programs usually operate with a high degree of program autonomy and a minimum of the red tape and bureaucracy often present in schools. Each early care and education program can establish its own unique place in the community and pursue its own unique vision (Morgan, 1995). Programs can be tailored to varied communities, cultural backgrounds, and families. The opportunity to shape each program independently has resulted in a wide variety of approaches and offers the possibility of families finding a match between their values and the programs that will care for their children. Third, deeply ingrained in the field are the assumptions that children are, first and always, members of families and communities and that early care and education works best in close partnership with both. And fourth, early care and education efforts tend to be holistic and developmental in their orientation, coupled with a commitment to constructivist education.

The Players in Change

Sweeping reform in early care and education will require the carefully orchestrated efforts of a range of individuals, organizations, and institutions.

To the President, Congress, and the Federal Government:

- Make significant increased funding of early care and education a priority. Disavow inequitable access and assure all families with young children quality early care and education.

- Assure worthy wages for early care and education staff, which are commensurate with experience, education, and training.
- Lead efforts to specify which level of government does what, to avoid gaps and overlap.
- Lead and coordinate the movement to build consensus on child results—the knowledge and skills preschool-age children need to be ready for school. Establish broad goals to guide states in the development of standards for child results and communities in the development of benchmarks to meet state standards and national goals.
- Provide incentives for states to establish governance structures for early care and education, such as state early care and education boards and local early care and education boards described in Chapter Seventeen.
- Develop guidelines for facility standards, with broad-based input, for state consideration and adoption.
- Coordinate the collection of uniform data on child results nationwide.
- Facilitate state and local networking to exchange information on best practices.
- Fund innovative research, demonstration, and evaluation.

To the Governors, State Legislators, and Facility Licensers:

- Create state-level governance structures for early care and education, such as the state early care and education boards described in Chapter Seventeen.
- Institute an ongoing, consolidated state-planning process to improve the quality and coordination of early care and education services. The process should include a structure for determining how to distribute funds to help parents pay for programs, how to offer parents paid parental leave, and how to divide funds for the infrastructure between the state and localities.
- Establish a quality early care and education infrastructure at the state level, particularly facility licensing and individual licensing.

For facility licensing, pilot and evaluate streamlined standards that give programs options for ways to organize children and staff.

For individual licensing, pilot full-fledged systems that include individual licensing laws and state licensing boards to oversee the process.

- Ensure that an organization or collaborative of organizations exists in every community to support family child care providers.
- Establish state standards for results for preschool-age children in early care and education settings.
- Discern the process and the criteria for providing incentives to high-performing local early care and education boards.

To Local Elected Officials and Community Leaders:

- Create local governance structures for early care and education in every school district or county, such as the local early care and education boards described in Chapter Seventeen.
- Set in motion a durable planning process that assesses community needs for early care and education services and matches resources to needs.
- Improve the quality of early care and education by building, maintaining, and funding the local infrastructure.
- Establish performance benchmarks for services that align with state standards for child results.
- Establish mechanisms and processes to assure community and consumer involvement in all planning and accountability efforts.

To Parents:

- Secure the knowledge and take the time to find quality programs for young children. Parent selection drives our market-based early care and education system.
- Be partners in your children's programs, participating on a regular basis in ways that meet your needs as well as those of your children and the programs themselves.

- Work together with other parents and with early care and education professionals to advocate for a quality early care and education system.

To the Business Community:

- Contribute funds directly to a quality early care and education system.
- Provide family-friendly workplaces.

To Early Care and Education Advocates at the National, State, and Local Levels:

- Work collaboratively and simultaneously toward a shared vision of a quality early care and education system. Each organization needs to fulfill its unique mission, as it also works collaboratively toward coordinated reform. Systemic and durable reform will require the cooperative support of all the organizations in the field.
- Work with the media to spur reform.
- Work for reform in the courts.

To Practitioners and Administrators of Early Care and Education Programs:

- Assist with the identification of child results and then work toward these results day-to-day with children. Use information about child results to improve pedagogy and instruction. Share information with parents.
- Help develop positive organizational climates in all early care and education programs, climates that nurture staff, parents, and families. In particular, work to form mutually supportive relationships with parents.
- Help nurture the cultural, racial, ethnic, and linguistic diversity of the children and families with whom you work. Learn about their cultures by respectfully asking questions, spending time in the community, and learning about and questioning your own biases.
- Help promote a quality infrastructure. Early care and education practitioners and administrators are powerful in their

own right and also in their potential to inform and mobilize parents.

- Help integrate services for children and families in communities.

To Early Care and Education Professional Organizations:

- Create model standards and exams for individual licenses.
- Expand the capacity to accredit all early childhood education and child development college programs, both two- and four-year.
- Develop leadership and management-training programs.

To Trainers of Early Care and Education Practitioners:

- Offer more training in working with mixed-age groups, facilitating the development of larger numbers of children, engaging and supporting families, developing multiculturalism, and observing and assessing children.
- Work to increase the credit-bearing training available to practitioners and administrators and to make articulation agreements among two- and four-year colleges the norm.
- Create mechanisms to grant credit for demonstrated knowledge and skills gained from direct experience with children and from previous noncredit training.

To Researchers:

- Expand research on individual classrooms and family child care homes to consider the quality of organizational climates and to consider quality from children's and parents' perspectives. Link assessments of program quality to the achievement of child results. What characteristics of quality programs—not just individual classrooms—lead to the specified child results? How are gains sustained over time as children and families traverse institutions? What infrastructure is needed to support quality early care and education programs?
- Support efforts to specify child results. Provide the detailed knowledge of human development and assessment to guide national, state, and local efforts to determine the child results to be achieved.

- Broaden the range of researchers studying young children. Attract researchers from a variety of domains—including economics, political science, and public health—to study young children and early care and education.

To the Private and Philanthropic Sectors:

- Support the development of model early care and education systems that integrate all the essentials of the infrastructure. Support the creation of quality community-wide and statewide early care and education systems that can be models for states and communities across the country. Develop an initiative to investigate and support comprehensive funding and financing reform for early care and education.

Conclusion

The unprecedented proliferation of innovative efforts in early care and education constitutes a nascent reform movement (Kagan, 1994), which can be harnessed to create and maintain a quality early care and education system. The rough planks for a change agenda and a quality system are already in place—isolated and idiosyncratic, to be sure, but promising nevertheless. Five or ten years ago, there was little talk of an early care and education system; few dared to look beyond individual programs to discern the field's common infrastructure needs. Today, communities and states across the nation are beginning to address issues such as parent engagement, professional development, licensing and accreditation, governance, and financing. These disparate efforts must be heralded, supported, and linked to create a coherent movement for change in the early care and education field.

With all of this attention, early care and education has become a fishbowl, magnetizing attention and evoking curiosity for some and confusion for others. The nature of current opportunity is different from any in the past. Though challenges and barriers abound, early care and education has a unique opportunity to move forward. Now is the time to create a coherent, high-quality early care and education system that supports all of the nation's children. The question is no longer whether a reform movement in early care and education is going to take place. A movement is already under way in communities and states across the nation. The question is: Will reform remain essentially unplanned and loosely organized, or will it harness the crucial supports needed to surge forward with coherent intention and strategy? We hope that this volume and the work it has fueled suggest concrete next steps toward the latter.

References

Committee for Economic Development. (1993). *Why child care matters: Preparing young children for a more productive America.* New York: Committee for Economic Development.

Doe v. *Obledo,* 756 F. 2nd. 713 (9th circuit, 1985).

Kagan, S. L. (1994). Early care and education: Beyond the fishbowl. *Phi Delta Kappan, 76,* 184–188.

Morgan, G. (1995). *Licensing and accreditation: How much quality is "quality?"* Paper prepared for an Invitational Conference sponsored by the Robert McCormick Tribune Foundation and the National Association for the Education of Young Children. Wheaton, Ill.

O'Brien, K., & Stevenson, C. (1994). Child care under the family support act: Ripe for reform. *Clearinghouse Review,* May, 12–20.

Schweinhart, L. J., & others. (1993). *Significant benefits: The High/Scope Perry preschool study through age 27.* Ypsilanti, Mich.: High/Scope Press.

Name Index

Subject Index